Nine-Headed D

Peter Matthiessen, novelist, naturalist and explorer, won the National Book Award in 1978 for *The Snow Leopard*. His books include *Blue Meridian*, about the search for the great white shark, *Sand Rivers*, *The Tree Where Man Was Born*, *In the Spirit of Crazy Horse* and *Indian Country*, a powerful and meticulously researched appeal for the rights of North America's Indians to preserve their traditions. He has also written five novels. Peter Matthiessen lives on Long Island, New York.

NINE-HEADED DRAGON RIVER

ZEN JOURNALS

Peter Matthiessen

Flamingo

First published by Collins Harvill 1986
This Flamingo edition first published
in 1987 by Fontana Paperbacks
8 Grafton Street, London W1X 3LA

Flamingo is an imprint of
Fontana Paperbacks, part of
the Collins Publishing Group

Made and printed in Great Britain by
William Collins Sons & Co. Ltd, Glasgow

To my excellent teacher and kind friend Bernard
Tetsugen Glassman-sensei, with admiration,
gratitude, and deep affection.

The great way of the buddhas is profound, wondrous, inconceivable;
how could its practice be easy? Have you not seen how the ancients
gave up their bodies and lives, abandoned their countries, cities, and
families, looking upon them as like shards of tile? After that they passed
eons living alone in the mountains and forests, bodies and minds like
dead trees; only then did they unite with the way. Then they could use
mountains and rivers for words, raise the wind and rain for a tongue,
and explain the great void. . . .

Shobogenzo
—EIHEI DOGEN

CONTENTS

Tiantong's first phrase of winter:
Old plum tree, bent and gnarled,
all at once opens one blossom, two blossoms,
not proud of purity,
not proud of fragrance;
falling, becoming spring,
blowing over grasses and trees,
balding the head of a patched-robe monk.
Whirling, changing into wind, wild rain,
falling, snow, all over the earth.
The old plum tree is boundless.
A hard cold rubs the nostrils.

from *Treasury of the True Dharma Eye*
—NYOJO ZENJI

FOREWORD

The poem by Tendo Nyojo Zenji from *Treasury of the True Dharma Eye* expresses the very spirit of what his student, Dogen Zenji, thoroughly penetrated with his entire being, skewering the lives of the Buddhas and Patriarchs with one new stem of the old plum tree, and, thus, beginning Japanese Soto Zen.

As Peter Muryo Matthiessen points out, numerous attempts have been made in Japan to elucidate Dogen Zenji's writings from various perspectives: philosophical, literary, historical, psychological, and so forth. These contributions have inspired an increasing number of Western scholars and practitioners to study Dogen Zenji. Zen has entered a new realm in the West. The spreading roots of Zen *are* the lives of those born here who diligently, with whole body and mind, practice the Way.

Reflecting upon the diversity of the social, cultural, traditional and spiritual climate in which we breathe, I note the richness, both evident and potential. Among my own students are Jews and Catholics, Protestants and atheists, physicists, carpenters, nurses, artists, doctors, teachers and so on. Each discipline and tradition has its own perspectives and ways of exploring the universe. My first Dharma successor, Bernard Tetsugen Glassman Sensei, a former mathematician, observes Jewish traditions with his family. Peter Matthiessen himself is an innately gifted, stubbornly talented Protestant, an established author, naturalist, explorer and hunter of the treasures of life, and is now close to completing his formal training as a Zen teacher under Glassman Sensei. I, though a naturalized American citizen for some twenty-five years, am Japanese by birth and was raised in my father's temple. When we ignore this cultural and spiritual complex and attach blindly to Japanese tradition, we drown in stagnant water; yet, if we ignore tradition, we will be swept away in the torrential onslaught of ideas and notions. Nonetheless, what I see around me are students of the Way, "uncountable blossoms" in varieties found nowhere in Japan.

> *When Gautama's eyeball vanishes,*
> *plum blossoms in snow, just one branch,*
> *becomes thorn bushes, here, everywhere, right now.*
> *Laughing, spring wind blowing madly.*
> —Nyojo Zenji

In order to realize our own true nature, we have to vanish Gautama's eyeball. When we vanish it, our lives are revealed as the plum blossoms and our everyday life becomes thorn bushes.

When the plum blossoms open spring, spring permeates the whole world and the whole world opens up as the lotus blossom. It is the old plum, and it is the uncountable blossoms, buddhas, and all beings, birth and death, delusion and enlightenment, mountains and rivers, moon and clouds.

It is my wish that those like Peter Matthiessen, who have gone through a severe winter of snowstorms and frosty winds, realize themselves as the timeless spring already here. The ten directions are the boundless blossoms, in no way proud of their fragrance. It is my earnest wish that this new era of practice open the door of the "Treasury of the True Dharma Eye" on this continent, and throughout the Western world.

> *Nyojo Zenji celebrates,*
> *The first day of the year is auspicious.*
> *Myriad things are all new.*
> *In prostration the great assembly reflects.*
> *Plum blossoms open early spring.*

Hakuyu T. Maezumi
Zen Center of Los Angeles
January 1, 1986

PREFACE

THE unwary reader has in hand a "Zen book" composed against the best instincts of its author, who has no business writing upon a subject so incompletely understood—far less a subject such as Zen, which is fundamentally impossible to write *about*.

Journals kept during fifteen years of practice provide a rickety armature for Zen poems, stories, and teachings, those luminous expressions of deep insight by Zen masters, past and present, which have delighted me and refreshed my life. This book will only justify itself if it transmits enough of that delight so that others may be drawn toward the path of Zen.

It is my hope that my deep gratitude to my teachers in the Rinzai and Soto sects will be made clear in this book, which is not "my book" but a compendium of teachings, and the property of the Zen Community of New York. In my life there have been many other teachers who were not Zen masters; I thank them, too, with all my heart. Many were Dharma sisters, Dharma brothers, in various Zen groups in America, and some were insightful friends and strangers, American Indians, sherpas, commercial fisherman, spontaneously leading a "Zen" way of life.

Zen has been called "the religion before religion," which is to say that anyone can practice, including those committed to another faith. And the phrase evokes that natural religion of our early childhood, when heaven and a splendorous earth were one. But soon the child's clear eye is clouded over by ideas and opinions, preconceptions and abstractions. Simple free *being* becomes encrusted with the burdensome armor of the ego. Not until years later does an instinct come that a vital sense of mystery has been withdrawn. The sun glints through the pines, and the heart is pierced in a moment of beauty and strange pain, like a memory of paradise.

After that day, at the bottom of each breath, there is a hollow place that is filled with longing. We become seekers without knowing that we seek, and at first, we long for something "greater" than ourselves, something apart and far away. It is not a return to childhood, for childhood is not a truly enlightened state. Yet to seek one's own true nature is, as one Zen master has said, "a way to lead you to your long-lost home."

To practice Zen means to realize one's existence moment after moment, rather than letting life unravel in regret of the past and daydreaming of the future. To "rest in the present" is a state of magical simplicity, although attainment of this state is not as simple as it sounds. At the very least, sitting Zen practice, called *zazen*, will bring about a strong sense of well-being, as the clutter of ideas and emotions falls away and body and mind return to natural harmony with all creation. Out of this emptiness can come a true insight into the nature of existence, which is no different from one's Buddha nature. To travel this path, one need not be a "Zen Buddhist," which is only another idea to be discarded, like "enlightenment" and like "the Buddha" and like "God."

AUTHOR'S NOTE

SINCE Western Zen had its origins in Japan, most American students are familiar with Japanese Zen terms, names, and usages. Therefore the names of Chinese Ch'an (Zen) teachers in this book appear in the Japanese transliteration (Rinzai, Joshu, Unmon). When the Chinese name (Hui Neng, Huang Po) seems more familiar, these names may appear in parentheses on the first occasion when the name is mentioned. Chinese names accompany their Japanese counterparts in the chart on page 264.

Foreign words and esoteric Zen expressions have been kept to a minimum in this book, but a number of important terms, in the absence of any satisfactory translation, will inevitably be adopted by American Zen. Those used here, in my opinion, are preferable to their English renditions, which tend to be diffuse and weak as well as incorrect. Most of these terms are defined on their first appearance in the text, and all may be located in the Glossary.

The Japanese language has no plural, and therefore it is incorrect to write *sesshins, roshis, koans,* and the like. Assuming, however, that such words will be incorporated in our language, it makes sense to do so, and for the most part, this practice has been followed here.

Out of respect, such titles as "roshi" (senior teacher) and "sensei" (teacher), when not used by themselves as a form of address, are always appended to Zen masters' names. In the present text, where their constant repetition would make the prose laborious and the style cumbersome, they are sometimes dispensed with, without disrespect: these well-earned titles are always there in spirit, whether they appear or not.

ACKNOWLEDGMENTS

I am especially indebted to my teachers—the late Soen Naka-gawa-roshi, Shimano Eido-roshi, Taizan Maezumi-roshi, and Tetsugen Glassman-sensei—whose insight and embodiment of the teachings lie at the heart of this book. Tetsugen-sensei's strong support, good counsel, and encouragement made much easier the assembling and editing of these notes and journals.

Helen Glassman, Lou Nordstrom, and Ken Wilber offered excellent ideas for deletions and additions to the text, and Dr. Nordstrom (a Buddhist scholar) also contributed the glossary of terms in the appendix. A number of Zen students, notably Wendy Megerman, Bryan Rich, Janet Skelton, and Lana McCalley, cheerfully typed, processed, and otherwise attended to the in-numerable drafts—my warm thanks to these friends, and also to Peter Cunningham, whose fine photograph for the book's jacket was but one of the many taken during the journey to Japan, and Henry Mende, who drew the map that appears in the appendix.

Finally, my sincere thanks to the book's editor, Emily Hil-burn Sell, for the intelligent and patient work that turned this book away from the brink of chaos.

AMERICA

RINZAI JOURNALS 1969–1976

The zazen I speak of is not learning meditation. . . . It is the manifestation of ultimate reality. . . . Once its heart is grasped, you are like the dragon when he gains the water, like the tiger when he enters the mountain. Forms and substance are like the dew on the grass, destiny like the dart of lightning—emptied in an instant, vanished in a flash.

Why leave behind the seat that exists in your own home and go aimlessly off to the dusty realms of other lands? . . . Do not be suspicious of the true dragon. Devote your energies to a way that directly indicates the absolute [and] gain accord with the enlightenment of the buddhas.

A Universal Recommendation for Zazen
—EIHEI DOGEN

CHAPTER ONE

ON an August day of 1969, returning home to Sagaponack, Long Island, after a seven-month absence in Africa, I was astonished by the presence in my driveway of three inscrutable small men who turned out to be Japanese Zen masters. Hakuun Yasutani-roshi, eighty-four years old, was a light, gaunt figure with hollowed eyes and round, prominent ears; as I was to learn, he had spent much of that morning upside down, standing on his head. Beside him, Nakagawa Soen-roshi, slit-eyed, elfin, and merry, entirely at ease and entirely aware at the same time, like a paused swallow, gave off emanations of lightly contained energy that made him seem much larger than he was. The roshis were attended by Tai-san (now Shimano Eido-roshi), a compact young monk with a confident, thick-featured face and samurai bearing. Though lacking the strange "transparent" presence of his teachers, Tai-san conveyed the same impression of contained power.

3

The teachers were guests of my wife, Deborah Love, a new student of Zen, but I was ignorant of this as of much else on that long-ago summer day. Because of my long absence and my unannounced return, the atmosphere between Deborah and me was guarded, and my first meeting with Zen masters was even less auspicious than an encounter that almost certainly took place in the 1890s between the first Zen Master in America, Soyen Shaku, and the senior partner in his host's manufacturing firm who, as karma would have it—and the Dharma, too—was none other than my forebear, Frederick Matthiessen. (This problematical meeting was at best unpromising, since it passed unrecorded in the annals of either side.) No doubt I revealed what I presume was my great-grandfather's wary attitude toward unanticipated Orientals in outlandish garb. For years thereafter, Tai-san would relate how Soen and Yasutani, perceiving my unenlightened condition at a glance, had shaken their shining heads and sighed, "Poor Debbo-lah."

For the next few years, I was often away on expeditions. Even when I was at home, my wife kept me well away from her Zen practice, not wishing to contaminate the zendo atmosphere with our dissension. Yet a seed had sprouted all the same, those men in my driveway knew something that I wished to know. I poked about in the Zen literature and pestered her for inside information.

In December of 1970—perhaps hoping to nip that bad seed in the bud—Deborah took me along to a weekend *sesshin*, or silent retreat, at the New York Zendo. I had had no experience or training in *zazen*—literally, "sitting Zen"—and suffered dreadful pain in the cross-legged posture, which I maintained, with the stubbornness of rage, for twelve hours daily for two days, weeping in pure shock during the rest periods. Though I won high praise from the zendo masochist, Monk D., I swore that this barbaric experience would never be repeated; in addition to all that pain, it had been so *boring*! A week later I departed gladly for Italy, Africa, and Australia, where I accompanied a more prudent

4

group of human beings underwater in quest of the first film of the great white shark.

That winter, to my own astonishment, I found myself doing zazen every day, not only in my Australian hotel room but on shipboard. The following summer I was working for a while in California, and in a vague impulse toward pilgrimage, I went on foot over the mountains from Carmel Valley to the San Francisco Zen Center's retreat at Tassajara. Shunryu Suzuki-roshi (whose wonderful *teisho*, or "Dharma talks," had recently been collected in *Zen Mind, Beginner's Mind*) walked about softly in white T-shirt and white sitting pants, puttering with garden pots, approving our repair of his cottage roof, and giving teisho on Zen Mind in the summer evening. Though he seemed frail, he did not comport himself like a man who was to die a few months later.

I have often tried to isolate that quality of "Zen" which attracted me so powerfully to its literature and later to the practice of zazen. But since the essence of Zen might well be what one teacher called "the moment-by-moment awakening of mind," there is little that may sensibly be said about it without succumbing to that breathless, mystery-ridden prose that drives so many sincere aspirants in the other direction. In zazen, one may hope to penetrate the ringing stillness of universal mind, and this "intimation of immortality," as Wordsworth called it, also shines forth from the brief, cryptic Zen texts, which refer obliquely to that absolute reality beyond the grasp of our linear vocabulary, yet right here in this moment, in this ink and paper, in the sound of this hand turning the page.

Later that summer, all but inexplicably, my wife and I at last embraced each other's failings. Happily she invited me to join a reconnaissance led by Soen-roshi and Tai-san of a tract of mountain land at Beecher Lake, in the headwaters of the Beaverkill River in the Catskills. This beautiful place would be chosen as the site of Dai Bosatsu (Great Bodhisattva), the first Zen monastery ever constructed in America.[1] What struck me most forcibly during our visit was the quiet precision, power,

5

and wild humor of Soen-roshi, who became my Zen teacher even before I realized that I was a student.

Both Soen-roshi and Yasutani-roshi had come to America in direct consequence of the pioneering efforts of the afore-mentioned Soyen Shaku, abbot of Engaku-ji, in Kamakura, and the first Zen master to visit and teach in the United States. In Soyen Shaku's opinion, Zen Buddhism had grown hollow and decrepit in Japan, and no longer reflected the great Dharma, or teaching, perceived in the enlightenment experience of Shak-yamuni the Buddha (the Awakened One) in the sixth century B.C. In its original Theravada form, Buddhism had traveled south from India to Ceylon and east to Burma and Thailand; the Mahayana Buddhist teachings that developed in the first century A.D. spread north and east to China, Korea, Japan, and Tibet. (An extraordinary, mysterious, and profound infusion of reli-gious and cultural energy remained behind even in those coun-tries where Buddhism was later suppressed, or died away; it has been said that in Japan a whole culture owes its character to Zen.)

A Mahayana teaching with a strong Taoist infusion, Ch'an or Zen cast off the dead weight of priestly ritual and mindless chanting of the sutras or scriptures—the records of the Buddha's teachings—and returned to the simple zazen way of Shakya-muni. In a statement attributed to the First Chinese Patriarch, Bodhidharma, an old monk from India who is loosely associated with the birth of Zen, the new teaching was described as "a special transmission outside the scriptures, not founded upon words or letters. By pointing directly to man's own mind, it lets him see into his own true nature and thus attain Bud-dhahood."

The illustrious teacher from India was soon summoned to an audience with the Emperor Wu, a devout Buddhist and teacher of the sutras who built temples and supported monks, and was therefore honored as the "Buddha-Mind Emperor." (One mean-ing of the Chinese character *wu* signifies "absolute being"; another denotes "awakening" or enlightenment.) Relating all he had studied and accomplished, Wu asked modestly, "What merit will there be?"

Bodhidharma said, "No merit."

In answering in this abrupt sharp way, the old Indian teacher points directly at the absolute, in which there is no merit to be given, and neither giver nor receiver. From the relative point of view, there is no merit either, so long as Wu clings to the concept of merit: true merit derives from seeing into one's own true nature or Buddha-nature, manifesting one's own free merit-less nature, moment after moment, like a fish or bird—just Wu, just bird.

Doubtless taken aback, the Emperor demands, "If all that has no merit, then what *is* the primary meaning of the holy truth?" Presumably the Emperor refers to the non-duality of universal and everyday truth, the fundamental identity of relative and absolute that underlies Mahayana Buddhist doctrine. And perhaps he is challenging the old villain to present the essence of this teaching. But Bodhidharma, correctly interpreting this sutra teacher's degree of spiritual attainment, recognizes a purely doctrinal question inviting exposition on the Dharma, and so, once more, he points directly at the realm of the Absolute or Universal.

"*No* holiness," says he. "Vast emptiness."

This ringing answer instantly established the spare uncompromising tone of the Zen teachings. It also carried great mystery and power, for this "emptiness" was neither absence nor a void. Its Chinese character was *ku*, which also signifies the clear blue firmament, without north or south, future or past, without boundaries or dimension. Like the empty mirror on which all things pass, leaving no trace, this *ku* contains all forms and all phenomena, being a symbol of the universal essence. Thus this emptiness is also fullness, containing all forms and phenomena above and below Heaven, filling the entire universe. In this universal or absolute reality, there is no holiness (nor any non-holiness), only the immediacy of sky *as-it-is* in this present mo-

7

ment, with or without clouds or balloons, kites or fireworks, birds or snow or wind.

Bodhidharma is not criticizing holiness. Religion is a precious concept, and concepts are crucial to the relative or "practical" aspect of our life, which is the ground of Zen. ("Rice in a bowl, water in a pail: how do you like these common miracles?") But when we are mired in the relative world, never lifting our gaze to the mystery, our life is stunted, incomplete; we are filled with yearning for that paradise that is lost when, as young children, we replace with words and ideas and abstractions—such as merit, such as past, present, and future—our direct, spontaneous experience of the thing itself, in the beauty and precision of this present moment. We identify, label, and interpret our surroundings as abstract concepts, quite separate from yet another concept, which is our own separate identity and ego. Even holiness is removed from us, a Heaven up there with a God in it.

One can certainly sympathize with the Buddha-Mind Emperor. Here he is, anticipating homage, only to be confronted with this old wretch saying *No merit!* to all of his good deeds, his imperial handiwork, saying *No holiness!* to his big question about holy truth—an outrageous scene, and a tremendous one. To judge from his portraits, Bodhidharma was as vital and ferocious as he was short-spoken, and he was fearless; he might have had those bristling brows plucked one by one. Cowled, round-shouldered, big-headed, bearded, broken-toothed, with prominent and piercing eyes, sometimes said to be blue—one can all but smell his hard-patched robes, stained with ghee butter from India, the wafting reek of cooking smoke and old human leather. One imagines him slouched there scratching and belching, or perhaps demanding, *What time do we eat?*

And Wu demands to know, *Who stands before me?*

Wu is after all an advanced student of the Buddha Dharma, and perhaps he has glimpsed something. All the same, he is a bit put out. And so this question must mean something like, You say no holiness, yet you present yourself as a holy man from

India! Or, If all is emptiness, then who is this terrible old person standing before me? He does not yet see the Oneness of existence, the One Body, that Bodhidharma points to, he is still stuck in the relative world, the delusion of the self as a complete entity, separate from like entities: *Who stands before me?!* And no doubt he is shaken, reassembling his dignity.

Bodhidharma has no wish to expound. He is bringing the Dharma from India to China, and as he is already one hundred and ten years old, time is not on his side. He says simply,

I know not.

This answer is the ultimate answer in Zen. It is "not-knowing," a response that echoes "vast emptiness," yet goes still deeper to the unnameable source where there is nothing-to-know, where nothing exists outside the *doing* and *being* of this present instant without past or future, an instant no more measurable than the flight of a bird from a limb. (Where to begin? Do we measure the relaxing of the feet? The moment when the eye glimpses the hawk, when instinct functions? For in this pure action, this pure moving of the bird, there is no time, no space, but only the free doing-being of this very moment—*now!* Unencumbered by concepts—such as emptiness, such as enlightenment—the bird is gone. To be at one with our element, like that bird—*that* is the Absolute, that is our enlightened Buddha-nature. The instant we are *conscious* of that element, we stand apart from our own true nature, our Buddha-nature, we are back in the relative world of time and space, of life and death. This world is real, too, but its reality is partial.

Like emptiness, this not-knowing is very close to us, therefore hard to see. It is the source or essence of our life, and of Zen practice. In zazen, all "knowing" falls away; we simply *are*. And that is the enlightened state, whether or not the practitioner has had a so-called "enlightenment experience."

Bodhidharma went north across the Yangtze River to Shorin Temple and spent nine years in zazen, "facing the wall." When the old monk had gone, Wu's minister, the venerable Shiko, told the Emperor gently that this old teacher was a manifestation of the great compassionate Bodhisattva Avalokiteshvara (Padmapani in India, Kuan Yin in China, Kwannon or Kannon in Japan) transmitting the Buddha Mind. Wu, dismayed, wished to send after him, but Shiko dissuaded him: how can you seek outside yourself for your own Buddha Nature? How can you send for the Lord Who Is Seen Within?

After Bodhidharma's death, Wu wrote a poem:

> I saw him without seeing, encountered without meeting.
> Now as before, I regret and lament.

Zen Master Setcho, who included this encounter in the eleventh-century koan collection called *Hekigan Roku* (the Blue Cliff Record), commented that Wu, however wise, still saw unclearly, still contaminated the vital nature of this very instant by clinging to the past. "Give up regret!" Master Setcho said. "How limitless is the pure wind circling the earth!"

Here in North America, the Anishinabi (Ojibwa) Indian people had arrived at the same insight:

> Sometimes I go about in pity for myself, and all the while
> A great wind is bearing me across the sky.

Bodhidharma's arrival was followed by four centuries of great Zen prosperity in China, and its establishment in Korea and Japan. But in recent ages, almost everywhere, the Buddha Way had withered in the grasp of its own priesthood, and Master Soyen believed that the time had come for the teachings to travel eastward to the New World. There Emerson and Thoreau, with their transcendentalist movement, had led the way in a wider study of what Emerson called "the wise silence, the universal beauty, to which every part and particle is equally related, the eternal One." Emerson confessed to a "sky-void idealism," in apparent reference to the Mahayana concept of universal "emptiness," the Oneness that includes everything; this sky-void he equated with "the Eternal Buddha." Thoreau, inspired by

10

"my Buddha," wished "to go soon and live away by the pond, where I shall hear only the wind whispering among the reeds. It will be a success if I shall have left my self behind." In this same period, as a muse, perhaps, Gustave Flaubert kept a gold Buddha on his desk.

Soyen Shaku, a fierce, venturesome teacher (of himself, he said, "My heart burns like fire but my eyes are as cold as dead ashes"), went to Ceylon to study Theravada, then represented Zen Buddhism at the World Conference of Religions in Chicago in 1883. From there he proceeded to LaSalle, Illinois, at the invitation of Dr. Paul Carus, author of *The Gospel of Buddha* and more than fifty other books on related topics. Carus was editor of *Open Court*, a leading journal of the day which claimed Bertrand Russell and John Dewey among its contributors. The founder of the Open Court Publishing Company was his father-in-law, Edward Hegeler (my great-grandfather's partner in zinc manufacture), who was keenly interested in ecumenical advances and also in any reconciliation of science and religion, which had parted on bad terms at the time of the industrial revolution. Buddhism, which did *not* depend upon faith in a deity, the supernatural, or the occult, seemed very well suited to these worthy purposes. As Soyen Shaku wrote, "Religion is not to go to God by forsaking the world but to find Him in it. Our faith is to believe in our essential oneness with Him. 'God is in us and we in Him' must be made the most fundamental faith of all religions."

Four years later Soyen Shaku, whose articles on war in *Open Court* were much admired by Count Leo Tolstoy, sent his young disciple Teitaro Suzuki to Illinois to help Carus with his translation of the *Tao Te Ching* as well as with the editing of his magazine. Before leaving Engaku-ji, Suzuki had attained a profound "opening" or enlightenment experience, at which time he was given the Dharma name Dai-Setsu, or "Great Stupidity" (from *setsu*, "unskilled" or "stupid": the sense here is "not-knowing" mind, or free, spontaneous mind, unhindered by concepts and illusions). He used this name for the remainder of his life. In

11

1905 and 1906, during Soyen-roshi's visits to America, Suzuki served as a translator for his lectures; otherwise, he spent eleven years in this small community south of Chicago. Here he began "The Outlines of Mahayana Buddhism," the first of numerous books and articles under the name D. T. Suzuki which would lay the foundation for the spread of Buddhism to the West.

"The Occidentals, as far as I can judge," Soyen Shaku wrote, "seem to be fond of making a full display of all their possessions with the frankness of a child; and they are prone to a strenuous and dissipating life which will soon drain all the nervous force at their command. . . . They are indeed candid and open-hearted—traits which sometimes seem wanting in Orientals. But they certainly lack the unfathomableness of the latter, who never seem to be enthusiastic, clamorous, or irrepressible. . . . Of course, there are exceptions in the West as well as in the East."[2]

In 1905, when Soyen Shaku traveled to San Francisco to give Zen instruction to an American couple who had visited him in Engaku-ji, he was attended by another student, Nyogen Senzaki, who took a job as a servant in that household. This young monk had had a flimsy start in life as a foundling abandoned to the Siberian winter (possibly his real father was Russian), and his Dharma name, Nyo Gen, "As If a Phantasm,"[3] well expressed his notion of himself as a homeless wanderer, "a mushroom without a very deep root, no branches, no flowers, and probably no seed." When he turned up at Engaku-ji in 1896, at the age of twenty, he was very ill from tuberculosis, and he asked Soyen Shaku, "What if I should die?" This teacher of "severe penetrating eyes and stern mouth" advised him, "If you die, just die." Hastening to recover, Nyogen joined life in the monastery, where he shared a room with the young lay student Teitaro Suzuki. After five years of study with Soyen-roshi, he left Engaku-ji in order to found a nursery school. He did not attempt religious instruction of the children, but "guided and watched over them, helping them learn about nature while they were playing."

12

The title of Nyogen's early writings, *A Grass in the Field*, conveys his longing to efface himself, and although Soyen Shaku, in a foreword, strongly supports this "nameless and penniless monk who goes unrecognized both in and out of monasteries, who has only an aspiration for loving-kindness, with which no honored position can compare," he never seems to have acknowledged him as a student, perhaps out of respect for Nyogen's own ideal of rootlessness. In fact, he appears to have met Nyogen's lifelong devotion with something less than loving-kindness, though doubtless the matter was well understood between them. When Nyogen was dismissed from his job as houseboy—he worked hard but was inexperienced and spoke no English—Soyen Shaku escorted him toward a Japanese hotel in San Francisco. While walking through Golden Gate Park, the master came to an abrupt halt, saying, "This may be better for you instead of being hampered as my attendant monk. Just face this great city and see whether it conquers you or you conquer it." Taking his leave, he walked away into the evening; his disciple never saw him again.

After Soyen Shaku's death in 1919, Nyogen commemorated his teacher every year with verses of gratitude. "Thirty years in America I have worked my way to answer him, cultivating a Buddhist field in this strange land," he wrote in 1935, not long after setting up a "floating zendo" in Los Angeles. "This autumn—the same as in the past—I have no crop but the growth of this white hair. . . ." He also wrote, "I was left in America to do something for Buddhism, but my work goes slowly, since I have neither an aggressive spirit . . . nor an attractive character for drawing crowds. If my teacher were still living, he would be disappointed in me."

Nyogen was both strict and outspoken. "Many Americans are currently seeking Truth, visiting classes in philosophy one after another, and studying meditation under various Oriental teachers. But how many of these students are either willing or able to cut through to the tree's very core? Scratching half-heartedly around the surface of the tree, they expect someone

13

else to cut the trunk for them. Such people should stay in church where they belong, praying to the Supreme Being so that It will do their work for them. Zen wants nothing to do with such mollycoddles!" Yet he was convinced that Zen was well suited to the American mind and would prosper in America, which was "fertile ground for Zen," he said, because its philosophy was rational and practical, with ethics rooted in individual morality and a notion of happiness in universal brotherhood. Also, most Americans were optimistic, informal, nature-loving, and—being both practical and efficient—capable of the simple living that lends itself best to sustained Zen practice.[4]

Despite strict avoidance of title, ceremonies, and priestly trappings, Nyogen-sensei (*sensei* means teacher) was revered by his American students. He was the first teacher in America to emphasize zazen, which is not merely sitting "meditation" but a silent training directed toward unification of body, mind, and spirit with the universal consciousness sometimes referred to as Oneness, Zen Mind, Buddha-nature. Zazen had been the foundation of the Buddha's practice. "Dhyana [zazen] strives to make us acquainted with the most concrete and withal the most universal fact of life," Soyen Shaku had written. "It is the philosopher's business to deal with dry, lifeless, uninteresting generalizations. Buddhists are not concerned with things like that. They want to see the fact directly and not through the medium of philosophical abstractions. There may be a god who created heaven and earth, or there may not; we could be saved simply by believing in his goodness, or we could not. . . . True Buddhists do not concern themselves with propositions such as these. . . . Buddhists through dhyana endeavor to reach the bottom of things and there to grasp with their own hands the very life of the universe, which makes the sun rise in the morning, makes the bird cheerfully sing in the balmy spring breeze, and also makes the biped called man hunger for love, righteousness, liberty, truth, and goodness. In dhyana, therefore, there is nothing abstract, nothing dry as a bone and cold as a corpse, but all animation, all activity, and eternal revelation."[5]

But Soyen Shaku gave no zazen instruction to Americans and neither did Sokei-an, a disciple who in the 1930s became the first Zen teacher in New York City. Sokei-an did not believe that Westerners would willingly sit still for an extended period, and he limited his Zen instruction to teisho or talks on the Dharma, and *dokusan*, or "private confrontation" with the teacher.[6] As for D. T. Suzuki, he was primarily a Zen scholar, and while he stressed the significance of the enlightenment experience (in Japanese, *satori* or *kensho*—literally, "seeing into one's own [true] nature"), from which Shakyamuni's teachings had derived, he rarely discussed the zazen training that almost always preceded its attainment.

In 1934, Nyogen-sensei was struck by the quality of verse contributed to one of the numerous Japanese magazines devoted to haiku poetry by a young monk named Soen Nakagawa, who lived as a hermit on Dai Bosatsu Mountain, near Mount Fuji. The two struck up a twenty-year correspondence that was interrupted only by World War II, when Nyogen was interned in a "relocation camp" for American Japanese at Heart Mountain, Wyoming; not until April 8, 1949, did they meet face to face on a pier in San Francisco. Thus Nyogen Senzaki brought about the first visit to America of a man now recognized as one of the great Zen masters of the day and an inspired pioneer in the establishment of Zen practice in the Western world. On this occasion Monk Soen wrote:

> No matter how much I contemplate this tea bowl
> It is still—a tea bowl!
> Thus I arrive in San Francisco.

"The summer breeze from the south has brought two wandering monks to San Francisco," Nyogen said, introducing his friend, then forty-two years old, to a meeting of the Theosophical Society. Soen discussed Soyen Shaku's statement upon *his* arrival in this city, nearly a half century before, that after forty years of studying Buddhism he had only recently begun to understand that "after all, I do not understand anything." This teaching referred to Bodhidharma's "not-knowing," or utterly free, spontaneous mind—called in Tibetan Buddhism "the crazy wisdom —but Monk Soen, understandably misunderstood, was laughed at by a disappointed audience. Quoting from Goethe's *Faust*— "I lead up and down, across, and to and fro my pupils by the nose—and learn that we in truth can nothing know"—Soen explained that this not-knowing was "the point of Zen," the banishment of fleeting and illusory clouds of ideas and emotions in order to reveal the brilliant moon of universal Mind. "Nowadays," he observed in that cryptic, idiosyncratic English that would serve him so well in the New World, "there is no one capable of being dumbfounded."

The following year, when Soen-roshi was installed as abbot of Ryutaku-ji (Dragon-Swamp Temple) under Mount Fuji, several of Nyogen's American students went to the temple to study with him. In the counterculture period after World War II, a number of Americans were interesting themselves in Zen, including the "Beat Zen" of such writers as Allen Ginsberg, Jack Kerouac, and Gary Snyder.[7] There were also the spurious Zen-type teachings of the spiritual hustlers who preyed on the yearnings of love-addled youth throughout the sixties. Ignoring the excellent lessons of Dr. Suzuki (a "Profile" of Dr. Suzuki appeared in *The New Yorker* in August 1957), these people twisted the dramatic teaching methods of the great masters, giving Zen an undeserved reputation for cultish obscurity, wild mystical excess, and eccentricity which plagues it to the present day.[8]

Far from being "eccentric" in any sense, Zen is (as Dr. Suzuki wrote) "the ultimate *fact* of all philosophy. That final psychic fact takes place when religious consciousness is heightened to extremity. Whether it comes to pass in Buddhists, in Christians, or in philosophers, it is in the last analysis incidental to Zen." Indeed, Zen shares its holistic perception of the universe, of "a reality even prior to heaven and earth,"[9] with almost all of mankind's most traditional faiths.

After World War II, Dr. Suzuki had lectured on Buddhism in Hawaii and California, and for some years after 1951, he was a professor at Columbia University in New York City. Already his admirers in Europe included Jung, Heidegger,[10] and Arnold Toynbee (who felt that the transmission of Buddhism to the West would someday be seen as one of the most significant events in history). In the United States, Aldous Huxley, Karen Horney, and Erich Fromm attributed much of their insight to his teachings; his students the composer John Cage and the painter Mark Tobey believed that Zen's influence on their work had been profound. Dr. Suzuki's combination of vast erudition, playfulness, and a serene and gentle manner attracted great interest not only to his classes but to the Zen teachings embodied by his presence, and a Zen Studies Society was set up in New York City to support his efforts.

As Thomas Merton once remarked, "In meeting him one seemed to meet that True Man of No Rank[11] that one really wants to meet. Who else is there? In meeting Dr. Suzuki and drinking a cup of tea with him I felt I had met this one man. It was like finally arriving at one's home." Jack Kerouac, who visited him with Ginsberg, yelled at him, "I would like to spend the rest of my life with you!," to which Dr. Suzuki, holding up one finger, giggled, "Sometime!" In 1959, Suzuki returned to Japan, where he kept a cottage at Engaku-ji and established a comprehensive Buddhist library in his house down the hill in Kamakura.

In 1955, after a half century in America, Nyogen Senzaki had also returned to Engaku-ji, on a pilgrimage to Soyen Shaku's grave, but most of his brief visit to Japan was spent at Ryutaku-ji, where he persuaded Soen-roshi that the future of Zen lay in the West. Three years later, at the age of eighty-two, Nyogen Senzaki died in America. Part of his ashes were sent to Soen-roshi and the rest were buried "in some unknown, uncultivated field. . . . Do not erect a tombstone! The California poppy is tombstone enough. . . . I would like to be like the mushroom in the deep mountains: no flowers, no branches, and no root;

I wish to rot most inconspicuously. . . ."[12] Nyogen Senzaki wished to leave no trace of his passage through this life, but to blow away into eternity, light as the dust of that old brown mushroom in the woods.

Soen-roshi came to Los Angeles for the simple funeral, and subsequently led two memorial sesshins, or intensive training periods—the first full seven-day sesshins ever conducted in America, according to Nyogen's student Robert Aitken (now Aitken-roshi), who served Soen as *jisha*, or attendant. In 1960 Soen sent his disciple the monk Tai-san to help Aitken establish his own zendo in Hawaii, and two years later Soen encouraged a series of sesshins in America led by his friend Hakuun Yasutani-roshi, with whom, at Soen's recommendation, Aitken and an American businessman, Philip Kapleau, had recently been study-ing in Japan.

At seventy-seven, Yasutani was still a strict, powerful teacher who emphasized kensho, or enlightenment experience, and ac-cording to Tai-san, the first sesshin in America (in Hawaii in 1962) was "as hysterical as it was historical." Nevertheless, five students experienced some degree of kensho, and Yasutani's vigorous methods were soon famous among the few Zen students in America, which he visited seven times between 1962 and 1969. (*The Three Pillars of Zen*, edited by Kapleau, is based on his teachings.) On these sesshin journeys his translator and jisha was Tai-san, who remained in New York after 1965 and resur-rected the Zen Studies Society, set up originally to support the work of Dr. Suzuki. Tai-san also established what is now the New York Zendo, with Soen-roshi as honorary abbot. By this time such Rinzai Zen teachers as Joshu Sasaki and Isshu Miura were already established in America, and so were the Soto Zen teachers Taizan Maezumi, Shunryu Suzuki, and Dainin Katagiri. There was also Seung Sa Nim, a Korean Zen master, and Chö-gyam Trungpa, Rinpoche, one of a distinguished company of Tibetan lamas.

Although Yasutani-roshi had come regularly to the United States after 1962 (for a while he intended to come here for good), Soen-roshi's duties as abbot of Ryutaku had kept him in Japan; his visit to America with Yasutani in the summer of 1968 was his first since the funeral of Nyogen Senzaki. Yasutani led a sesshin for Maezumi-sensei's Soto Zen group in Los Angeles, then visited the San Francisco Zen Center's mountain retreat at Tassajara, in the California Coast Range, where Soen spoke about his late friend Nyogen. Subsequently, Yasutani led two sesshins for Tai-san's Rinzai students near New York, where he and Soen would preside at the opening of the New York Zendo a few weeks later (September 15, 1968). The following year, both teachers returned to the United States, where a visit to students on Long Island brought about the first of the encounters with Zen teachers, past and present, which form the heart and marrow of this book.

Gaining enlightenment is like the moon reflecting in the water.
The moon does not get wet, nor is the water disturbed.
Although its light is extensive and great . . .
The whole moon and the whole sky are reflected
in a dew-drop in the grass, in one drop of water.
Enlightenment does not disturb the person,
just as the moon does not disturb the water.
A person does not hinder enlightenment, just as a dew-drop
does not hinder the moon in the sky.
The depth of the drop is the height of the moon.

Actualization of the Koan
—EIHEI DOGEN

CHAPTER TWO

IN mid-November of 1971, Deborah and I attended a weekend sesshin at the New York Zendo. For two months Deborah had been suffering from pains that seemed to resist all diagnosis, and she decided to limit herself to the Sunday sittings. On Saturday evening, meeting me at the door of our apartment, she stood there, smiling, in a new brown dress, but it was not the strange, transparent beauty in her face that took my breath away. I had been in zazen since before daybreak, and my mind was clear, and I saw Death gazing out at me from those wide, dark eyes. There was no mistaking it, and the certainty was so immediate and shocking that I could not greet her. In what she took as observance of sesshin silence, I pushed past quietly into the bathroom, to collect myself in order that I might speak.

On Sunday, Deborah chanced to sit directly opposite my own place in the two long lines of buddha figures that faced each other. During morning service, still resisting what I had perceived the night before, and upset that this day might exhaust her, I chanted for her with such intensity that I "lost" myself, obliterated my *self*—a function of the ten-line *Kannon Sutra*, dedicated to the bodhisattva Avalokiteshvara, which is chanted hard, over and over, thirty-three times, with wood gong and bells, in mounting volume and intensity. At the end, the chanters give one mighty shout of *MU!*—a mantric word corresponding to *Om*, which symbolizes the Absolute, eternity—this followed instantly by a great hush of sudden, ringing silence, as if the universe had stopped to listen. But on this morning, in the near darkness—the altar candle was the only light in the long room—this immense hush swelled and swelled and kept on swelling, as if this "I" were opening out into infinity, in eternal amplification of my buddha being. There was no hallucination, only awe, "I" had vanished and also "I" was everywhere.

Then I let my breath go, gave my self up to immersion in all things, to a joyous *belonging* so overwhelming that tears of relief poured from my eyes. For the first time since unremembered childhood, I was not alone, there was no separate "I." Wounds, anger, ragged edges, hollow places were all gone, all had been healed; my heart was the heart of all creation. *Nothing was needed*, nothing missing, all was already, always, and forever present and forever known. Even Deborah's dying, if that had to be, was perfectly in place. All that day I wept and laughed.

Two weeks later, describing to Tai-san what had happened, I astonished myself (though not my teacher, who merely nodded, making a small bow) by a spontaneous burst of tears and laughter, the tears falling light and free as rain in sunlight.

The state of grace that began that November morning in the New York Zendo prevailed throughout the winter of my wife's dying, an inner calm in which I knew at once what must be done, wasting no energy in indecision or regrets. When I told Tai-san about this readiness and strength, and confessed to a kind of crazy exaltation, he said quietly, "You have transcended." I supposed he meant "transcended the ego," and with it all horror and remorse. As if awakened from a bad dream of the past, I found myself forgiven, not only by Deborah but by myself.

Rohatsu sesshin, commemorating the Buddha's enlightenment, took place in the first eight days of December. The day before sesshin, Deborah entered Roosevelt Hospital for medical tests, and a bone biopsy was performed on December 1; consequently I came and went during the sesshin. On the morning of December 4—the same day that Suzuki-roshi died in San Francisco—I told Tai-san the good news that the biopsy report was negative. I also told him that two weeks earlier, on November 20, in a knowing that was not the same as knowledge, I had perceived that Deborah was dying.

The day after sesshin, with cancer suspected but undiagnosed, I took Deborah home to Sagaponack, where she went straight to bed, exhausted. Within a few days, two small lumps developed under her skin, and on December 14 the local hospital reported metastatic cancer. On December 16, when I told Tai-san the bad news, we sat together a few minutes in dead silence. Then he said quietly, "Oh, Peter," and offered his beautiful red fan as a gift for Deborah. The fan calligraphy, done by Soen-roshi, meant "Going Home."

Deborah was teaching at the New School for Social Research, and brought books with her to Memorial Hospital in New York City. A fortnight later the books were still untouched. Meekly she sewed at a Christmas stocking provided the patients by the recreation staff, and seeing this, I realized for the first time how much the disease and its violent therapy had stunned her.

On Christmas Eve I drove home to Sagaponack to pull together some sort of Christmas for the children. Deborah was to be taken out on Christmas Day by our friend Milly Johnstone and their Cha No Yu (Japanese tea ceremony) master, Hisashi-san. But she felt too weak and sick to go, and the day after Christmas, with Zendo friends—Milly, Tai-san and his wife, Yasuko, and Sheila Curtis—we put together a champagne-and-oyster party in her room, the first good time she had had in weeks and the last celebration of her life. Tai-san honored her fierce sincerity as a Zen student, giving her the Buddhist precepts and a Dharma name. He had brought to the hospital a brown robe for zazen and the bib-like garment known as a *rakusu*, inscribed with the characters Ho Ko (Dharma Light). Sheila gave us a poem by the Japanese poet Chora:

> *I fell in love with the wings of birds*
> *The light of spring on them!*

Under the covers, Ho Ko was already an old woman, her hips and beautiful legs collapsed, black and blue from needles, but she was still lovely when propped up in bed, and she wore her rakusu like a proud child. I watched our friends' faces admiring the brave, calm, smiling woman in the bed. I admired her, too, putting out of my mind those other days when her dying was neither calm nor lovely, those days that no one knew about but the nurses and me.

With the turn of the year, she retreated swiftly, battered insensible by radiation and chemotherapy. I could not ease her pain or fear or loneliness, or enter the half world of shadows closing around her. On January 3 there were serious complications that almost killed her, and by the time her downward progress stabilized again, her mind was disintegrating in feverish mutterings about going on a journey, and the raging paranoia of death fear and too much pain.

Tai-san spoke to me about Soen-roshi's mother, who had died of cancer at Ryutaku-ji without sedation rather than cut off awareness of life and death, but seeing Ho Ko on January 18 for the first time since the Christmas party, he wept and said no more. Like a mad old woman, recognizing no one, anticipating pain, she fought away those who tried to help her. Most of the few people I permitted into the room, remembering an entirely different person, went red in the face or burst into tears at the first sight of her.

Zen students[1] volunteered as nurses, and the presence of

23

Zen people always calmed her, even when she appeared to be lost in coma. The head nurse, dealing with the tense, desperate confrontations between living and dying in the hushed rooms rank with flowers up and down the corridor, told me that in all her years in the cancer ward, she had never known such an atmosphere of support and love. "I don't know what you Zen people do," she said, "but you're doing *something* right." Bending all rules, she taught me to use the mucus respirator to clear my wife's throat when she was strangling, let me sleep in the room overnight and bathe her and carry her on the last diminishing journeys to the toilet, where her weight had to be held above the seat to keep her from crying out in pain. Finally I put a stop to the doctors' obsessive tests and weighing, which were excruciating, humiliating, useless. Deborah's great courage had worn out at last, and she cowered and whined whenever she was lifted. The last tubes were attached, and she never left her bed again.

For the first time in two weeks, I went home to see our little boy. After hours of driving that cold January night, I could not clear my nostrils of the stink of flowers in the cancer ward, the floor shine on that corridor of death. Then a rabbit ran across the frozen country road, in the winter moon. In that instant my head cleared; I was back in life again and ready to deal with whatever I met with when I returned to the city the next day.

Deborah was far away in what the doctors told me was her terminal coma. She would not come to again and would almost certainly be dead in the next few days. But early Wednesday morning, January 20, a nurse rang from the hospital; my wife wished to speak with me on the telephone! I said there must be some mistake, and she said the staff was just as astonished as I was. Then the voice of Deborah as a young child said, "Peter? I have something to tell you. Peter? I'm very very sick! Come right away!" In tears, I ran all the way to the hospital through the daybreak streets, but by the time I arrived she had sunk again into her nether world.

Two days later, at weekend sesshin, I was given a place close to the door so that I could come and go inobtrusively to the hospital. Ordinarily Tai-san remained silent in the first hours of sesshin, as people calmed themselves, but this day he spoke out suddenly, very slowly, in the middle of the first period of sitting. "A few streets away, our beloved sister Ho Ko lies *dying*! The pain of your knees is nothing like the pain of *cancer*! She is still teaching us, still helping us, and by sitting with great concentration—*Mu!*—we will help her to erase her evil karma." After dedicating the sesshin to Ho Ko, Tai-san paused for a long time, then resumed quietly. "Last month, during our Rohatsu sesshin, Suzuki-roshi died of cancer. This month Debby Matthiessen dies of cancer!" Again he paused for long taut seconds. "Who among you . . . will be *next*? Now . . . *sit!*"

Tai-san shouted the words *next* and *sit*; they resounded in the zendo like two cuts of a whip, and the whole place stiffened. Later all present would agree that the sittings that afternoon and evening were the most powerful in memory. At dawn next morning, everyone chanted with furious intensity, ending with a mighty shout of MU! Immediately afterward I went to the hospital, where the bewildered nurses said that my wife was conscious.

Deborah's face was clear and lovely; she smiled softly and said, "I love you," and actually found strength to put her arms around my neck. Tai-san brought Maurine Freedgood, Ruth Lilienthal, and other senior students, still in their robes. Deborah recognized and embraced them all. Happy and radiant in her awakening after three days and nights of torment and delirium, of raving about death and journeys, she blessed everyone with a smile of childlike sweetness, murmuring, "Oh, I love you so!" Later she asked me shyly, "Will I die?," and when I repeated the question—"Will you die?"—to make sure she wished to hear the answer, she nodded without fear and moved gently away from the whole matter, as if to spare me. Next day she was still calm and happy, though less clear, and on Monday morning she smiled at me, whispering, "Peter." Deborah never spoke again, but neither did she return to the wild fear and distress of earlier days. She seemed to be in a blessed state, and

Tai-san wondered if she had not had a spontaneous kensho. That afternoon she returned into the coma, and she died peacefully three nights later, with Tai-san and I holding her cooling hands. After three suspended pauses between breaths, my beautiful wife—how incredible!—made no effort to inhale again. We sat with her for two more hours until her body was removed for autopsy.

To the great annoyance of the mortuary and crematorium attendants, who hurried and chivied us from start to finish, Tai-san and I accompanied Ho Ko right to the oven door of a strange, windowless temple far out in the winter wastes of the huge gray cemetery in Queens. She wore her beads, brown linen robe, and rakusu for the great occasion. Years ago in Paris I said goodbye to my infant son by touching kissed fingers to his forehead, at a small service in the hospital yard conducted by a wine-spotted cleric and two conscripted witnesses, still clutching brooms. But New York law forbids the touching of the deceased by the unlicensed; two gay attendants in tight, broad-shouldered suits hissed like cobras as I put forth my hand. Under their disdainful gaze, as the stretcher slid into the oven, we chanted the Four Vows, as we had done at the moment of her death. Then the iron door rang to on the regal, gray-faced form, reassembled so skillfully after an autopsy that had traced her cancer even to the brain.

We bowed to Ho Ko and departed under a full moon in the old gray sky of New York winter afternoon. By now the foulmouthed mortuary driver had divined that something not so ordinary was in the wind, and was circumspect, asking shy questions, all the way back into the city.

To tell eight-year-old Alex that his mother had died, I took him for a walk on the winter beach. Alex assured me she could not be dead. "If she was dead," he explained, hoping to comfort us, "I would be crying."

In the grayest part of the empty months that followed, my heart was calm and clear, as if all the bad karma of our past together had been dissolved on that early morning of November.

Toward that experience that prepared me for my wife's death I was filled with gratitude, which had nothing to do with the thankfulness I felt toward Tai-san and our Zen community, toward kind family and friends and children. I could scarcely feel grateful to *myself*, yet there it was: where could that Buddha-self reside if not in my own being? Chanting the *Kannon Sutra* with such fury, I had invoked Avalokiteshvara Bodhisattva, but I paid no attention to the words. All energy was concentrated upon Deborah, who sat in the line of buddha forms across the way. Avalokiteshvara was also Deborah, also myself—in short, what Meister Eckhart meant: "The eye with which I see God is the Eye with which God sees me." Or Jesus Christ: "I and my Father are one." Surely those Christian mystics spoke of the Lord Who Is Seen Within.

Almost another year had passed before something said by an older student made me realize what must have happened. At dokusan, Tai-san confirmed it. But an opening or kensho is no measure of enlightenment, since an insight into one's "true nature" varies widely in its depth and permanence. Some may overturn existence, while others are mere fragmentary glimpses that "like a mist will surely disappear." To poke a finger through the wall is not enough—the whole wall must be brought down with a crash! The opening had been premature, and its power seeped away, month after month. This saddened me, although I understood that I had scarcely started on the path; that but for Deb's crisis, which had cut through forty years of cynicism and defensive encrustations, I might never have had such an experience; that that small opening was very far from great enlightenment, *dai kensho*, in which the self dissolves without a trace into the One.

February sesshin, a few weeks later, was dedicated to Ho Ko, whose bones and photograph shared the altar with fat white carnations. At morning service on the second day, Tai-san repeated the dedication to Deborah, after which the sangha—the community of Buddhist followers—chanted the *Kannon Sutra*

27

thirty-three times with mounting intensity, followed by the shouted MU! Because this was dawn of a Sunday morning, great care had been taken to shut all doors so as not to rouse the neighborhood against weird Zen practices. There was no draft whatever in the windowless room, where the service candle always burned without a tremor. But this morning, in the ringing hush that falls after such chanting, the candle suddenly flared wild and bright, remaining that way for at least ten seconds before diminishing once more to its normal state.

Don Scanlon, sitting near the altar, had always been incorrigibly curious and missed nothing, but later, when I whispered to him about the candle, he assured me that I was going nuts. Discovering that no one else had seen that flaring, I realized that Don must be right. But at dokusan, when I said I was disturbed by something that occurred after the shouted Mu, Taisan nodded and smiled before I could finish. "The candle," he murmured. We gazed at each other and said nothing more.

In March, 1972, the first Dai Bosatsu sesshin was held in the old lodge on Beecher Lake. In the small upstairs zendo, the Buddha silhouette was black against the brilliant winter pane; the woods sparkled with snow blossoms of ice and sun. During this week, using a pick-axe, I dug a hole at the foot of a lichened boulder in the wild meadow, and on the last day of sesshin, in a ceremony that consecrated the new graveyard, a lovely urn containing half of Ho Ko's bones became the first ever interred in what is now the "sangha meadow" at Dai Bosatsu. (Marsha Feinhandler, who had made the urn, said she had felt the clay breathing in her hands—a nice experience!) I covered the hole with a small capstone, then a large flat stone, and scattered pine boughs over the fresh earth. By the time those boughs rotted, there would be no trace of Deborah Love's return into the earth.

The remaining bones went home to Sagaponack, where on May 4, with Alex, I dug a grave in the old cemetery, choosing a spot where a robin had left a wild blue egg in the spring grass.

Together we planted the grave with heath and marigold. All day it had been very dark, but as we finished, a bright storm light illumined the pale chickweed blossoms scattered like light snow in the cemetery. On the spring wind, the winter geese were restless; an indigo bunting came to the copper leaves of an old cherry. I went for a long walk along the dunes.

On May 6, Tai-san arived with his Dharma brothers Do-san and Dokyu-san (now Kyudo-roshi) and a few Zen students. My four children participated in the simple service, taking turns tossing earth into the hole. (Alex said, "I liked the shoveling the best! It made me feel just like a workman!" He was later observed showing his mother's grave to friends, his arm slung companionably around the headstone.) In the afternoon we went clamming in Northwest Harbor. On no occasion before or since have I seen Tai-san so relaxed and joyful as he was that day, digging clams with his brother monks from Ryutaku-ji. Later that year he would receive from his teacher *inka*, or "seal of approval," and already Soen referred to him as Eido-shi, which is short for Eido-roshi.

We celebrated something at our seafood supper. Tai-san said to me quietly, "So . . . it's over now," but of course it wasn't. Still clinging, I had saved out a brown bit of bone, which I taped to Ho Ko's small memorial plaque in our small zendo. The following week, grief took me by surprise during Ozu's great film, *Tokyo Story*, when the old country people, packed off to a garish and noisy modern seashore hotel for their vacation when they attempt to visit their married children in Tokyo, agree shyly that they are homesick for their country village.

> Here I am in Sagaponack,
> Yet my heart longs for Sagaponack.

Just understand that birth and death itself is nirvana, and you will neither hate one as being birth and death nor cherish the other as being nirvana. Only then can you be free of birth and death.

This present birth and death is the life of Buddha. If you reject it with distaste, you are thereby losing the life of Buddha. If you abide in it, attaching to birth and death, you also lose the life of Buddha. But do not try to gauge it with your mind or speak it with words. When you simply release and forget both your body and your mind and throw yourself into the house of Buddha, then with no strength needed and no thought expended, freed from birth and death, you become Buddha. Then there can be no obstacle in any man's mind.

There is an extremely easy way to become Buddha. Refraining from all evil, not clinging to birth and death, working in deep compassion for all sentient beings, respecting those over you and pitying those below you, without any detesting or desiring, worrying or lamentation—this is what is called Buddha. Do not search beyond it.

Birth and Death
—EIHEI DOGEN

CHAPTER THREE

IN the summer of 1972, Soen-roshi came back to America and led a "week's holiday, the best sesshin now taking place in world!" at the Catholic retreat house in Litchfield, Connecticut. He was accompanied by the bamboo flute master Watazumi-sensei, who played every morning and evening in the zendo. In "Mind and Moon," the flute drew forth a rough, wild wind, then a tree and a bamboo stalk in the wind, then calm as the crickets sang with him in the long twilight. A white moth came, just at dusk, to tighten the shadows in front of my black cushion.

Watazumi-sensei spoke about the similarity of flute music and Zen as manifestations of true self. Since he usually practiced alone, even in secret, his playing was to be considered not as a musical performance but as an expression of the Buddha-nature all around us. To coax his instrument to fulfill itself as it had in "Mind and Moon," he said, required seventeen years—a Zen lesson, since almost all his efforts went unheard, and since he had found no student able to succeed him. We were fortunate to hear such a great master's flute, Soen-roshi said, because few of the master's own students had ever heard him play.

At dokusan, the Roshi bowed and said, "Eido-shi told me about your wife. It is all right. You live near ocean . . . the waves come and go, but the ocean is still there, You die, I die"—we smiled, nodded, and bowed—"it is all right, too. The ocean is still there."

In his first teisho, Soen-roshi spoke of "coming and passing, passing and coming, the pure wind, ho-o-o-o-o!" He urged us to "*truly* hear the crickets; that is the same as doing zazen." And later, during walking meditation, he instructed us to chant this *Ho* (Dharma) that is chanted by the monks of Ryutaku-ji, walking the roads with *takuhatsu* bowls, receiving offerings. Our voices rose shy and soft at first, then louder and wilder as people dropped their masks and let anger and pain and grief and laughter flow.

Soen-roshi talked about driving to sesshin in California, and an ancient auto running out of gas in open country, and the whole group chanting the *Kannon Sutra*, over and over, empowering the car to go on for mile after mile on an empty tank, refusing to quit until just the moment that it coasted into an Enco station. "In Japan, this word *enko* means 'out of commission,' as in no gas, car breakdown—won-derful? But even if car had stopped too soon, it is *still* won-derful practice, everybody doing *Kanzeon* together, nobody mad at the driver. Every day there is such a situation in our life."

The Roshi had come by car across the country, visiting the Grand Canyon ("Perhaps this is the first time tea has been offered to Grand Canyon? Next morning we went to a certain point to watch the sun come up; I shed a tear") and Yellowstone Hot Springs ("Chauffeur say it is against American rules, but Eido-shi became naked, drived in, and I and Do-san drived in too, won-derful! And finally driver drived in too!"). He was delighted by a night-blooming cereus in the zendo that blossomed in the dusk and was dead by morning; he jumped up on the windowsills in celebration of its death and life. "Life and death are the same! Only the words are different! Cereus not so-called beautiful! Not so-called ugly! Those are just *words*! Cereus comes from universe, you come from universe, all comes from universe—clouds, sky, fire, rain, stone, self! Flower reflect something beautiful in *you*!"

Soen-roshi has written:

> All are nothing but flowers
> In a flowering universe.

All week the Roshi shimmered and danced with a wild joy that pervaded the dokusan room ("When you are happy at do-kusan, I wish only to dance with you!") and his teisho, too. *Tei* means "to carry," *sho* "to declare." According to Soen's teacher, Yamamoto Gempo-roshi, teisho only occurs when the teacher can carry and declare the essence of the Buddha Dharma in a live, direct way, without the "dead" explanations and analysis of the ordinary lecture. Soen-roshi spoke highly of the great Chinese master Joshu, whose famous "MU!" (in answer to the monk's question "Does the dog have Buddha-nature?") has been used since the ninth century as a teaching word, a mantric equivalent of Mind or Buddha-nature, of the universal essence, before heaven and earth. ("This is Joshu, of that terri-bell story. Let us *kill* such a dog!") Even those not working on this classic koan were fiercely exhorted to concentrate on Mu with every breath, in and out of the zendo. "To call it Mu is to violate its unnameable nature, yet . . . inhale this universal essence: MU! Exhale the self into the universe: MU!"

"When you are in airplane, do not read a magazine! Look out! Won-derful! Everything is very important, in any event, in any moment, everything this MU! Everything is right-here-now! We are all Buddhas, all bodhisattvas, all mis-er-robble creatures—away with this mis-er-robble word *kensho*! If I wish to be a thief, I just steal! If I wish to be a buddha, I just *do* it! *Be* the Buddha! No need to be so serious. Be light, light, light—full of light!"

At dark, Soen-roshi leads us outside, points at Orion; he loves to celebrate the night and sun and water. "Swallow the stars," he murmurs, "until you are one with the universe, with all pervading universal life!"

At dawn sitting, I imagine myself a deer in the early woods. The hard autumn bell note of a blue jay tingles the hairs of the deer's dew-silvered hide, its steps are crisp and sure yet soundless in the leaves. Such images help concentrate my breathing, make me taut and aware. Later they will fall away like armatures, like scaffolding, I will not need them. At dokusan, I ask Soen-roshi if it is all right to use such devices, or should I struggle to empty out my mind? He says it is all right: "There is no such thing as 'empty mind.' There is only *present* mind."

I bow, expecting him to ring the bell, but he says quietly, "Coming across the country, I thought of won-derful Dharma name—I Shin. One Mind. Uni-versal Mind. Won-derful name! Say it!" (I say it: I Shin!) "I asked Eido-shi who should receive it, and he said nothing. But last night we talked again, and we decided it will be given to you." Unaccountably, my eyes mist. I do a full bow, leave the room as the roshi sits smiling in the sunlight.

At rest period I walk in the pine woods and meadows, in the breath of chickory and early aster, hot summer goldenrod. Everything seems perfectly in place, just-as-it-is, precisely "right," as in Deborah's favorite Zen expression, "No snowflake falls in an inappropriate place."

I litter these notebooks with small verse:

> *Crows plotting in hot August woods:*
> *Caw! Caw!*
> *Who is It?*

On the final morning of sesshin, the white moth visited me on my black cushion, fluttering against my head to focus my attention. I ran lightly up the stairs for my last dokusan with Soen-roshi. He met me on the landing, grabbed me, spun me, and pointed through the window at the rising sun, roaring like fire through a tall black burning pine. I glimpse Who-it-is who has glimpsed that long-lost home, and the healing tears stream down my face, in the overwhelming clarity and simplicity of this moment. A hard-eyed man who, not so long ago, had scarcely wept for twenty years wept throughout the sitting, the tears alternating with delicious silent laughter. At breakfast I got laughing so hard that I had to stop eating and bite my lip to avoid unraveling the strong sesshin atmosphere for others.

In the midmorning sittings, I become a sapling pine, warmed by the sun, swaying in wind, inhaling wind, water, minerals, exhaling warm, fragrant amber resin. Tough roots budge subterranean rock, the trunk expands, sinewy limbs gather in sunlight far above, new needles shining in new sun, new wind, until the great pine is immovable, yet flexible and live, the taproot boring ever deeper into the earth. Then the tree evaporates, and there is nothing, and nothing missing, only emptiness and light.

"Be light, light, light," whispers Soen-roshi. "Full of light."

Somewhere far off in a golden haze, the roshi is saying, "So this is not 'last day,' it is everlasting day, beginning day."

Sesshin ended with a purification service and a talk on the ten Buddhist precepts, which resemble the Ten Commandments. "Sesshin is nothing else but purification," Soen-roshi said. "The best zazen is our everyday life, which cannot be spent on a black cushion. Listen to people. Do not talk too much about your wonderful experience in sesshin; perhaps it will show in your behavior, your presence."

I try to confine my "wonderful experience" to these journals, but so far as I can tell, this experience has done nothing at all to alter my old patterns of what the Purification Gatha calls "greed, anger, and folly." However, my children claim to detect a difference, and perhaps without the purification of sesshin, I might have stiffened into place like an old barnacle, winter already in my heart.

In early September of 1972, Shimano Eido-roshi was installed as abbot of New York's Shobo-ji and also of International Dai Bosatsu Zendo, in impressive ceremonies led by Soen-roshi, who had given up the abbotship of Ryutaku-ji to come to America as honorary founder of these temples. Among his attendants was a young Soto Zen teacher from Los Angeles, Maezumi-sensei. In this period, the ground for the new monastery was broken on a forest hillside overlooking Beecher Lake.

With the wistful light of Indian Summer days, the blowing milkweed silk and silent silver crows, came loneliness. On the first day of fall Soen-roshi came to Sagaponack with Eido-shi and a small group of Zen students to hold a memorial service for Ho Ko in the little tearoom zendo that she had created upstairs. At supper he gave me a shiny plum pit like varnished wood with the *Kannon Sutra* inscribed on it in tiny characters. At dawn next day he held another service. When we visited Ho Ko's grave in the old cemetery, three swans flew over with whistling wings as he gave the blessing.

That morning the roshi laid out his scroll paper, ink, and brush on the living room floor. Instructing us to chant, he gathered himself for a long time, then uttered a cry and flew at the paper, creating in seconds a wonderful Mu calligraphy for the upstairs zendo. Afterward, to relieve the pressure, he drank off a jigger of every liquor in the house. "You must not discriminate," he warned us, addressing himself bravely to the last one, an exceedingly bitter aperitif best saved for hangovers. "This animal does not understand me," Soen-roshi said, his invisible eyebrows raised in alarm on his high forehead. But since waste offended him, he instantly dipped his finger into the jigger glass and used the dark stuff as ink, drawing a smiling face on a *shikishi*—a stiff card used for calligraphy—with a masterly flourish

35

and inscribing it "Before Christ, Before Buddha." He then bowed to this useful substance and signed the shikishi with the last of it.

At a ceremony before October sesshin, Eido-shi gave me the Buddhist precepts and a rakusu with a calligraphy of my Dharma name, I Shin. I was proud to wear a rakusu, but after a few sittings I took it off. I had been a Zen student for only one year, whereas Deborah had been a sincere practitioner for five years before receiving the precepts a few weeks before her death. I had not earned lay ordination, being so scattered, so far from the condition of "One Mind."

At dokusan, Eido-shi asked sharply why I wore no rakusu, and I reminded him of what he had told us in teisho of his own recent status as a roshi, forced on him early, so he said, by Soen-roshi because of his status as temple abbot and Zen teacher here in New York. Though he had completed koan study several years before, he had not felt ready to receive inka, or seal of approval, as a "senior teacher." While Nyogen Senzaki had been a "true-ue-ue roshi!" without ever receiving inka from a recognized teacher, he considered himself still "a technical roshi," a "yellow-green-apple roshi," who one day hoped to become mature and red.

How often this man had disarmed us with humility just when we thought him arrogant and egotistical! But after the first of the year, he said, he would answer no longer to "Tai-san"; he is now Eido-shi or Eido-roshi. Yellow-green or not, he has seemed very well since receiving inka, more gentle, more humorous, less autocratic, and somehow more spiritual into the bargain, though no doubt the mirror would be polished more before he attained the transparent aura of his teachers.

Nodding, he tells me to wear my rakusu when I am ready, and I put it away.

Going home on Saturday night of November sesshin, I felt a presence, as if Deborah might open the door as she had the year before, on the mid-sesshin night when I knew that she was dying. Inside, the presence was much stronger, and soon, al-

36

though the lights were on, a suffused glow approached the bed-side and remained there for some time. There was nothing scary here, but on the contrary, something gentle and approving. I invited Deb to manifest herself, convey a message, but she did not. The light withdrew from the bedside, then vanished, and this "dream" of her presence, if that is what it was, never came again.[1]

Once a monk asked, "I hear you have said All the universe is one bright pearl. How can I gain an understanding of that?" The master said, "All the universe is one bright pearl. What need is there to understand it?"

One bright pearl is able to express reality without naming it, and we can recognize this pearl as its name. One bright pearl communicates directly through all time. . . . While there is a body now, a mind now, they are the bright pearl. That stalk of grass, this tree, is not a stalk of grass, is not a tree; the mountains and rivers of this world are not the mountains and rivers of this world. They are the bright pearl.

Being essentially unobscured from first to last, the pearl is the original face and the enlightened eye. . . . Therefore the reality and beginninglessness of the bright pearl are beyond grasp. All the universe is one bright pearl—we do not speak of two pearls or three pearls. . . . Your whole body is a radiant light. Your whole body is Mind in its totality. . . your whole body knows no hindrance. Everywhere is round, round, turning over and over. . . .

One Bright Pearl
—EIHEI DOGEN

CHAPTER FOUR

IN the winter of 1972/1973, in New York, then Dai Bosatsu, Eido-roshi led two arduous winter sesshins. In Japan, Rinzai students sit day and night for the full eight or ten days of Rohatsu, although they are permitted to doze on their cushions between 1:00 and 3:00 A.M. Our American schedule is much less strict, though we sit in zazen fourteen hours a day, not counting meals, on our black cushions in the zendo. Each afternoon we recite from the *Diamond Sutra*. Each evening at 6:30, Monk Do-san reads from the *Hakuin Jishu*, the zazen exhortations of the great Rinzai master Hakuin Ekaku, who was honorary founder of Ryu-taku-ji in the same way that Soen-roshi is honorary founder of his disciple's temples in America. Eido-shi's teisho are based on *The Iron Flute*—an upside-down iron flute without holes or mouthpiece, which one plays as a mosquito bites an iron bull. (Both images are Zen metaphors for the vain attempt to "solve" the secret of our existence with logic.)

At morning service, in dim candlelight, we chant thirty-three fierce *Kanzeons* and bellow MU! as Eido-shi goes up and down the lines, yelling, "Louder! Louder!" The black-robed silhouette with its upraised stick dances on the walls; he whacks our shoulders with his *keisaku* (the flat-bladed "warning stick" used to offset stiffness and sleepiness and urge the student on).

In dawn zazen, I get concentrated quickly by becoming an eagle on a mountain ridge, entirely alert and full of its own eagle-ness. Blood traces on leg feathers and gleaming talons, wind lifting dark plumes as the fierce head turns downwind, gold eye fixed on the first streak of dawn on the ridge horizon. . . . And gradually breathing subsides, becomes "natural," until I subsist on sips of air, and all is still. With this altered state, breathing takes over, the universe takes over. In a rush of immanence comes the *knowing* that everything-is-right-here-now, there is nothing outside this present moment. At the same time this "everything" is gathering, "something" is happening—

"Sit still!"

Eido-shi shouts this at a restless student, and whatever this "something" was withdraws. I am high, with a racing heart, for the next three days. I feel like a tuning fork about to be struck, like a diamond at the point of shattering. At the same time I am easy and loose, untroubled by noise, distractions, even pain. There is only this calm tautness, this soft intensity, this wild imminence of immanence with every breath. At dokusan, accepting my koan answer, Eido-shi smites me with his keisaku to urge me on, then touches his own forehead to the ground.

In teisho, he speaks of the *Diamond Sutra* scholar who is refused cake in an inn until he answers an old woman's question: If, as you say, past, present, and future cannot be grasped, which one do you eat your cake in? Assigned this question as a koan, I exclaim rudely at next dokusan, "Away with such stale cake!" Eido-shi laughs, and spontaneously we chew a little while on the fresh cake of this *now*, regarding each other in silent confrontation. "It's good, is it not?" he says at last. For the rest of the day, in happy tears again, I am filled with gratitude, and not simply to the teacher: *who* is this who is grateful here, and to whom, for what?

Next day in the zendo I am flat, a little sad; I had felt so close, and now feel far away. Eido-shi parodies the master's reprimand from *The Iron Flute*: "Your hair is getting white and your teeth sparse, and *still* you tell me that one day your practice is wonderful, the next day terrible?" He bursts out laughing, and I do, too, but sadness lingers all the same.

This winter's second Rohatsu sesshin, at Dai Bosatsu, is the anniversary of the last week of Ho Ko's life. It is warm January weather, and with Merete Galesi I walk the two miles uphill to the snowfield at Beecher Lake. There Don and Marsha, who gave eulogies to Ho Ko at the memorial service less than a year ago, are paying respects at her boulder gravestone. We chant together, under a daylight moon. Later I build a small snow Buddha on the boulder, then return to the road bridge over the stream which pours down to the Beaverkill and watch the mist and snow return into Beecher Lake.

> *Night mists cross the moon shadow on the white lake.*
> *You speak of Mu?*

Eido-shi continues teisho from *The Iron Flute*. He also quotes the wonderful haiku of the great poet Basho, who is much admired by Soen-roshi. " 'There is no one on this road but me this autumn evening.' Seen one way, this is true of Zen. You are alone. The zazen is yours, the pain is yours, the attainment is yours. I am your guide to the mountain peak, but you must walk up there on your own legs."

Basho again: "'The cicada's voice: no intimation of mortality.' The cicada knows no death, no haiku, nothing but *b-z-z-z*! Nothing but Mu! The purpose of Zen is to be a cicada! Every exhalation, *b-z-z-z*! Every exhalation Mu! So-called quiet sitting is not enough—stone Buddhas can do that! It must be *live* zazen!"

Dark, blowing clouds of snow over the mountain, and a snowy sunlight in the skeletal hickories—how do you like these common miracles!

The winter thunder is the budge of the lake ice, in winter thaw. On the fourth day I am deep into sesshin, letting everything go, welcoming pain, in what Soen-roshi calls "diamond-hard pain *samadhi*." One evening I am inspired to sit through supper, and am deep in profound zazen when Bruce R. comes bounding back upstairs, hunting his eating bowls. People downstairs eating sensible supper, and here I am, poor foolish Zen student, seeking the Absolute! Eating and the Absolute!—not different! I laugh out loud, jump up, and go down to supper, then run out through the night woods, hollering MU! At dokusan, Eido-shi warns me, "Pain and Mu are very good, but it is possible to be too intense, to expect too much."

In teisho next morning, Eido-shi spoke of the head monk at a Tokyo temple who remained there thirteen years without an absence, so immersed was he in the koan Mu. Seeing him sweeping leaves in the temple cemetery, Eido-shi had been moved by his beauty of demeanor and was astonished when the old man said he had never had kensho. What is better, Eido-shi demanded, a superficial kensho after a few months of sitting, or this moment-by-moment enlightenment in everyday life?

And yet, he said, urging us on, Zen cannot be truly apprehended without kensho.

I vowed to myself for the hundredth time that I would burst the iron wall of "self," through moment-by-moment emptying of mind. But I could not stifle my "monkey mind" and was exasperated with myself—who is this idler, thinking about Mu, not *becoming* Mu? Then a load of melting ice fell off the roof with a loud crash, startling me so that I had to fight not to burst out laughing. So exhilarated was I that I sat in full lotus through two periods without moving my legs, using the pain to focus my breath-body-mind to a shimmering point. Somebody else was panting with pain, and I said to myself, Give me your pain too!, and my own pain vanished.

When I finally stand, no wiser than before, the pain unravels with such violence that, during walking meditation (*kinhin*), my teeth are chattering. Even lying down in rest period, my knees hurt. Then I open this notebook to set down my folly, and my child's photograph drops onto the bed—just . . . Alex! Nothing in the world but . . . ALEX! It is as if dark glasses had been snapped away. So startled am I that I burst out with a great laugh, awakening monks Don and Bruce. Silly idiot, cracking his knees off for a glimpse of "truth," and here is truth smiling up at him from his own bed! ("Not knowing how near the truth is, we seek it far away," Hakuin says in *The Song of Zazen*.) Something has fallen into place, though I can't think what. In the next sitting, I perceive Eido-shi as an old man, as a young boy, and as he is right now, all in an instant.

In a winter evening full of storm and significations, I run swiftly down the long woods road. I am leery of night graves and make my way in excited trepidation through the rough field to the rock that rises up against the dark wall of the pines. I ask Deborah to manifest her presence, as she has before, but not to scare me. However, I can sense no presence, the night rock is the night rock, nothing more. Or perhaps I am no longer open to her, for I never had a sign again.

I walk alone on the night road, dark clouds rushing overhead. Each night, each day, the mountain weather, changing. By morning there is light snow, followed by blizzard.

Zendo stillness: to be aware without being aware of it, like the eagle on the peak, like the wary deer, like the Zen monk who is "just sitting" in *shikan-taza*. At dokusan, straightening after my bows, I am transfixed in confrontation with Eido-roshi. For minutes we gaze into each other's eyes, unblinking, and finally he whispers, "So-o-o . . . You know what zazen is." I nod, saying how foolish I now feel about all my big talk of "samadhi" in the past. (In early Zen practice, if one sits hard, one is soon so full of clarity and power that one imagines one is doing shikan-taza, that profound samadhi has already been attained.) "Still," he murmurs, "you had a taste of it today." When I ask how he knows, he smiles. "I know. Your bearing, how you make your bows. Your face."

At March sesshin at Dai Bosatsu, Eido-shi spoke of Yasu-tani-roshi. ("Sitting in solitude like a mountain—this alone is required," Yasutani used to say.) On that same day, March 28, 1973, although Eido-shi would not know it until after sesshin, Hakuun Yasutani, aged eighty-nine, died in Japan.

"The mind of a buddha," Yasutani once said, "is like water that is calm, deep, and crystal clear, and upon which 'the moon of truth' reflects fully and perfectly. The mind of the ordinary man, on the other hand, is like murky water, constantly being churned by the gales of delusive thought and no longer able to reflect the moon of truth. The moon nonetheless shines steadily upon the waves, but as the waters are roiled, we are unable to see its reflection. Thus we lead lives that are frustrating and meaningless. . . .

"So long as the winds of thought continue to disturb the water of our Self-nature, we cannot distinguish truth from un-truth. It is imperative, therefore, that these winds be stilled. Once they abate, the waves subside, the muddiness clears, and we perceive directly that the moon of truth has never ceased shining. The moment of such realization is kensho, enlighten-ment, the apprehension of the true substance of our Self-nature. Unlike moral and philosophical concepts, which are variable, true Insight is imperishable."[1]

At daylight and dusk the hollow tokking of the wood block, or *han*, urges the student to clarify this great matter of life and

43

death: Be diligent (*tok*), be diligent (*tok*), for life is passing (*tok, tok, tok, tok, tok*) very, very fast.

After three days, my breath is natural like the deep breathing of the sea, the wave washing softly up the beach, and washing back, more and more softly, more and more minute, scarcely breathing at all, like a hibernating lizard under a desert rock. Then, in the great stillness, I am no longer breathing, I am being breathed. "That is your natural mind," Eido-shi murmurs, "that we have lost and is so hard to find again." A luminosity, sunlight and gold, a round, light, golden buddha, all mortality gone. What was "I" is now transparent, now invisible. "I" is nothing but soft tears, soft laughter, "I" knows no longer who is weeping, laughing, as birdsong, light, and bells come pouring through.

A tree frog or "spring peeper" has replaced the white moth as my sentinel. It bounces down the silent row of bodhisattvas, bounces back again with a minute *pum, pum, pum*, seeking the dark. Where is the door to Zen? Do you hear the peeping of a tree frog? Begin there! Or there! Or there! (Shunryu Suzuki-roshi said, If you have truly understood a frog, you have understood everything.) Zen is life, each moment of our life, thus Zen is everywhere.

Lao Tzu said, When your mind is empty like a valley or a canyon, *then* you will know the power of the Way. A Zen master says, How can I fill your cup until you empty it? In zazen, one opens to this emptiness, to the great stillness of our true nature, which is also the foundation of the universe. Then pure tears fall in utter relief at finding the way home.

The zazen of even one person at one moment invisibly accords with all things and fully resonates through all time. Thus in the past, future and present of the limitless universe this zazen carries on the buddha's teaching endlessly. Each moment of zazen is equally wholeness of practice, wholeness of realization.

This is not only practice while sitting, but it is like a hammer striking emptiness—before and after, its exquisite peal permeates everywhere. How can it be limited to this moment? . . .

Sit zazen wholeheartedly . . . letting all things go. Then you will go beyond the boundary of delusion and enlightenment, and being apart from the paths of the ordinary and sacred, immediately wander freely outside ordinary thinking, enriched with great enlightenment. If you do this, how can those who are concerned with the fish trap or hunting net of words and letters be compared with you?

On the Clarification of the Way
—EIHEI DOGEN

CHAPTER FIVE

AT a memorial service in New York on April 9, 1973, Eido-shi would reflect that he had been thinking about his old teacher throughout March sesshin. Due to "karmic relations," he believed he had spoken of Yasutani on the day he died. Today he read one of Yasutani's poems, which for me recalled a summer morning of 1969 and an old man with big ears and wide eyes observing me calmly from the back seat of a car: this was the only time I ever saw him.

> *Year after year, year after year.*
> *And yet I like to fly above the clouds*

I am only skin and bones, like an old crane.

In June 1973, with Don, Merete, and two other students, I traveled abroad for sesshin with Soen-roshi at Ryutaku-ji. Powerful as that sesshin was, it did not seem to me I had made much progress as a Zen student, and at August sesshin at Dai Bosatsu, I discussed with Eido-shi the fact that recent sesshins had been mostly "flat" and uneventful, with little of the tears, laughter, and small miracles of earlier sesshins. He replied that sesshin phenomena tended to diminish after a time, even as sesshin effects became more profound, and warned me again that perhaps I was too anxious for "progress." I asked about greed as opposed to zeal, and he said that desire of attainment was only greedy when it impinged on others, whereas zeal was never entirely selfless. To be emancipated from the idea of enlightenment, he said, took a long time, and that was the true enlightenment. He told me to keep deepening my samadhi, expecting nothing.

> *No coming and no going.*
> *Just at dark,*
> *A white moth comes to my black cushion,*
> *Goes.*

In the next sittings, I gave up "forcing" Mu. Gradually my zazen cleared, until it seemed clear, clear, clear and effortless, absorbing and yet reflecting everything, abiding nowhere. Whoever it is who sits here on this cushion, at the very center of a sphere of light that fills the sunny room to bursting, is not separable from the pain, the cooking smells, the insect ringing. During kinhin on the grass, the refreshing tears of the early days returned, as light came glancing from the hard wing of a crow across the lake, and once again the husk of intellect opened outward. The following day, in celebration, I wore my rakusu for the first time.

Despite the general calm of August sesshin, I had no feeling of disappointment—a common experience when the "miraculous" early sesshins that characterize the beginning of Zen practice fail to culminate in an opening or kensho.

> Slap!—*the beaver's tail*
> *casting circles on the black lake.*
> *Deep mountain stillness.*

In November I traveled to India and Nepal, a pilgrimage to Bodh Gaya where Shakyamuni had attained enlightenment, and a two-hundred-mile trek across high passes of the Himalaya to the Crystal Monastery, an ancient Buddhist shrine on the Tibetan Plateau. Eido-shi gave me a new koan for the journey: All the peaks are covered with snow—why is this one bare? One Zen master, he said, had achieved great enlightenment after five years of intense struggle with this koan.

The journey across the Himalaya was full of astonishment and wonder, but the year that followed—1974—was a very dark one. Eido-shi had sent me off with the instruction "Expect *nothing*," but failing to heed him, or unable to do so, I had clung to the hope that the great clarity and insights of hard snow mountain samadhi would culminate in a profound enlightenment. When this failed to occur, I was cast down. I resumed fierce attendance at every sesshin, although I had a young child at home and lived one hundred miles out of the city. I also continued with tea lessons at the Urasenke Tea School in New York. But my spirits wandered in some low, dark place, especially after the news came that my older son, Luke, was a victim of an incurable eye disease that might one day blind him. I went through the vague, dim motions of my life, like a sick bird.

In February 1974, Soen-roshi came to America by sea, escorted by Eido-shi from Yokohama to Seattle (where they met a man who had known Nyogen Senzaki and Soen in 1949, in Los Angeles, and who had named his son Zen in commemoration). In February sesshin at the New York zendo, I resumed koan study with Soen-roshi, who also gave teisho. Soen disliked

the self-conscious spirituality, "the stink of Zen," that he thought
he detected in the sesshin participants, and his most inspired
teaching was to hang out his long underwear in the small stone
garden, in secret, to startle us into imagining that an outrage
against the teacher had been committed. (On another occasion,
he put a large pumpkin on the roshi's cushion in the dokusan
room, then hid behind the door, snickering wickedly as earnest
students prostrated themselves before the pumpkin, only to hear
the laughter of the bell that ended their "confrontation with
the roshi" and sent them packing back downstairs to their black
cushions.)

In March 1974, Soen-roshi leads his first sesshin at Dai
Bosatsu. It is still winter, and in the woods that shut away the
outside world, the snow is thick. It falls in darkness as sesshin
begins, to shroud the past and purify the world. But by morning
the mountain weather has changed and the white ice of the lake
sparkles in sun.

Deer tracks lead through the white woods to the bronze
statue of the Buddha; an owl hoots at the north end of the pond.

> *Owl on a snow-thick limb*
> *shifting soft feathers.*
> *Snow falls on snow.*

In the evening rest, I go to the south meadow and stand
before Deborah's boulder. On the frozen road come footsteps,
and in the late winter sun—the days are longer now—I am
joined by Soen-roshi, in thin robes and low black shoes that fill
with snow. Is this where Debbo-lah is buried? I nod. We chant
there, in the silence of the mountain. Then we retrace our
footsteps to the road and, standing on the bridge over the dam,
chant again into the winter sun, low in the trees. Then the
roshi returns along the road, a small brown figure, the lone
monk of ages. Moved, I bow, although he would ignore this,
for Soen-roshi never says goodbye. By next evening it is snowing

again, and as I stand on the bridge at dusk, with mountains breathing, my thought dissolves, my head becomes transparent, and snow blows through the emptiness where it had been.

When I told him at dokusan how I had become invisible on the bridge, with snow blowing right through the erstwhile Ishin, Soen-roshi said gently, with great kindness, "Take good care of yourself." He teaches us in everything he says, but I did not know why he said this at this moment. Eido-roshi says that sometimes for months afterward he does not understand this master's teachings.

Snow morning. In the warmed snow outside the kitchen, crisp jays and chickadees share this first day of spring. Just two years ago, in winter dusk, as I set out to dig Deborah's grave in the south meadow, a chickadee flickered onto the handle of my pick, and afterward, in granite earth that was locked in snow and ice, the very first swing of the pick discovered the soft hollow between rocks where her urn would lie.

Across the wind an early redwing sings, undaunted, though its forage lies beneath yesterday's snow. In the long sittings I am having pain, and this bird's cheery acceptance of hard going gives me courage.

> *Torn blackbird*
> *blown to the white birch by the white lake*
> *sings*
> Redwing!

Each evening I go to the great granite in the meadow and listen to the wind in the dark pines. Wild geese are passing overhead, from south to north.

My work assignment is assistant to Marsha, who is *tenzo* (cook). I peel vegetables, smack garlic, core onions, heed the wok (when it sizzles, greens are burning), mix Chinese cabbage with peppers, ginger, tree fungi, and mushrooms, knead dough

49

for bread: "When it comes alive in your hands," says Marsha, a gifted potter who made Deborah's urn, "then you know that the kneading is done." I make purée, cut vegetables, grate cheese.

The doing, the doing—how hard it is to drop the idea of attainment! A monk asked Unmon, What is individual samadhi? Unmon answered, Rice in a bowl, water in a pail. ("*Just* rice! *Just* water!" Soen-roshi comments. "All the rest is extra!")

Every morning in rest period I go along the snow road to do bows to the great Buddha in the woods. Each evening I visit my wife's grave and bow in the direction of the sunset. Sometimes I run through the snowy woods or do solitary *t'ai chi* on the dark road.

> *On the east mountain, snow*
> *afire,*
> *Bare trees, in the striped light—*
> *I cough!*
> *Who hears that? The spring*
> *tiger?*

Soen relates how once, in London, he was on the point of entering the bathroom when Christmas Humphreys, passing by, said it was occupied. The roshi waited there politely for a long time before he became concerned, after which he knocked, then opened the door. "Nobody there!" He laughed delightedly. "Wait as long as you like! *Never* anybody there! From the beginning!"

With his wonderful tales, he is telling us that we must not cling to the idea of self, not to speak of others, far less cling to our own concepts—our idea of "good" zazen or "bad" zazen, our notion of Mu or of the Buddha. Even a notion of "sincere" practice that one clings to is already polluted. "Do not analyze the condition of your zazen! When you are climbing a steep cliff, do you analyze your climbing condition? No! You climb! When you vomit, do you stop to analyze? No! You vomit! Just *do* zazen! Just march ahead! Do not be a slave to your moods

50

and your emotions. It is sunny, then it is cloudy; do not cling to either. Just march on!"

The true miracle, the true enlightenment—he says this in different ways, over and over—is awareness of this present moment, moment after moment. In seeking the Buddha, seeking the Dharma, seeking so-called enlightenment, one imposes an extra head on top of one's own. The Zen expression "Kill the Buddha!" means to kill any concept of the Buddha as something apart from oneself. To kill the Buddha is to *be* the Buddha.

Like Eido-shi, Soen quotes over and over from the *Rinzai Roku*:

> Do you know where the disease lies that keeps you learners from reaching true understanding? It lies where you have no faith in your Self. When faith in your Self is lacking you find yourselves hurried by others in every possible way. At every encounter you are no longer your master; you are driven about by others, this way and that.
>
> All that is required is all at once to cease leaving your Self in search of something external. When this is done you will find your Self no different from the Buddha or the patriarch.
>
> Do you want to know who the Buddha or patriarch is? He is no other than the one who is, at this moment, right in front of me, listening to my talk on the Dharma. You have no faith in him and therefore you are in quest of someone else somewhere outside. And what will you find? Nothing but words and names, however excellent. You will never reach the moving spirit in the Buddha or patriarch. Make no mistake.[1]

Shakyamuni allegedly declared at birth, "Alone above and below heaven, I am the honored one"—that is, the universe is not different from myself, it does not exist apart from me in this present moment. At the moment of his enlightenment, he cried, "How wonderful! How miraculous! All things are enlightened!," which is another way of saying the same thing.

Under the lid of a golden box containing the Buddha's ashes (Soen says) is the inscription *Atha dipa, Ana sarana, Anana*

51

sarana: You are the light, You are the refuge, There is no place to take shelter but yourself.

On the morning of Soen-roshi's birthday, I am *junkei*, or monitor, walking around with upraised keisaku. When I pass the Roshi, he raises his hands in *gassho* (palms together) and removes his rakusu, in sign that he wishes to be struck, something I have never seen a roshi do. (Eido-shi describes his first impression of Soen, the only one in a group of Rinzai roshis to whom the young monk Tai-san was serving tea who would acknowledge the lowly monk by raising his hands in gassho. Unlike most roshis, Soen did zazen and morning service with his monks and even ate with them.) Soen looks very small and frail, his little shoulders are a poor target, I am afraid of hurting him and also afraid he will think me a poor junkei. But I hit him smartly enough, and he does not wince, and I feel honored, though I know he has asked for the keisaku for my sake, not for his own. Later, seeing him upstairs gazing quizzically at his giant American birthday cake, I am not touched but *moved* by the ancient and innocent child in Soen-roshi, who looks like some ancient seer from the Gobi Desert.

In this sesshin, the roshi has extended his Namu Dai Bosa chanting ("Be One with the Great [Kwannon] Bodhisattva") into Namu Dai Bosa "dancing" in the kinhin line between sitting periods. No one quite understands this wild leaping and swaying. Perhaps it is only another way of banishing the hated "stink of Zen" by undoing our great spiritual dignity.

On the last morning of March sesshin, Soen-roshi leads a ceremony of purification of the new monastery now rising from the rubble of concrete and mud in the winter woods on the west side of the lake. The roshi is resplendent in the heavy gold brocaded robes of Soyen Shaku, which had been presented to the Zen Studies Society by D. T. Suzuki.

By June the monastery windows are going in and the ceramic shingles are in place. The Japanese roof is very beautiful.

We install fiberglass insulation around the windows, a dirty job that is extremely satisfactory. Yet the new monastery is in serious debt, and there will have to be extensive fund-raising. I am asked to organize the campaign. I work with Lou N. on an emergency letter to be sent to all the Zen community, and ask others to work on various ideas after the sesshin. (But at a second work sesshin, in August, helping unload Tasmanian oak for the monastery floors, I am filled with doubt, wondering why such exotic materials are needed.) Meanwhile we plan a maple syrup operation as a zendo livelihood.

One evening I take the canoe to the north end of the lake to see the beavers, which have returned for the first time in decades—an auspicious sign for the founding of the new monastery. But Eido-shi is opposed to beavers because, he says, they kill all the young trees beside the lake. He wants them shot, the resident students say, or at least trapped and removed. However, most of the dead saplings show no sign of gnawing, and in my opinion, these young trees are being killed by the high water caused by the raised dam, which Eido-shi ordered to enlarge the lake and replace the weedy margin of wild shore with the formal edge of a Japanese water garden.

The beleaguered creatures have not given up. I am elated to see one swimming with a new green branch, and another circles the canoe, slapping the water with its tail, which it would not do unless defending a home territory. Later I say respectfully to Eido-roshi that we have no right to drive away these beavers, far less kill them. They were here long before we were, with the mountains and the deer, and we should be happy they have returned with our own arrival, since they will bring new life to the deep lake by creating beaver pools and swampy edges.

Eido-shi is angered by my insurrection and will scarcely answer. He knows that many of the students hold such views, and no doubt perceives me as the ringleader. The following day we moved our large bronze Buddha to a new site on a rock outcrop across the lake, only to find that the wise rodents had chosen the cleft right behind the Buddha rock for their new abode, which was already half constructed. Word came that this lodge should be destroyed too, but no one would have a hand in that, and one student informed Eido-shi that if the beavers were destroyed, he would resign as a Zen student. Delighted by the beauty of the Buddha image on its rock throne, reflected in the lake, our teacher did not enforce his edict, speaking instead of the beavers' "remarkable" skills of construction, and so, for the moment, our Buddha and his buck-toothed Dharma guardians reside together.

With Paul S., whom I knew first at Ryutaku-ji, I work on a forest trail along the shore, exploring ways to span the swamp streams at the beaver pools. We build bridges, to complete a circuit of the lake.

Clear, still evenings, with trout leaping; bats and swallows join these fish that are hunting insects in the air. A teal like a swift leaf in storm hooks down between the trees into the beaver pools at the north end, and at dusk a wood thrush tests its flute notes in the silence. Spotted newts, large-eyed and silent, are orange on land and greenish in the water.

A half day to myself. I climb the west ridge and work my way around the mountains, toward the east. In a cool glade of the high forest stands an elegant woodland grass, a solitary blade, dead still, as if caught listening.

In the meadow a brown-spotted frog transfixed on a warm rock awaits me. Shifting flat stones to make a rock path to the grave, I find small snakes—two adult red-bellies, young watersnakes, young blacksnakes—and a beautiful green tree snake, killed on the road. I make a small snake terrarium for the kitchen, returning the snakes to the meadow at week's end.

In August the newts return into the water and hang suspended at all depths in the black pond. Each day the deer drift to the lake edge, red does and spotted fawns, and the beaver are active, rebuilding their lodges for the coming winter. At dusk a long, delicate feather parts the lake where a beaver swims northward. On the first night, I sleep outside, under a sky live with shooting stars and brown bats that flicker from the eaves.

We clear the windfall in the woods, burn brush. I bake bread, fetch milk from a dying farm, and carve and sand a pair of cedar chopsticks. One evening I walk with Merete to the small lake up the logging road, to westward. One night I meet a bobcat on the moonlit road.

> *Black-and-gold finches*
> *in gold black-eyed susans*
> *— south summer wind!*

September. The weathers change, the clouds blow in mists across the mountain pond. I pick blueberries in the waiting meadow. At twilight, a wild wind spins the lake, and rain and thunder come as sesshin begins.

Each morning after work period, I slip the canoe from the bank and drift along the lake. In the stillness of the trees, red autumn leaves of the swamp maple float on a black mirror. After three days of sesshin, my eye is opening, and all things in nature stand forth in four dimensions, clear and ringing. On the dark bottom of the lake, a pale newt, belly up, lies side by side with a pale leaf, all color gone.

Now a beaver, like a spirit of the lake, splits the surface with its coarse-haired head as water pours from the blunt snout —*slap!* All is still again. Where the spirit vanished, a circle is spreading out across the world.

Days pass, and the beavers draw near. Are they drawn to a stillness in the canoe that was not there before? The ringing and luminosity of the first days of sesshin seem to have vanished, as if an intensity had gone, or is it that I grow accustomed to fresh ways of seeing and take it now for ordinary perception? Before sesshin, the mountain is the mountain; then the mountain seems extraordinary, more than the mountain; today the extraordinary and the ordinary are not different, and the mountain is the mountain once again.

In the night window of the zendo, a full moon appears among the clouds that cross the eastern ridge. Now the moon goes. A white moth comes out of the night. The white moth goes.

In zazen, one is one's present self, what one was, and what one will be, all at once. I have a glimpse of the Mahayana teaching known as nondiscrimination, perceiving that this black cushion, candle flame, cough, belch, Buddha, incense smell, wood pattern on the floor, pine branch, sharp pain—and also awareness of these phenomena, of all phenomena—are all of equal significance, equal value. And the next day, what resolves in my mind like a soft soap bubble swelling and soundlessly bursting is that "my" mind and all minds everywhere are manifestations of One Mind, Univeral Mind, like myriad birds flying as one in a swift flock, like so many minute coral animals, in the sway of tides on a long reef, not the same and yet not different, feeding as one great creature with a single soul.

The stars grow colder, and each morning a mist shrouds the lake until Indian summer sun burns it away. At the north end a feeding beaver lifts its forepaws from the water, calmly observing, and the silent hickories are observing, too, in red-gold light. The canoe slips ashore on the far bank, and I swim out naked into the shining mist.

A heavy rain at night, clear blue at dawn. Sesshin passes. In greatest contentment, ease, simplicity, I wash lettuce by the waterfall.

Before going away, I sit by the lake with Eido-roshi, enjoying the fair white clouds that cross the mountains. "Who is it that is looking at the clouds?" he says. "Do you know who?" I shake my head. Laughing, we lie back in the warm grass and watch these clouds that have never been anywhere else in all the world.

At November weekend sesshin, Eido-shi discussed Master Rinzai, who was "plain and direct in manner, very simple and obedient. The wonderful thing was that when the head monk told him to go back to Obaku a second time, then a third, he did not say, Why?—he just went. And he also went south to another teacher, a journey of months, because Obaku told him to."

I worry that I lack Master Rinzai's attitude. The unquestioning obedience taken for granted by all Japanese teachers is very difficult for Western students, at least those like myself who are not devotional by nature and tend to resist figures of authority. This may be a weakness (or strength) of American Zen.

At Rohatsu sesshin in New York I am in charge of the garden zendo (the second zendo). Eido-roshi is demanding double sittings, seventy minutes or more—known as "killer sittings" to the shocked participants—but Soen-roshi's "diamond-hard pain samadhi" sees me through, and after four days my mind, or what is left of it, is dancing.

My koan is the one attributed to the Sixth Chinese Patriarch, Daikan Eno (Hui Neng): Is it the flag that moves? Is it the wind? No, it is your mind. There are two ways to answer almost any koan in a way the teacher must take seriously until he is sure that the student has more koan "style" than understanding. The first is to vividly present a key word, such as "flag," that is, BE the flag in all its flag-ness, just-as-it-is. The second is a forceful shout of MU!, which symbolizes this suchness, this ever-present Buddha-nature, this eternal *now*! However, it is not enough to present the flag, or present Mu with a shout. One must *become* it, there must be no separation. As for a "correct" koan response, it is utterly meaningless unless infused with *prajna* wisdom—the experiential insight, the noncerebral *knowing* that arises from the depths of profound samadhi.

Eido-shi says he can always tell if a student is merely giving a "Zen" answer. Not until the sixth day of sesshin, after many dokusans, does he pass me on this koan, which I intuited from the first day, yet could not present freely and forcefully, with my whole being. He gives me two whacks with his keisaku and a new koan.

Each afternoon, when we chant from the *Diamond Sutra*, I am reminded that the Sixth Patriarch, a simple woodcutter entirely ignorant of formal practice, attained great enlightenment upon hearing the Diamond Sutra's phrase about the mind that abides nowhere, clings to nothing. Thus—I tell myself—the mind need not alight on pain, as mine is doing. It helps, up to a certain point, to regard pain as "just pain," without judgment of "good" or "bad." Pain is simply *there*, like the tatami mat, the bells, the cooking smell, the sun in the garden window. Perceived that way, it is bearable, and bearing it, I manage to stay light, breath after breath, until breath itself all but disappears. The emptied mind is no longer aware of sounds and smells since it is part of them, bouncing lightly along in the great flux like an escaped bubble, alighting nowhere, on the point of dissolution. At the same time this mind is clear and precise as a laser, a new point. The lightness and precision (or the lack of them) are very critical when one serves as junkei, for the keisaku must fall sharply and clearly, with the stroke pulled at the same time, so that the recipient is stimulated rather than stung.

This Rohatsu is a strong one, although not spectacular; my days of sesshin miracles are perhaps over. Yet I feel that I understand much better how my practice is impeded by my yearning for emancipation, by my spiritual ambition, by addiction to "knowledge" and these sesshin notes. It is time to dispense with notes, like Master Tokusan. This great explicator of the *Diamond Sutra* burned all his notes and all the written teachings, which when compared with the teaching in this moment were "like tossing a hair into the sky or a drop of water into the ravine." (Tokusan had had a deep awakening, but nevertheless he was thought to be still "green," as is said in Zen. There was nothing wrong with the notes themselves, only with his clinging to them.)

Ten days after sesshin came a dream of kensho. I was walking up a street when very suddenly all broke apart, and all was light. All aspects and fragments of the world were of equal significance, and everything was full to bursting, brimming with its own shimmering particularity. From a luminous earth, awakening, I disappear without impediment into the sky.

In January 1975, Rohatsu sesshin is held at Dai Bosatsu. There we sleep on the dusty concrete floor of the new monastery, which Eido-shi is inspired to call Kongo-ji, Diamond Temple, after the *Diamond Sutra*. The monastery's first chanting service is held in the unfinished Dharma Hall.

As usual I sit beside Min Pai, a Korean master of the martial arts. Min and I like this arrangement, we think we give each other the energy that we shall need. This Rohatsu will be strict; we are not to lie down during rest periods, Min says. As usual, I am gloomy, with a headache, on the first day of a long sesshin, but I accept this, knowing it will pass—that from a Zen point of view, it is already passing.

After supper on the first day, I dig a snow path to Deborah's grave. Returning, I stand on the road bridge by Beecher Lake and observe the soft light of the old lodge through fat, soft snow. It looks like a house of childhood fairy tales. Snowflakes melt upon my face, a lifetime passes, and no time at all: this man on the bridge has been here always, seeking his long-lost home.

At teisho next day, Eido-shi is transfigured in a golden light against the snow light in the sunny window. Once again he quotes the simple passage from the great thirteenth-century master Dogen Zenji:

> *To study the Buddha Dharma is to study the self*
> *To study the self is to forget the self*
> *To forget the self is to be enlightened by all things.*

Do not think that this silence is useless and empty. Entering the monastery and doing zazen in silence, or leaving the monastery and going all about are both the form of the continuous practice of the monastery. This continuous practice . . . is the realm of freedom from conditions, in the same way that the sky is free from the tracks of flying birds; it is the realm where one is completely one with the whole universe. . . .

Don't idle away the time needed for practice, but rather practice in the spirit of a person trying to extinguish a blaze in his hair. Do not sit and wait for enlightenment, for great enlightenment is to be found in everyday activities such as eating, or drinking tea. . . . The person who lives in his old home should leave it; the person who has thoughts and desires should get rid of them. The famous person should abandon fame, and the person who has benefited materially should get rid of his goods. The person with fields and gardens should part with them, and the person with a family should leave it. You should renounce them even if you do not possess them. What should be clear in this matter is the principle of being free from them whether you have them or not. That is the continuous practice of being free from everything whatever it is. . . .

This life of one day is a life to rejoice in. Because of this, even though you live for just one day, if you can be awakened to the truth, that one day is vastly superior to an eternal life. . . . If this one day in the lifetime of a hundred years is lost, will you ever get your hands on it again?

Unbroken Practice
—EIHEI DOGEN

CHAPTER SIX

AFTER four years of hard zazen, my right knee is suddenly so sore that I must tape it. I use aspirin, heat pads, liniment, but cannot bring myself to do zazen in a chair. Alas, this is no evidence of grit or dedication but only ineradicable male vanity.

To permit myself a chair would be to relax my fierce grip on the ego, but I do not do it. For seven months I have avoided sesshin, and in recent weeks I have scarcely sat at all, which suits a cynical festering of mood.

At Dai Bosatsu, in late August, the doors and the wood floors are in, there is one coat of paint, but the huge building still looks like a raw eruption on the scraped hide of the mountain woodland. Indoors the atmosphere is worse. Eido-roshi, whose comportment (which will not be the business of this book) has caused dismay among his students, is racked with uneasy ill-nesses, bad gums. The head of the Buddha, say the residents, fell to the floor during its installation in the Dharma Hall, and other evil portents followed. The zendo atmosphere is dark, distempered, and most of Eido-shi's senior students have only come out of loyalty to Soen-roshi, who is here to lead the first sesshin in the new monastery.

A number of students have brought their anger and distress to Soen-roshi, and as a consequence, our old teacher seems shy and a bit distant. Finding him alone in the Dharma Hall, I approach quietly and wait. When he looks up from his reverie, I tell him how happy we are to see him. "I am happy too," he declares bravely. He shows me photos of the murals for the Dharma Hall being executed by his friend the Greek Orthodox priest Father Maxima. "Here soon!" He smiles. But when I ask about the many-fingered Kwannon at Ryutaku-ji, which two years earlier, in Japan, he had promised would soon be sent to Dai Bosatsu, he frowns and shakes his head. "Too many fingers," he snaps cryptically.

Soen-roshi says he wishes to come visit me again out on Long Island, and I ask about his recent journey to the Gobi Desert, where I have always wished to go. He laughs, saying he has gone "far beyond" the Gobi Desert. Too distracted to see that he tests my understanding, I ask foolishly if he means Central Mongolia. "No, no! *Far* beyond!" He waves his arm in a great circle, like the bold circle of emptiness in his calligraphy. This time I laugh, and bow, and let him go.

In opening ceremonies for the new Dharma Hall, Soen-roshi says, "I look in the *Rinzai Roku* and there is no word there: *where* is Master Rinzai? Who dares represent him before me?" Eido-shi goes forward, saying, "How do you do." They bow, and his teacher felicitates him on the opening of the new monastery. But Soen's teisho afterward seems weak and rambling, and his favorite small Noh play with his robes over his head and his red demon mask lacks his usual spirit. As if weary of his own clowning, he sighs and removes the mask, paraphrasing the teaching of Soyen Shaku: "For more than forty years I studied the Dharma and went about preaching it here and there, and only quite recently did I understand. And all I understood was that I understood nothing at all." There is great sadness (do I imagine it?) in the way he speaks.

Cleaning the zendo after evening sitting, I find Soen alone in the shadows at the end of the empty row, in the stillness of zazen. He is the archetypal old monk of the paintings, ancient as death, burning with life. I dust around him. These days his joy in life is dark; he refers gleefully to "the majority," as he calls the dead. He is shaken profoundly, yet he struggles to carry on as if nothing has happened. Each day he reminds us that, despite all the tumult and delusion of our life, our true nature is always there, like the sun or moon above black wind and clouds. "The sun is shining; the sun is *always* shining. The sun is enlightenment; *everything* is enlightenment!" He dabbles his fingers in a water bowl. "Do you hear? *That is enlightenment!*" At one point he reads his own new haiku:

> In the midst of winter
> I find in myself at last
> Invincible summer.

Intending some sort of confrontation, I go to dokusan with Eido-roshi, who greets me simply, with great warmth and friendliness. How can I ignore his strength and compassion at the time of Deborah's death, or my high opinion of him as a teacher? I cannot repudiate him, yet how insincere I feel when I say nothing! Many of his students are as torn as I am. We hope he will deal candidly with all the protest, but he does not; his shouts at dokusan, driving a student from the sesshin, carry downstairs. Returning to the zendo, his face full of anger, he announces that no one should go to dokusan with Soen-roshi who is not "an advanced student of the Dharma." Clearly this is some sort of sarcastic challenge. Though scarcely "advanced," I go in a mutinous spirit. Soen-roshi tests me and accepts my answer.

Two days later, Soen himself announces that there will be no more dokusan: "You must meet your *self* before you meet roshi at dokusan!" Unable to maintain this severe tone, he says more gently, "You must burn like a fire—hot, hot, hot! Do not compare to anybody else: do your own zazen. Some young, some old: just do your best! Do not compare elephant and flea! The elephant walks—Mu! Mu! Mu! Mu!—but the flea can *spring*!" He made a springing motion. "Both flea and elephant are best in world!"

Soen-roshi spoke of the old-time monk[1] who burned a wooden image of the Buddha to keep warm while others cried *Ho! What? Hey!* "You are infinitely more precious than a wood Buddha! Even more precious than the great Buddha at Nara! You are living bodhisattvas, endless dimension universal human beings!

"At this moment, what more is there to say? More foolish talk of 'truth' "—he snapped out the fatty word almost with hatred—"by this talkative lazy monk?" He whacked the lectern with his stick, making his glass of water jump. "The truth is *here*! A piece of paper, a drop of water!"

"There are no Zen masters," said Master Rinzai's teacher, Master Obaku. "There is only Zen." Shakyamuni himself said, "When you meet a teacher who expounds the matter of supreme *bodhi* [enlightenment], you should not . . . pay any heed to his shortcomings, or criticize his actions."[2] (One student abandoned Yasutani-roshi because that old master was too fond of marshmallows.) But for idealistic American Zen students, seeking respite from our own disorderly lives, this practice had seemed a clear oasis where life could be kept pure, spare, and simple, as in the Buddhist image of the white lotus rising from the muddy water. Now the image had been muddied, messy "real life" had come flooding in, and we wrestled with "oughts" and "shoulds" on our black cushions; we had forgotten that the lotus needs the nourishment of mud, that it cannot grow in clean "pure" water.

Out of doors again, a warm Indian Summer day all around me, I visited the new beaver ponds at the north end of the lake, studied wildflowers of late summer—self-heal and speckled touch-me-not, goldenrod and black-eyed susan, asters and pearly ever-lasting. The early, infatuated days of my Zen practice had come to an end, the flowers were just flowers once again.

I saw Eido-shi next almost a year later, at the sesshin that preceded the formal opening of International Dai Bosatsu Zendo on July 4, 1976. On the afternoon of my arrival, I met with my teacher to explain my withdrawal as his student, saying I hoped that things would work out in the future. He bowed a little, saying, "Let us hope . . ." Afterward I visited Deborah's grave with a senior student who was in her own process of painful separation. Eido had announced that Soen-roshi would attend the inaugural sesshin as honorary abbot, but Soen had not an-swered the invitation, and would not appear. "I am glad Soen-roshi refused to come," she said, in tears. "He did not do what appearances demanded but what was right." Standing before the boulder in the field, I wondered what Deborah would have thought of the whole sad business.

Accounting for his teacher's absence, Eido-roshi advised the sesshin participants that Soen-roshi had not recovered from one of his mysterious illnesses. In a bewildered and uncertain talk, he said that "this little crazy monk" would have to offer teisho instead ("But . . . if it were not for this craziness . . . perhaps we would not be here?"). In a later teisho, he looked discolored, feverish, insisting that gratitude to one's teacher was more important than kensho. Seeing this gifted teacher give such feeble teisho before all his peers, my heart went out to him, yet it was clear that what he wished was not loyal friendship but unquestioning submission. The frank discussion of his actions which his American Zen students were demanding he apparently perceived as anarchy and loss of face which, in terms of Japanese student–teacher relationships, it doubtless was. Once he had told us that he still felt "very green, very immature," and "neither American nor Japanese"—a touching admission, apparently sincere, that partly accounted for his own confusion as well as ours.

The new zendo was fresh with the grassy fragrance of new tatamis, reminding me of Ryutaku-ji. The last places were filled by roshis, monks, priests, and visitors from other Zen centers, and everyone hoped that the atmosphere would be purified by the strong zazen of all these teachers. Eido's Dharma brothers from Ryutaku-ji, Sochu-roshi and Kozen-roshi, both offered dokusan, using Monk Do-san as interpreter. Sochu-roshi (who had replaced Soen as abbot) would not give me a new koan: "Work with Mu!" he said. "Then a baby will be born." And his stern face collapsed in a great smile. (At subsequent dokusan, he simply shouted, "More, more! Harder, harder!" and rang me out of the room with his little bell.) As if guessing my intentions, Kozen-roshi said simply that I must "go deeper," that I must now apply my practice to my life, not reserve it for "quiet places" such as this one. And of course the application of zazen to the "ordinary" world is the real point of this extraordinary practice.

After sesshin, I enjoyed good talks with Robert Aitken-roshi from Hawaii (who received Dharma transmission from Yasutani's disciple, Koun Yamada-roshi, in 1974) and also with Kobin Chino-sensei from Los Altos. On the list of sesshin participants, Chino was called *roshi*, but he said he felt himself unready to take this title, which tends to be forced on teachers prematurely by American students. Gently smoothing matters in his meetings with Eido's students, Chino-sensei said that it was our zazen that must concern us; that our teacher, too, would surely grow in this wonderful spiritual atmosphere at Dai Bosatsu;

that perhaps Soen-roshi was teaching from afar by sending us two bodhisattvas, Sochu and Kozen.

At the end of sesshin, on the Fourth of July, the rain came crashing as Shimano Eido-roshi opened the great doors of Dai Bosatsu. The ceremony has been well described in a recent book:

The sesshin began like every other sesshin—with the deep hollow sound of the bell—and it continued for seven days like every other sesshin, with alternating periods of sitting and walking, eating formally in the zendo, working for short periods at manual labor, *sanzen* (*dokusan*) with the roshi, and a few hours of sleep. But instead of one roshi, like most sesshins, this one had more than twenty roshis and dharma teachers in attendance. [In fact, four roshis attended sesshin, and "more than twenty" came to the opening ceremony on the final day.]

The sesshin had been held to mark the opening of Dai Bosatsu, the first traditional Japanese-style Zen monastery in America. Richard Baker-roshi had come from San Francisco for the opening ceremony, Sasaki-roshi and Maezumi-roshi from Los Angeles, Takeda-roshi from Mexico City, and Philip Kapleau-roshi from Rochester. Seung Sahn not a Japanese or American Zen master, but a Korean Zen master, had come up from Providence, and then there was a large contingent of visiting roshis from Japan. There was even a Tibetan, who had incorporated certain elements of Zen into his teaching, Chögyam Trungpa, Rinpoche, the Eleventh Trungpa Tulku, not wearing his best robes like the roshis, but a dark suit of English cut. . . . A contingent of Shinto priests wearing pointed wizard hats chanted and made offerings, and somebody rang the big brass bell on the hill for the first time, with a log wrapped in red, white and blue for the occasion. There was a speech in Japanese and then Baker-roshi said a very few words in English, and Eido-roshi mentioned someone who should have been there, but wasn't. Though he didn't use his name nearly everyone there knew he meant Nakagawa Soen-roshi, who was considered eccentric even for a Zen master and who always did what he pleased without worrying about social niceties.[3]

As it happened, the "somebody who rang the big brass bell" was me. My vantage point on the hill platform provided a fine view of all the dignitaries assembled on the broad entrance steps of the new monastery, in fitting tribute to Zen's herald in America, Master Soyen Shaku, whose golden robes were worn that day by Eido-roshi. But the strongest presence was the absence of Soen-roshi, which Eido-roshi now referred to as a "silent teaching."

For more than two years after this sesshin, I did not return to Dai Bosatsu. Polishing my Himalayan journals[4] had become my practice, taking the place of the intense sesshin attendance of the past four years.

NEPAL

HIMALAYAN JOURNALS 1973

The great Master Unmon has said, "The East Mountain moves over the water. . . ." We should realize that . . . "the East Mountain moving over the water" is the very bones and marrow of the Buddhas and Patriarchs. All the waters are appearing at the foot of the East Mountain, and therefore the mountains mount the clouds and stride through the heavens. The mountains are the peaks of the waters . . . the tips of the mountains' feet walk across the waters, setting them dancing; therefore, walking extends freely in all directions. . . .

From time immemorial the mountains have been the dwelling place of the great sages; wise men and sages have all made the mountains their own chambers, their own body and mind. And through these wise men and sages the mountains have been actualized. However many great sages and wise men we suppose have assembled in the mountains, ever since they entered the mountains no one has met a single one of them. There is only the actualization of the life of the mountains; not a single trace of their having entered remains.

Mountains and Rivers Sutra
—EIHEI DOGEN

CHAPTER SEVEN

A HIMALAYAN pilgrimage undertaken in the autumn of 1973 had its inception on the path of Zen taken years earlier, as well as in a lifelong attraction to wild places. In the rigors of hard travel on foot, in the monumental landscapes, the calm of ancient peoples and wild creatures, lay a simplicity and silence which restored perspective to the death of my wife the year before. The journey exposed me to Tibetan Buddhism as practiced in a remote region of the Tibetan Plateau, and in particular to an ancient "Zen-like" sect, Karma-Kagyu, which is now well established in America.

Work on the journals of this quest (set down eventually in a book, *The Snow Leopard*) occupied several years after my return from Nepal, and the following excerpts concerning Buddhism and meditation in the Himalayas represent a period of transition between Rinzai Zen and the Soto Zen studies that commenced with my first sesshin at the Zen Center of Los Angeles in early 1977.

Despite the stern injunction of Zen teachers to seek nothing, to keep one's feet upon the ground, I was still stuck in that wide-eyed early stage of practice in which one yearns for "miraculous" experience of the universal self, for so-called "enlightenment." And the journals reflect the inevitable struggle to apply such insights as have been attained on the black cushion to the more rigorous Zen of everyday life.

In late September of 1973, I set out with G.S. (the zoologist Dr. George Schaller) on a journey to the Crystal Mountain, walking west under Annapurna and north along the Kali Gandaki River, then west and north again, around the Dhaulagiri peaks and across the Kanjiroba, two hundred and fifty miles or more to the Land of Dolpo, on the Tibetan Plateau.

Twelve years before, on a visit to Nepal, I had seen those astonishing snow peaks to the north; to close that distance, to go step by step across the greatest range on earth to somewhere called the Crystal Mountain, was a true pilgrimage, a journey of the heart. Since the usurpation of Tibet by the Chinese, the Land of Dolpo, all but unknown to Westerners even today, was said to be the last enclave of pure Tibetan culture left on earth, and Tibetan culture was the last citadel of "all that present-day humanity is longing for, either because it has been lost or not yet been realized or because it is in danger of disappearing from human sight: the stability of a tradition, which has its roots not only in a historical or cultural past, but within the innermost being of man. . . ."[1] The lama of Shey, the most revered of all the rinpoches, the "precious ones," in Dolpo, had remained in seclusion when a scholar of Tibetan religions[2] reached the Crystal Monastery seventeen years ago, but surely our own luck would be better. . . .

Wildflowers and painted stones are set among the buttressed roots, to bring the traveler good fortune, and stone terraces are built up around the trunks in such a way that the shade-seeking traveler may back up and set down his load while standing almost straight. These resting places are everywhere along the trading routes, some of them so ancient that the great trees have long since died, leaving two round holes in a stonework oval platform. Like the teahouses and the broad stepping stones that are built into the hills, the rest walls impart a blessedness to this landscape, as if we had wandered into a lost country of the golden age.

The fire-colored dragonflies in the early autumn air, the bent backs in bright reds and yellows, the gleam on the black cattle and wheat stubble, the fresh green of the paddies and the sparkling river—over everything lies an immortal light, like transparent silver.

In the clean air and absence of all sound, of even the simplest machinery—for the track is often tortuous and steep, and fords too many streams to permit bicycles—in the warmth and harmony and seeming plenty, come whispers of a paradisal age. Apparently the grove of sal trees called Lumbini, only thirty miles south of this same tree, in fertile lands north of the Rapti River, has changed little since the sixth century B.C., when Siddhartha Gautama was born there to a rich clan of the Shakya tribe in a kingdom of elephants and tigers. Gautama forsook a life of ease to become a holy mendicant, or "wanderer"—a common practice in northern India even today. Later he was known as Shakyamuni (Sage of the Shakyas) and afterward as the Buddha—the Awakened One. Fig trees and the smoke of peasant fires, the greensward and gaunt cattle, white egrets and jungle crows are still seen on the Ganges Plain where Shakyamuni passed his life, from Lumbini south and east to Varanasi (an ancient city even when Gautama came there) and Rajgir and Gaya. Tradition says that he traveled as far north as Kathmandu and preached on the hill of Swayambhunath, among the monkeys and the pines.

In Shakyamuni's time, the disciplines called yogas were already well evolved. Perhaps a thousand years before, the dark-skinned Dravidians of lowland India had been overcome by nomadic Aryans from the Asian steppes who were bearing their creed of sky gods, wind, and light across Eurasia.[3] Aryan concepts were contained in their Sanskrit Vedas, or knowledge—ancient texts of unknown origin which include the *Rig Veda* and the *Upanishads* and were to become the base of the Hindu religion. To the wandering ascetic named Shakyamuni, such epic preachments on the nature of the universe and man were useless as a cure for human suffering. In what became known as the Four Noble Truths, Shakyamuni perceived that man's existence is inseparable from sorrow; that the cause of suffering is craving; that peace is attained by extinguishing craving; that this liberation may be brought about by following the Eightfold Path: right attention to one's understanding, intentions, speech, and actions; right livelihood, effort, mindfulness; right concentration, by which is meant the unification of the self through sitting yoga.

The Vedas already included the idea that mortal desire—since it implies lack—had no place in the highest state of being; that what was needed was that death-in-life and spiritual rebirth sought by all teachers, from the early shamans to the existentialists. Shakyamuni's creed was less a rejection of Vedic philosophy than an effort to apply it, and his intense practice of meditation does not content itself with the clarity of yoga states but goes beyond, until the transparent radiance of stilled mind opens out in prajna, or transcendent knowing, that higher consciousness or "Mind" which is inherent in all sentient beings, and which depends on the unsentimental embrace of all existence.

In the fifth century B.C., near the town of Gaya, south and east of Varanasi, Shakyamuni attained enlightenment in the deep experience that his own "true nature," his Buddha-nature, was no different from the nature of the universe. For half a century thereafter, at such places as the Deer Park in Sarnath, and Nalanda, and the Vulture's Peak near present-day Rajgir, he taught a doctrine based upon the impermanence of individual existence, the eternal continuity of becoming, as in the morning river that appears the same as the river of the night before, now passed away. At the age of eighty, he ended his days at Kusinagara (the modern Kusinara), forty miles east of Gorakhpur and just west of the Kali Gandaki River.

In what is now known as Bodh Gaya—still a pastoral land of cattle savanna, shimmering water, rice paddies, palms, and red-clay hamlets without paved roads or wires—a Buddhist temple stands beside an ancient pipal, descended from that *bodhi* tree, or "enlightenment tree," beneath which this man sat. Here in a warm dawn, ten days ago, with three Tibetan monks in maroon robes, I watched the rising of the morning star and came away no wiser than before. But later I wondered if the Tibetans were aware that the bodhi tree was murmuring with gusts of birds, while another large pipal, so close by that it touched the holy tree with many branches, was without life. I make no claim for this event: I simply declare what I saw there at Bodh Gaya.

October 2

The sherpas are alert for ways in which to be of use, yet are never insistent, far less servile; since they are paid to perform a service, why not do it as well as possible? "Here, sir! I will wash the mud!" "I carry that, sir!" Yet their dignity is unassailable, for the service is rendered for its own sake—it is the task, not the employer, that is served. As Buddhists, they know that the doing matters more than the attainment or reward, that to serve in this selfless way is to be free. Because of their belief in karma—the principle of cause and effect that permeates Buddhism and Hinduism (and Christianity, for that matter: as ye sow, so shall ye reap)—they are tolerant and unjudgmental, knowing that bad acts will receive their due without the intervention of the victim.

October 9

Our speculations about the Crystal Monastery have led inevitably to talk of Buddhism and Zen. G.S. refuses to believe that the Western mind can truly absorb nonlinear Eastern perceptions; he shares the view of many in the West that Eastern thought evades "reality" and therefore lacks the courage of existence. But the courage to be, right here and now and nowhere else, is precisely what Zen, at least, demands: eat when you eat, sleep when you sleep! Zen has no patience with "mysticism," far less the occult, although its emphasis on the enlightenment experience is what sets it apart from religions and philosophies.

I remind G.S. of the Christian mystics such as Meister Eckhardt and Saint Francis, Saint Augustine, and Saint Catherine of Siena, who spent three years in silent meditation: "All the way to Heaven is Heaven," Saint Catherine said, and that is the very breath of Zen, which does not elevate divinity above the common miracles of every day. G.S. counters by saying that all these people lived before the scientific revolution had changed the very nature of Western thought, which of course is true, but it is also true that in recent years Western scientists have turned with new respect toward the intuitive sciences of the East. Einstein repeatedly expressed suspicion of the restrictions of linear thought, concluding that propositions arrived at by purely logical means were completely empty of reality even if one could properly explain what "reality" means; it was intuition, he declared, that had been crucial to his thinking. And there are close parallels in the theory of relativity to the Buddhist concept of the identity of time and space, which, like Hindu cosmology, derives from the ancient teaching of the Vedas.

"Nothing exists but atoms and the void"—so wrote Democritus. And it is "void" that underlies the Eastern teachings —not emptiness or absence, but the Uncreated that preceded all creation, the beginningless potential of all things.

> Before heaven and earth
> There was something nebulous
>   silent isolated
>   unchanging and alone
>   eternal
>   the Mother of All Things
> I do not know its name
> I call it Tao[4]

Darkness there was, wrapped in yet more Darkness. . . . The incipient lay covered by the Void. That One Thing . . . was born through the power of heat from its austerity. . . . Where this Creation came from, He who has ordained it from the highest heaven, He indeed knows; or He knows not.[5]

The mystical perception (which is only "mystical" if reality is limited to what can be measured by the intellect and sense) is remarkably consistent in all ages and all places, East and West, a point that has not been ignored by modern science. The physicist seeks to understand reality, while the mystic is trained to experience it directly. Both agree that human mechanisms of perception, stunted as they are by screens of social training that close out all but the practical elements in the sensory barrage, give a very limited picture of existence, which certainly transcends mere physical evidence. Furthermore, both groups agree

77

that appearances are illusory. A great physicist extends this idea: "Modern science classifies the world . . . not into different groups of objects but into different groups of connections. . . . The world thus appears to be a complicated tissue of events in which connections of different kinds alternate or overlap or combine and thereby determine the texture of the whole."[6] All phenomena are processes, connections, all is in flux, and at moments this flux is actually visible: one has only to open the mind in meditation or have the mind screens knocked awry by drugs or dreams to see that there is no real edge to anything, that in the endless interpenetration of the universe, a molecular flow, a cosmic energy shimmers in all stone and steel as well as flesh.

The ancient intuition that all matter, all "reality," is energy, that all phenomena, including time and space, are mere crystallizations of mind, is an idea with which few physicists have quarreled since the theory of relativity first called into question the separate identities of energy and matter. Today most scientists would agree with the ancient Hindus that nothing exists or is destroyed, things merely change shape or form; that matter is unsubstantial in origin, a temporary aggregate of the pervasive energy that animates the electron. And what is this infinitesimal non-thing—to a speck of dust what the dust speck is to the whole earth? "Do we really know what electricity is? By knowing the laws according to which it acts and by making use of them, we still do not know the origin or the real nature of this force, which ultimately may be the very source of life and consciousness, the divine power and mover of all that exists."[7]

The cosmic radiation that is thought to come from the explosion of creation strikes the earth with equal intensity from all directions, which suggests either that the earth is at the center of the universe, as in our innocence we once supposed, or that the known universe has no center. Such an idea holds no terror for mystics; in the mystical vision, the universe, its center, and its origins are simultaneous, all around us, all within us, and all One. What the Buddha perceived was his identity with the universe; to experience existence in this way is to be the Buddha. Even the brilliant "white light" that may accompany mystical experience (the "inner light" attested to by Inuit shamans) might be perceived as a primordial memory of Creation. "Man is the matter of the cosmos, contemplating itself," a modern astronomer has said;[8] another points out that each breath we take contains hundreds of thousands of the inert, pervasive argon atoms that were actually breathed in his lifetime by the Buddha, and indeed contain parts of the "snorts, sighs, bellows, shrieks"[9] of all creatures that ever existed, or will ever exist. These atoms flow backward and forward in such useful but artificial constructs as time and space, in the same universal rhythms, universal breath as the tides and stars, joining both the living and the dead in that energy which animates the universe. What is changeless and immortal is not individual body-mind but, rather, that Mind which is shared with all of existence, that stillness, that incipience which never ceases because it never becomes but simply IS. This teaching, still manifest in the Hindu and Buddhist religions, goes back at least as far as the doctrine of Maya that emerges in the Vedic civilizations and may well derive from much more ancient cultures. Maya is Time, the illusion of the ego, the stuff of individual existence, the dream of "reality" that separates us from a true perception of the whole. It is often likened to a sealed glass vessel that separates the air within from the clear and unconfined air all around, or water from the all-encompassing sea. Yet the water in the vessel is not different from the sea, and to shatter or dissolve the vessel brings about the reunion with all universal life that mystics seek, the home-going, the return to the lost paradise of our "true nature."

Today science is telling us what the Vedas have taught mankind for three thousand years, that we do not see the universe as it is. What we see is Maya, or Illusion, the "magic show" of nature, a collective hallucination of that part of our consciousness which is shared with all of our own kind, and which gives a common ground, a continuity, to the life experience. According to Buddhists (but not Hindus), this world perceived by the senses, this relative but not absolute reality, this dream, also exists, also has meaning; but it is only one aspect of the truth, like the cosmic vision of this goat by the crooked door, gazing through sheets of rain into the mud.

October 10

I wait, facing the north; instinct tells me to stand absolutely still. Cloud mist, snow, and utter silence, utter solitude: extinction. Then, in the great hush, the clouds draw apart, revealing the vast Dhaulagiri snowfields. I breathe, mists swirl, and all has vanished—nothing! I make a small involuntary bow.

A downward path is forged through the wet snows, striking a treeline of dwarfed cedar six hundred feet below and emerging at dusk on a saddleback ridge of alpine tundra where it is flat enough to pitch a tent. Just at darkness the clouds lift: at 12,500 feet, the campsite is surrounded by bright glaciers. The five peaks of Dhaulagiri shine in the black firmament, and over all this whiteness rings a silver moon, the full moon of October, when the lotus blooms.

October 14

Only the enlightened can recall their former lives; for the rest of us, the memories of past existences are but glints of light, twinges of longing, passing shadows, disturbingly familiar, that are gone before they can be grasped, like the passage of that silver bird on Dhaulagiri.

Thus one must seek to "regard as one this life, the next life, and the life between, in the Bardo." This was a last message to his disciples of Tibet's great poet-saint the Lama Milarepa, born in the tenth century, in the Male Water-Dragon Year, to a woman known as "the White Garland of the Nyang." Milarepa is called Mila Repa because as a great yogi and master of "mystical heat" he wore only a simple white cloth, or *repa*, even in deepest winter: his "songs" or hortatory verses, as transcribed by his disciples, are still beloved in Tibet. Like Shakyamuni, he is said to have attained nirvana in a single lifetime, and his teaching as he prepared for death might have been uttered by the Buddha:

> All worldly pursuits have but the one unavoidable and inevitable end, which is sorrow: acquisitions end in dispersion; buildings, in destruction; meetings, in separation; births, in death. Knowing this, one should from the very first renounce acquisition and heaping-up, and building and meeting, and . . . set about realizing the Truth. . . . Life is short, and the time of death is uncertain; so apply yourselves to meditation. . . .[10]

Meditation has nothing to do with contemplation of eternal questions, or of one's own folly, or even of one's navel, although a clearer view on all of these enigmas may result. It has nothing to do with thought of any kind—with anything at all, in fact, but intuiting the true nature of existence, which is why it has appeared, in one form or another, in almost every culture known to man. The entranced Bushman staring into fire, the Inuit using a sharp rock to draw an ever-deepening circle into the flat surface of a stone, achieves the same obliteration of the ego (and the same power) as the dervish or the Pueblo sacred dancer. Among Hindus and Buddhists, realization is attained through inner stillness, usually achieved through the samadhi state of sitting yoga.[11] In Tantric practice, the student may displace the ego by filling his whole being with the real or imagined object of his concentration; in Zen, one seeks to empty out the mind, to return it to the clear, pure stillness of a sea shell or a flower petal. When body and mind are one, then the whole being, scoured clean of intellect, emotions, and the senses, *experiences* that individual existence, ego, the "reality" of matter and phenomena are no more than fleeting and illusory arrangements of molecules. The weary self of masks and screens, defenses, preconceptions, and opinions that, propped up by ideas and words, imagines itself to be some sort of entity (in a society of like entities) may suddenly fall away, dissolve into formless flux where concepts such as "death" and "life," "time" and "space," "past" and "future" have no meaning. There is only a pearly radiance of Emptiness, the Uncreated, without beginning, therefore without end.

Like the round-bottomed Bodhidharma doll, returning to its center, meditation represents the foundation of the universe to which all returns, as in the stillness of the dead of night, the stillness between tides and winds, the stillness of the instant before Creation. In this "void," this dynamic state of rest, without impediments, lies ultimate reality, and here one's own true nature is reborn, in a return from what Buddhists speak of as "great death." This is the Truth of which Milarepa speaks.

October 16

Traversing the slope to its north ridge, I scan the valley that leads north to the Jang, then return slowly down the mountain. Phu-Tsering gives me warm chapatis, and hot water for a wash in the cold sun. He is wearing his amulets outside his shirt, but tucks them away, embarrassed, when I ask about them; they were given him by his lama, he murmurs, feeling much better when I show him that I, too, wear an "amulet," a talisman given to me by Soen-roshi, "my lama in Japan." He admires this smooth plum pit on which a whole ten-phrase sutra is inscribed in minute characters, and is awed when I tell him that the sutra honors the most revered of all those mythical embodiments of Buddhahood called bodhisattvas, the one known to Phu-Tsering as Chenresi, who is the Divine Protector of Tibet and is invoked by Om Mani Padme Hum. In the Japanese sutra inscribed upon this pit, this bodhisattva is Kannon, or Avalokiteshvara. Like all bodhisattvas, he represents "the divine within" sought by mystics of all faiths, and has also been called the Lord Who Is Seen Within.[12]

Like most good Buddhists, Phu-Tsering chants *Om Mani Padme Hum* each day, and in time of stress he also clings to fear of demons, and is frightened by the dark. Walking behind G.S. one night in eastern Nepal, he chanted this mantra so incessantly that G.S. longed to throw him off the cliff. But the faithful believe that the invocation of any deity by his mantra will draw benevolent attention, and since *Om Mani Padme Hum* is dedicated to the Great Compassionate Chenresi, it is found inscribed on prayer stones, prayer wheels, prayer flags, and wild rocks throughout the Buddhist Himalaya.

Pronounced in Tibet *Aum Ma Ni Pay May Hung*, this mantra may be translated: *Om!* The Jewel in the Heart of the Lotus! *Hum!* The deep, resonant *Om* is all sound and silence throughout time, the roar of eternity and also the great stillness of pure being; when intoned with the prescribed vibrations, it invokes the All that is otherwise inexpressible. The *mani* is the "adamantine diamond" of the Void—the primordial, pure, and indestructible essence of existence beyond all matter or even antimatter, all phenomena, all change, and all becoming. *Padme*—in the lotus—is the world of phenomena, *samsara*, unfolding with spiritual progress to reveal beneath the leaves of delusion the *mani*-jewel of nirvana, that lies not apart from daily life but at its heart. *Hum* has no literal meaning, and is variously interpreted (as is all of this great mantra, about which whole volumes have been written). Perhaps it is simply a rhythmic exhortation, completing the mantra and inspiring the chanter, a declaration of being, of Is-ness, symbolized by the Buddha's gesture of touching the earth at the moment of enlightenment. *It* is! *It* exists! All that is or was or will ever be is right here in this moment! *Now!*

I go down along the canyon rim and sit still against a rock. Northward, a snow cone rises on the sky, and snowfields roll over the high horizon into the deepening blue. Where the Saure River plunges into its ravine, a sheer and awesome wall writhes with weird patterns of snow and shadow. The emptiness and silence of snow mountains quickly bring about those states of consciousness that occur in the mind-emptying of meditation, and no doubt high altitude has an effect, for my eye perceives the world as fixed or fluid, as it wishes. The earth twitches and the mountains shimmer, as if all molecules had been set free: the blue sky rings. Perhaps what I hear is the "music of the spheres," what Hindus call the breathing of the Creator and astrophysicists the "sighing" of the sun.

Wind brings swift, soft clouds from the south that cast shadows on the snow. Close at hand, a redstart comes to forage in the lichens, followed soon by a flock of fat rose finches. I do not stir, yet suddenly all whir away in a gray gust, and minutely I turn to see what might have scared them. On a rock not thirty feet away, an accipitrine hawk sits in silhouette against the mountains, and here it hunches while the sun goes down, nape feathers lifting in the wind, before diving after unseen prey over the rim of the ravine. The great lammergeier comes, gold-headed and black-collared, a nine-foot blade sweeping down out of the north; it passes into the shadows between cliffs. Where the river turns, in a corner of the walls, the late sun shines on a green meadow, as if a lost world lay in that impenetrable ravine, so far below. The great bird arcs around the wall, light glancing from its mantle. Then it is gone, and the sun goes, the meadow vanishes, and the cold falls with the night shadow.

Still I sit a little while, watching the light rise to the peaks. In the boulder at my back, there is a shudder, so slight that at another time it might have gone unnoticed. The tremor comes again; the earth is nudging me. And still I do not see.

October 20

Before departing, I had taken leave of Eido-roshi, and spoke to him of odd death whispers that had come for several months.

He nodded: perhaps what such whispers anticipated was a spiritual "great death" and a rebirth. "The snow," he murmured, "may signify extinction, and renewal." After a pause, he warned me, "Expect nothing." The roshi was pleased that there would be but two of us—this seemed to him a condition of true pilgrimage. He instructed me to recite the *Kannon Sutra* as I walked among the mountains, and gave me a koan: *All the peaks are covered with snow—why is this one bare?*

The roshi rose from his black cushion and, taking me by the shoulders, touched my forehead three times with his own, then smote my back, and sent me on my way with a great shout.

"Expect nothing." Walking along, I remind myself of that advice; I must go lightly on my way, with no thought of attainment. Instead of the *Kannon Sutra*, I intone *Om Mani Padme Hum*, which is addressed to the same great bodhisattva and, when recited one word for each step, has a resonant and mighty sound much better suited to this slow tread up the mountain.

Aum . . . Ma-Ni . . . Pay-May . . . Hung! . . . Aum . . . Ma-Ni . . . Pay-May . . . Hung! . . .

Disputing the path is a great copper-colored grasshopper, gleaming like amber in the sun. So large is it, and so magical its shimmer, that I wonder if this grasshopper is not some holy man, advanced in the art of taking other forms. But before such a "perfected one" can reveal himself, the grasshopper springs carelessly over the precipice, to start a new life hundreds of feet below. I choose to take this as a sign that I must entrust myself to life, and thanking the grasshopper, I step out smartly on my way.

The Bheri River is far behind us and below, and a snow peak of the Kanjirobas is rising, quiet as a cloud, on the northern blue. A claterynge of choughs, lilting along upon the air currents, delights me, and for want of a fresh way to let well-being overflow, I talk to G.S. rapturously about my boots, which are broken in at last and give me no end of honest pleasure. Mildly alarmed by my euphoria, he goes on rapidly. Left to myself, I listen contentedly to the leather creak of my back harness and beloved boots, the steady thump of my faithful stave upon the mountain, feeling as indomitable as Padma Sambhava, who carried the Dharma from India to Tibet.

Upon the path, in the glint of mica and odd shining stones, lies the yellow and gray-blue feather of an unknown bird. And there comes a piercing intuition, by no means understood, that in this feather on the silver path, this rhythm of wood and leather sounds, breath, sun and wind, and rush of river, in a landscape without past or future, time, transience and eternity, death and life are one.

To the north, high on the mountain's face, has come in view the village called Rohagaon. The track passes along beneath wild walnut trees. The last leaves are yellowed and stiff on the gaunt branches, and the nuts are fallen; the dry scratch and whisper of sere leaves stir a vague melancholy of some other autumn, half remembered. The wildwood brings on mild nostalgia, not for home or place but for lost innocence—the paradise lost that, as Proust said, is the only paradise. Childhood is full of mystery and promise, and perhaps the life fear comes when all the mysteries are laid open, when what we thought we wanted is attained. It is just at the moment of seeming fulfillment that we sense irrevocable betrayal, like a great wave rising silently behind us, and know most poignantly what Milarepa meant: "All worldly pursuits have but one unavoidable and inevitable end, which is sorrow: acquisitions end in dispersion; buildings, in destruction; meetings, in separation; births, in death." Confronted by the uncouth specter of old age, disease, and death, we are thrown back upon the present, on this moment, here, right now, for that is all there is. And surely this is the paradise of children, that they are at rest in the present, like frogs or rabbits.

The trail meets the Suli Gad high up the valley, in grottoes of bronze-lichened boulders and a shady riverside of pine and walnut and warm banks of fern. Where morning sun lights the red leaves and dark, still conifers, the river sparkles in the forest shadow; turquoise and white, it thunders past spray-shined boulders, foaming pools, in a long rocky chute of broken rapids. In the cold breath of the torrent, the dry air is softened by mist; under last night's stars this water trickled through the snows. At the head of the waterfall, downstream, its sparkle leaps into the air, leaps at the sun, and sun rays are tumbled in the waves that dance against the snows of distant mountains.

Upstream, in the inner canyon, dark silences are deepened by the roar of stones. Something is listening, and I listen, too: who is it that intrudes here? Who is breathing? I pick a fern to see its spores, cast it away, and am filled in that instant with misgiving: the great sins, so the Sherpas say, are to pick wildflowers and to threaten children. My voice murmurs its regret, a strange sound that deepens the intrusion. I look about me—who is it that spoke? And who is listening? Who is this ever-present "I" that is not me?

The voice of a solitary bird asks the same question.

Here in the secrets of the mountains, in the river roar, I touch my skin to see if I am real; I say my name aloud and do not answer.

By a dark wall of rock, over a rivulet, a black-and-gold dragonfly zips and glistens; a walnut falls on a mat of yellow leaves. Seen through the mist, a water spirit in monumental pale gray stone is molded smooth by its mantle of white water, and higher, a ribbon waterfall, descending a cliff face from the east, strikes the wind sweeping upriver and turns to mist before striking the earth. The mist drifts upward to the rim, forming a halo in the guarding pines.

At daybreak, when I peek out at the still universe, ice fills my nostrils; I crouch back in my sleeping bag, cover my head.

At dawn the camp is visited by ravens. Then a cold sun rises to the rim of the white world, bringing light wind.

This morning we shall carry three more loads up to Kang La, and then three more. That will make nine; there are fourteen altogether. To avoid the bitter cold, we wait until the sun touches the slopes, then climb hard to take advantage of the snow crust, reaching the pass in an hour and a half. In the snowbound valleys to the north, still in night shadow, there is no sign of our companions, no sign of any life at all.

The sherpas start down immediately; they, too, seem oppressed by so much emptiness. Left alone, I am overtaken by that northern void—no wind, no cloud, no track, no bird, only the crystal crescents between peaks, the ringing monuments of rock that, freed from the talons of ice and snow, thrust an implacable *being* into the blue. In the early light, the rock shadows on the snow are sharp; in the tension between light and dark is the power of the universe. This stillness to which all returns is profound reality, and concepts such as soul and sanity have no more meaning here than gusts of snow; my transience, my insignificance are exalting, terrifying. Snow mountains, more than sea or sky, serve as a mirror to one's own true being, utterly still, utterly clear, a void, an emptiness without life or sound that carries in itself all life, all sound. Yet as long as I remain an "I" who is conscious of the void and stands apart from it, there will remain a snow mist on the mirror.

A silhouette crosses the white wastes below, a black coil dangling from its hand. It is Dawa Sherpa carrying tump line and headband, yet in this light a something moves that is much more than Dawa. The sun is roaring, it fills to bursting each crystal of snow. I flush with feeling, moved beyond my comprehension, and once again, the warm tears freeze upon my face. These rocks and mountains, all this matter, the snow itself, the air—the earth is ringing. All is moving, full of power, full of light.

In a dream I am walking joyfully up the mountain. Something breaks and falls away, and all is light. Nothing has changed, yet all is amazing, luminescent, free. Released at last, I rise into the sky. . . . This dream comes often. Sometimes I run, then lift up like a kite, high above earth, and always I sail transcendent for a time before awaking. I *choose* to awake, for fear of falling, yet such dreams tell me that I am a part of things, if only I would let go, and keep on going.

In recent dreams, I have twice seen light so brilliant, so intense, that it "woke me up," but the light did not continue into wakefulness. Which was more real, the waking or the dream?

*"The mind of the ancient Buddhas" should not be understood as some-
thing irrelevant to your experience, as some mind which exists from the
beginningless past, for it is the mind which eats rice gruel or tastes
other food in your ordinary everyday life, it is the mind which is grass,
the mind which is water. Within this life just as it is is the act of sitting
like a Buddha which is called "arousing the thought of enlightenment."*

*The conditions for arousing the thought of enlightenment do not come
from anywhere else. It is the enlightened mind which arouses the
thought of enlightenment. . . . One honors the Buddha with a grain of
sand, one honors the Buddha with the water in which rice has been
soaked. One offers a handful of food to living creatures.*

Arousing the Supreme Mind
—Eihei Dogen

CHAPTER EIGHT

November 2

AT ALMOST 15,000 feet, Shey is as high as the Jang Pass. It is
located in what has been described as Inner Dolpo, which is
walled off from eastern Dolpo by a surrounding crescent of high
peaks, and must be one of the highest inhabited areas on earth.
Its people are of pure Tibetan stock, with a way of life that
cannot differ much from that of the Ch'ang Tartars out of Central
Asia who are thought to have been the original Tibetans, and
their speech echoes the tongue of nomads who may have arrived
two thousand years ago. Dolpo was formerly a part of western
Tibet, and it is certain that some form of Buddhism came here
early. Beyond the Karnali River, to the north and west, the

Tibetan Plateau rises to Kailas, the holy "Mount Sumeru" or "Meru" of Hindus and Buddhists, home of Shiva and the Center of the World. From Mount Kailas, four great rivers—the Karnali, the Indus, the Sutlej, and the Brahmaputra—flow down in a great mandala to the Indian seas.

Shey Gompa (Crystal Monastery) is a temple of the Kagyu sect, which was established in the eleventh century as a departure from the Kalachakra Tantrism of the Old Sect, or Nyingma. Kalachakra (Circle of Time) came to Tibet in the same century. It traditionally derives from a Tantra or treatise known as *Journey to Shambhala*, which teaches the adept how to transcend time (death), and is supposed to be the Book of Wisdom that appears in portraits of the bodhisattva called Manjusri. In Kalachakra, the already numerous Buddha aspects are split once more into peaceful and wrathful forms of the same deity. Thus, Avalokiteshvara, the Great Compassionate One, is also perceived as Mahakala, or Great Time, the Lord of Death—the Tantric personification of the disintegrating forces of the cosmos, often depicted wearing skulls and human skins, brandishing darts, and stamping upon copulating humankind. Mahakala will liberate those who can die to their past in order to be reborn, and terrify those who cling to the worldly existence of samsara, the thirsting and quenching and thirsting anew that is symbolized by the priest's skull cup full of blood. For better or worse, the Kalachakra pantheon of peaceful-and-wrathful deities was retained by the "reformed" sects—the Kagyupas, the Sakyapas, and, much later, the Gelugpas, led by the Dalai Lamas, who have dominated Tibetan Buddhism since the sixteenth century.

The Kagyu sect was established by the great Lama Marpa, the "Translator," who made three trips to India to study with a famous teacher called Naropa. When Marpa returned to Tibet, he transmitted the Dharma to Milarepa. Subsequently, Milarepa's disciples split off from Kagyu as the Karmapas, and this new school, in the thirteenth century, was the first Tibetan sect to establish influence with the emperor of China, Kublai Khan. (Subsequently, according to the chronicles of Marco Polo, the

Khan's conversion was strengthened by a lama who triumphed over competing divines of Christian, Muslim, and Taoist persuasions by causing a cup to rise to the royal lips of its own accord.)

Gelugpa reforms since the sixteenth century have not changed the nature of Karma-Kagyu, or not, at least, in such far places as the Crystal Mountain. In its ascetic disciplines and spare teachings, which discourage metaphysical speculation in favor of prolonged and solitary meditation, Karmapa practice is almost identical with that of Zen, which also emphasizes intuitive experience over priestly ritual and doctrine. Both have been called the "Short Path" to liberation, and although this direct path is difficult and steep, it is also the pure essence of Buddhism with all religious trappings cut away. It seems to me wonderful karma that the Crystal Monastery belongs to this "Zen" sect, and that the Lama of Shey is a notable *tulku*, or incarnate lama, revered throughout the Land of Dolpo as the present reincarnation of the Lama Marpa. On my way here, I entertained visions of myself in monkish garb attending the lama in his ancient mysteries, and getting to light the butter lamps into the bargain; I suppose I had hoped that he would be my teacher. That the gompa is locked and the Lama gone away might be read as a karmic reprimand to spiritual ambition, a silent teaching to this ego that still insists upon itself, like the poor bleat of a goat on the north wind.

Although the monastery is locked tight, the two large stupas on the bluff over the river bridge give a clue to the iconography within. Perhaps thirty feet high, they have the typical square red base and red-garlanded white dome, with a tapering cone topped by a lunar crown and solar disc. On the four sides of the base are crude clay frescoes of symbolic creatures—elephants on the east face, horses south, peacocks west, and on the north face the garuda, or mythical hawk, here represented as a man with wings bearing what appears to be the sun and moon. The garuda, like the swastikas inside the stupa, is a pre-Buddhist symbol, and so is the yin-yang symbol on the door, which is thought to antedate the early Taoism of three thousand years ago in China.

November 4

Condemned by cold to spend twelve hours in my sleeping bag each night, I find myself inclined to my Zen practice. Each morning before daybreak, I drag my down parka into my sleeping bag to warm it, then sit up in meditation posture and perform a sutra chanting service for perhaps forty-five minutes. This morning service is lent dignity by a clay *ts'a ts'a* Buddha taken from piles of these small icons that littered the stupas visited at Ring-mo. I place the figure outside the tent on an altar of flat stone, where it will receive the first of the eastern light, down the White River, and I sit bundled up just inside the flap, for at this hour the temperature is never more than minus twelve degrees Centigrade. Sometimes I am joined for morning service by a hardy little bird that dwells in the brush piles on the roof of the pink stone house behind the tent. With flicking tail it hunts among the dung chips near the Buddha.

November 6

The nights at Shey are rigid, under rigid stars; the fall of a wolf pad on the frozen path might be heard up and down the canyon. But a hard wind comes before the dawn to rattle the tent canvas, and this morning it is clear again, and colder. At daybreak the White River, just below, is sheathed in ice, with scarcely a murmur from the stream beneath.

The sun rising at the head of the White River brings a

suffused glow to the tent canvas, and the robin accentor flits away across the frozen yard. At seven there is breakfast in the cook hut—tea and porridge—and after breakfast on most days I watch sheep with G.S., parting company with him after a while, when the sheep lie down, to go off on some expedition of my own. Often I scan the caves and ledges on the far side of Black River in the hope of leopard; I am alert for fossils, wolves, and birds. Sometimes I observe the sky and mountains, and sometimes I sit in meditation, doing my best to empty out my mind, to attain that state in which everything is "at rest, free and immortal. . . . All things abided eternally as they were in their proper places . . . something infinite behind everything appeared." (No Buddhist said this, but a seventeenth-century Briton.)[1] And soon all sounds, and all one sees and feels, take on imminence, an immanence, as if the universe were coming to attention, a universe of which one is the center, a universe that is not the same and yet not different from oneself, even from a scientific point of view: within man as within mountains there are many parts of hydrogen and oxygen, of calcium, phosphorus, potassium, and other elements. "You never enjoy the world aright, till the Sea itself flows in your veins, till you are clothed with the heavens, and crowned with the stars: and perceive yourself to be the sole heir of the whole world, and more than so, because men are in it who are every one sole heirs as well as you."[2]

I have a meditation place on Somdo Mountain, a broken rock outcrop like an altar set into the hillside, protected from all but the south wind by shards of granite and dense thorn. In the full sun it is warm, and its rock crannies give shelter to small stunted plants that cling to this desert mountainside—dead red-brown stalks of a wild buckwheat (*Polygonum*), some shrubby cinquefoil, pale edelweiss and everlasting and even a few poor wisps of *Cannabis*. I arrange a rude rock seat as a lookout on the world, set out binoculars in case wild creatures should happen into view, then cross my legs and regulate my breath, until I scarcely breathe at all.

Now the mountains all around me take on life; the Crystal

Mountain moves. Soon there comes the murmur of the torrent, from far away below under the ice. It seems impossible that I can hear this sound. Even in windlessness, the sound of rivers comes and goes and falls and rises, like the wind itself. An instinct comes to open outward by letting all life in, just as a flower fills with sun. To burst forth from this old husk and cast one's energy abroad, to fly . . .

Although I am not conscious of emotion, the mind-opening brings a soft mist to my eyes. Then the mist passes, the cold wind clears my head, and body-mind comes and goes on the light air. A sun-filled Buddha. One day I shall meditate in falling snow.

I lower my gaze from the snow peaks to the glistening thorns, the snow patches, the lichens. Though I am blind to it, the Truth is near, in the reality of what I sit on—rocks. These hard rocks instruct my bones in what my brain could never grasp in the *Heart Sutra*, that "form is emptiness, and emptiness is form"—the Void, the emptiness of blue-black space, contained in everything. Sometimes when I meditate, the big rocks dance.

The secret of the mountains is that the mountains simply exist, as I do myself: the mountains exist simply, which I do not. The mountains have no "meaning," they *are* meaning; the mountains *are*. The sun is round. I ring with life, and the mountains ring, and when I can hear it, there is a ringing that we share. I understand all this, not in my mind but in my heart, knowing how meaningless it is to try to capture what cannot be expressed, knowing that mere words will remain when I read it all again, another day.

November 9

From the path that leads beyond Tsakang, along the precipices of the Black River Canyon, there is a stirring prospect of the great cliffs and escarpments, marching northward toward the point where this Yeju-Kangju flows into the great Karnali River. The path is no more than a ledge in many places and, on the northward face of each ravine, is covered by glare ice and crusted snow. Even on the southward face, the path is narrow, and concentrating hard on every step, I come upon what looks like a big pug mark. Just at this moment, looking up, I see that G.S. has paused on the path ahead. As I approach, he points at a distinct cat scrape and print. The print is faded, but at least we know that the snow leopard is here. A little farther on there is another scrape, and then another, and G.S., looking ahead to where the path turns the cliff corner into the next ravine, says, "There ought to be a leopard scat out on that next point—it's just the sort of place they choose." And there it is, all but glowing in the path, right beneath the prayer stones of the stupa—the Jewel in the Heart of the Lotus, I think, unaccountably, and nod at my friend, impressed. "Isn't that something?" G.S. says, "To be so delighted with a pile of crap?" He gathers the dropping into one of the plastic bags that he keeps with him for this purpose and tucks it away into his rucksack with our lunch.

Across the next ravine is the second hermitage, of earth red decorated in blue-gray and white. It lacks stacked brush or other sign of life, and its white prayer flags are worn to wisps by wind. In the cliffs nearby are smoke-roofed caves and the ruins of cells that must have sheltered anchorites of former times; perhaps their food was brought them from Tsakang. This small gompa, half covering a walled-up cave, is tucked into an outer corner of a cliff that falls into Black Canyon, and like Tsakang it faces south, up the Black River. Because the points of the Shey stupas are just visible, its situation is less hallucinatory than the pure blue-and-white prospect at Tsakang, but the sheer drop of a thousand feet into the gorge, the torrent's roar, the wind, the high walls darkening the sky all around, make its situation more disturbing. The hermitage lies on the last part of a pilgrim's path that climbs from Black River and circles around the Crystal Mountain, striking Black Canyon once again on the north side of this point and returning to Shey by way of Tsakang. Most of this path is lost beneath the snows.

Taking shelter on the sunny step, leaning back into the

warmth of the wooden door, I eat a green disc of Phu-Tsering's buckwheat bread that looks and tastes like a lichened stone mandala from the prayer walls. Blue sheep have littered this small dooryard with their dung, a human hand has painted a sun and moon above the lintel, yet in this forlorn place, here at the edge of things, the stony bread, the dung and painted moon, the lonely tattering of flags worn to transparence by the wind seem as illusory as sanity itself. The deep muttering of boulders in Black River—why am I uneasy? To swallow the torrent, sun, and wind, to fill one's breath with the plenitude of being . . . and yet. . . . I draw back from that sound, which seems to echo the dread rumble of the universe. Perhaps I imagine things, but earlier on this same ledge, as if impelled, my boots sought out the loose stones and snow-hidden ice, and I felt dull and heavy and afraid; there was a power in the air, a random menace. On the return, an oppression has lifted, I am light and quick. Things go better when my left foot is on the outside edge, as it is now, but this cannot account for the sudden limberness, the pleasure in skirting the same abyss that two hours ago filled me with dread. Not that I cease to pay attention; on the contrary, it is the precise bite and feel and sound of every step that fills me with life. Sun rays glance from snow pinnacles above and the black choughs dance in their escadrilles over the void, and dark and light interpenetrate the path, in the all-pervading presence of this moment.

November 10

These days are luminous, as in those far October days in Tichu-Rong. There is no wisp of cloud—clear, clear, clear, clear. Although the shade is very cold throughout the day, and wind persists, the sun is hot—imagine a striped and shiny lizard above 15,000 feet, in deep November! For the first time in my life, I apprehend the pure heat of our star, piercing the frigid atmospheres of so many million miles of outer space.

Rock, and snow peaks all around, the sky, and great birds and black rivers—what words are there to seize such ringing splendor? But again something arises in this ringing that is not quite bearable, a poised terror, as in the diamond ice that cracks the stone. The brain veers; the sun glints like a weapon. The Black Canyon writhes and twists, and the Crystal Mountain looms as a castle of dread, and all the universe reverberates with horror. My head is the sorcerer's skull cup full of blood, and were I to turn, my eyes would see straight to the heart of chaos, the mutilation, bloody gore, and pain that are seen darkly in the bright eye of this lizard.

Then lunacy is gone, leaving an echo. The lizard is still there, one with its rock, flanks pulsing in the star heat that brings warmth to our common skin. Eternity is not remote, it is here beside us.

November 11

In the east, at dark, bright Mars appears, and soon the full moon follows the sun's path, east to west across a blue-black sky. I am always restless in the time of the full moon, a common lunatic, and move about the frozen monastery, moon-watching. Rising over the White River, the moon illuminates the ghostly prayer flag blowing so softly on the roof of the still hut, and seems to kindle the stacked brushwood; on its altar stone my small clay Buddha stirs. The snow across the river glows, and the rocks and peaks, the serpentine black stream, the snows, sky, stars, the firmament—all ring like the bell of the universal Buddha. *Now!* Here is the secret! *Now!*

In hope of seeing the snow leopard, I have made a wind shelter and lookout on this mountain, just at snowline, that faces north over the Black Canyon all the way to the pale terraces below Samling. From here the Tsakang mountainsides across Black River are in view, and the cliff caves, too, and the slopes between ravines, so that most of the blue sheep in this region may been seen should they be set upon by wolf or leopard. Unlike the wolves, the leopard cannot eat everything at once, and may remain in the vicinity of its kill for several days. Therefore our best hope is to see the griffons gather, and the choughs and ravens, and the lammergeier.

The Himalayan griffon, buff and brown, is almost the size of the great lammergeier. Its graceful turns against the peaks inspire the Tibetans, who, like the vanished Aryans of the Vedas, revere the wind and sky. For Buddhist Tibetans, prayer flags and wind bells confide spiritual longings to the winds, and the red kites that dance on holidays over the old brown city of Kathmandu are of Tibetan origin as well. There is also a custom called "air burial" in which the body of the deceased is set out on a wild crag such as this one, to be rent and devoured by the wild beasts; when only the bones are left, these are broken and ground to powder, then mixed into lumps of dough, to be set out again for passing birds. Thus all is returned into the elements, death into life.

Against the faces of the canyon, shadows of griffons turn. Perhaps the Somdo raptors think that this queer lump on the landscape—the motionless form of a man in meditation—is the defunct celebrant in an air burial, for a golden eagle, plumage burnished a heraldic bronzy-black, draws near with its high peeping, and a lammergeier, approaching from behind, descends with a sudden rush of feathers, sweeping so close past my head that I feel the break of air. This whisper of the shroud gives me a start, and my sudden jump flares the dark bird, causing it to take four deep, slow strokes—the only movement of the wings that I was ever to observe in this great sailer that sweeps up and down the Himalayan canyons, the cold air ringing in its golden head.

Dark, light, dark: a raptor, scimitar-winged, under the sun

peak—I know, I know. In such a light, one might hope to see the shadow of that bird upon the sky.

The ground whirls with its own energy, not in an alarming way but in a slow spiral, and at these altitudes, in this vast space and silence, that energy pours through me, joining my body with the sun until small silver breaths of cold, clear air, no longer mine, are lost in the mineral breathing of the mountain. A white down feather, sun-filled, dances before me on the wind: alighting nowhere, it balances on a shining thorn, goes spinning on. Between this white feather, sheep dung, light, and the fleeting aggregate of atoms that is "I," there is no particle of difference. There is a mountain opposite, but this "I" is opposite nothing, opposed to nothing.

I grow into these mountains like a moss. I am bewitched. The blinding snow peaks and the clarion air, the sound of earth and heaven in the silence, the requiem birds, the mythic beasts, the flags, great horns, and old carved stones, the rough-hewn Tartars in their braids and homespun boots, the silver ice in the black river, the Kang, the Crystal Mountain. Also, I love the common miracles—the murmur of my friends at evening, the clay fires of smudgy juniper, the coarse, dull food, the hardship and simplicity, the contentment of doing one thing at a time: when I take my blue tin cup into my hand, that is all I do. We have had no news of modern times since late September, and will have none until December, and gradually my mind has cleared itself, and wind and sun pour through my head, as through a bell. Though we talk little here, I am never lonely; I am returned into myself. Having got here at last, I do not wish to leave the Crystal Mountain. I am in pain about it, truly, so much so that I have to smile, or I might weep. I think of Deborah and how she would smile, too. In another life—this isn't what I know, but how I feel—these mountains were my home; there is a rising of forgotten knowledge, like a spring from hidden aquifers under the earth. To glimpse one's own nature is a kind of homegoing, to a place East of the Sun, West of the Moon— the homegoing that needs no home, like that waterfall on the

100

upper Suli Gad that turns to mist before touching the earth and rises once again into the sky.

Yesterday a circumambulating wolf left a whole circle of tracks around the prayer wall across the river, at the foot of the trail that climbs around the mountains to Tsakang, and this morning, on the trail itself, there are prints of leopard. As if seeking protection, the blue sheep feed close by the hermitage, where I go with Jang-bu to call on the Lama of Shey.

When we arrive, the lama is inside chanting sutras, but his attendant sits outside, cutting and sorting their small store of potatoes; he is an aspirant monk, or *trapa*, whose clear gaze makes him look much younger than he is. His name is Takla, he is twenty-two years old, and he comes from the great north plain of Tibet.

On the sunny ledge, under the bright blue window of the gompa, we listen to the murmurs of the lama and contemplate the prospect of the snows. Soon the mountains stir, then shift and vibrate—how vital these rocks seem, against blue sky! If only they would fly apart, consume us in a fire of white light. But I am not ready, and resist, in fear of losing my death grip on the world, on all that provides the illusion of security. The same fear—of loss of control, of "insanity," far worse than the fear of death—can occur with the hallucinogenic drugs. Familiar things, losing the form assigned to them, begin to spin, and the center does not hold, because we search for it outside instead of in.

When the lama appears, he seems glad of our visit, though we lack the gift of a *kata*, or ceremonial white scarf, that is customary on such occasions. He is an imposing man with the long hawk nose and carved cheekbones of a Plains Indian. His

101

skin is a dark reddish copper, his teeth are white, his long black hair is tied up in a braid, and he wears an old leather jacket with brass buttons, patched with burlap homespun of strange colors. When talking, he sits with legs crossed, barefoot, but puts on ancient laceless shoes when he moves around. In the doorway behind him hangs a wolf skin that he wears about his waist, indoors, to warm his back.

The lama of the Crystal Monastery appears to be a very happy man, and yet I wonder how he feels about his isolation in the silences of Tsakang, which he has not left in eight years now and, because he is crippled, may never leave again. Since Jang-bu seems uncomfortable with the lama or with himself or perhaps with us, I tell him not to inquire on this point if it seems to him impertinent, but after a moment Jang-bu does so. And this holy man of great directness and simplicity, big white teeth shining, laughs out loud in an infectious way at Jang-bu's question. Indicating his twisted legs without a trace of self-pity or bitterness—they belong to all of us—he casts his arms wide to the sky and the snow mountains, the high sun and dancing sheep, and cries, "Of course I am happy here! It's wonderful! *Especially* when I have no choice!"

In its wholehearted acceptance of *what is*, this is just what Soen-roshi might have said: I feel as if he had struck me in the chest. I thank him, bow, go softly down the mountain. Butter tea and wind pictures, the Crystal Mountain, and blue sheep dancing on the snow—it's quite enough!

Have you seen the snow leopard?
No! Isn't that wonderful?

November 15

The moon is waning, and the fine lunar clarity of life at Shey swiftly diminishes. A kind of power is winding down, a spell is broken.

102

I prepare to go, though I try hard to remain. The part of me that longs to see my children, to drink wine, make love, be clean and comfortable again—that part is already facing south, over the mountains. This makes me sad, and so I stare about me, trying to etch into this journal the sense of Shey that is so precious, aware that all such effort is in vain; the beauty of this place must be cheerfully abandoned, like the wild rocks in the bright water of its streams. Frustration at the paltriness of words drives me to write, but there is more of Shey in a single sheep hair, in one withered sprig of everlasting, than in all these notes; to strive for permanence in what I think I have perceived is to miss the point.

Near my lookout, I find a place to meditate, out of the wind, a hollow on the ridge where snow has melted. My brain soon clears in the cold mountain air, and I feel better. Wind, blowing grasses, sun: the drying grass, the notes of southbound birds in the mountain sky are no more fleeting than the rock itself, no more so and no less—all is the same. The mountain withdraws into its stillness, my body dissolves into the sunlight, tears fall that have nothing to do with "I." What it is that brings them on, I do not know.

In other days, I understood mountains differently, seeing in them something that abides. Even when approached respectfully (to challenge peaks as mountaineers do is another matter), they appalled me with their "permanence," with that awful and irrefutable *rock*-ness that seemed to intensify my sense of my own transience. Perhaps this dread of transience explains our greed for the few gobbets of raw experience in modern life, why violence is libidinous, why lust devours us, why soldiers choose not to forget their days of horror: we cling to such extreme moments, in which we seem to die, yet are reborn. In sexual abandon as in danger we are impelled, however briefly, into that vital present in which we do not stand apart from life, we *are* life, our being fill us; in ecstasy with another being, loneliness falls away into eternity.

Yet in other days, such union was attainable through simple awe.

My foot slips on a narrow ledge: in that split second, as needles of fear pierce heart and temples, eternity intersects with present time. Thought and action are not different, and stone, air, ice, sun, fear, and self are one. What is exhilarating is to extend the acute awareness of such split seconds into ordinary moments, as in the moment-by-moment experience of the lammergeier and the wolf, which, finding themselves at the center of things, have no need for any secret of true being.

In this very breath that we take now lies the secret that all great teachers try to tell us, what one lama refers to as "the precision and openness and intelligence of the present."[3] The purpose of meditation practice is not enlightenment; it is to pay attention even at unextraordinary times, to be of the present, nothing-but-the-present, to bear this mindfulness of *now* into each event of ordinary life. To be anywhere else is "to paint eyeballs on chaos."[4] When I watch blue sheep, I must watch blue sheep, not be thinking about sex, danger, or the present, for this present—even while I think of it—is gone.

November 16

Not a thousand feet above our tents at Shey, on the path that I walked yesterday, a leopard has made its scrape right in my boot print, as if in sign that I am not to leave. The leopard may still be present on this slope, for the rams are skittish. Even so, the rut is near, activity is constant, and G.S. scribbles in his notebook. "Oh, there's a penis-lick!" he cries. "A beauty!" The onanism is mingled here and there with fighting, especially among the older rams, which rear repeatedly on their hind legs; remarkably, another rears at the same instant, and the two run forward like trained partners, coming down together with a crash of heads. For most creatures, such an encounter would be fatal, but bharal are equipped with some two inches of parietal bone between the horns, together with a cushion of air space in the sinuses, thick woolly head hair, and strong necks to absorb the shock, and the horns themselves, on the impact side, are very thick and heavy. Why nature should devote so many centuries—thousands, probably—to the natural selection of these characters that favor head-on collisions over brains is a good question, although speaking for myself in these searching days, less brains and a good head-on collision might be just the answer.

November 17

I climb to my old lookout, happy and sad in the dim instinct that these mountains are my home. But "only the Awakened Ones remember their many births and deaths,"[5] and I can hear no whisperings of other lives. Doubtless I have "home" confused with childhood, and Shey with its flags and beasts and snowy fastnesses with some Dark Ages place of forgotten fairy tales, where the atmosphere of myth made life heroic.

In the longing that starts one on the way of Zen is a kind of homesickness, and some way, on this journey, I have started home. Homegoing is the purpose of my practice, of my mountain meditation and my daybreak chanting, of my koan: All the peaks are covered with snow—why is this one bare? To resolve that illogical question would mean to burst apart, let fall all preconceptions and supports. But I am not ready to let go, and so I shall not resolve my koan, or see the snow leopard, that is to say, *perceive it*. I shall not see it because I am not ready.

I meditate for the last time on this mountain that is bare, though others all around are white with snow. Like the bare peak of the koan, this one is not different from myself. I know this mountain because I am this mountain, I can feel it breathing at this moment, as its grass tops stray against the snows. If the snow leopard should leap from the rock above and manifest itself before me—S-A-A-O!—then in that moment of pure fright, *out of my wits*, I might truly perceive it, and be free.

In the cold wind, the track is icy even at midday, yet one cannot wander to the side without plunging through the crust. The regular slow step that works best on steep mountainside is difficult; I slip and clamber. Far above, a train of yaks makes dark curves on the shining ice. Soon a second herd overtakes me, the twine-soled herders strolling up the icy incline with hands clasped behind their backs, grunting and whistling at the heaving animals. Then black goats come clicking up the ice glaze, straight, straight up to the noon sky; the goat horns turn silver on the blue as, in the vertigo and brilliance of high sun, the white peak spins. The goatherd, clad from head to boots in blood-red wool, throws balls of snow to keep his beasts in line. Crossing the sun, the balls dissolve in a pale fire.

Eventually the track arrives at the snowfields beneath the summit rim; I am exhausted. Across the whiteness sails a lammergeier, trailing its shadow on the snow, and the wing shadow draws me taut and sends me on. For two more hours I trudge and pant and climb and slip and climb and gasp, dull as any brute, while high above, the prayer flags fly on the westering sun, which turns the cold rocks igneous and the hard sky to white light. Flag shadows dance upon the white walls of the drifts as I enter the shadow of the peak, in an ice tunnel, toiling and heaving, eyes fixed stupidly upon the snow. Then I am in the sun once more, on the last of the high passes, removing my woolen cap to let the wind clear my head. I sink to my knees, exhilarated, spent, on a narrow spine between two worlds.

To the south and west, glowing in snow light and late sun, the great white Kanjirobas rise in haze, like mystical peaks that might vanish at each moment. The caravans are gone into the underworld. Far behind me and below, in the wastes where I have come from, my companions are black specks upon the snow. Still breathing hard, I listen to the wind in my own breath, the ringing silence, the snow fire and soaring rocks, the relentless tappeting of prayer flags, worn diaphanous, that cast wind pictures to the northern blue.

I have the universe all to myself. The universe has me all to itself.

November 24

From the village, a southward path quits the main trail, descending through rocks and shining olives to a bridge on the green river. The portals of the bridge are carved in grotesque figures, yellow and red. Awaiting the others, I stand on the hot planks in the noon sun, overtaken by a vague despair.

Another hour passes; no one comes. Beside myself, I go on across the bridge and climb the bluff. A half mile below, the jade water of the snow peaks disappears into the gray roil of the Bheri River, which will bear it southward into lowland muds.

The track follows the Bheri westward in a long, gradual climb to the horizon, arriving at a village in a forest. In the cedars of Roman, a fitful wind whips the mean rags on the shrines, and phallic spouts jut from red effigies at the village fountains, and west of the village stand wild cairns and tall red poles. From fields below, a troupe of curl-tailed monkey demons gazes upward, heads afire in the dying light. Then the sun is gone behind the mountains.

I have a headache and feel very strange. The whole day has been muddied by a raging in my head caused by the tardiness of my companions, who were two hours behind me at the bridge—an echo of that grotesque rage at Murwa, where for want of unfrozen air in which to bathe, I vilified the sun that dodged my tent. I seem to have lost all resilience, not to mention sense of humor—can this be dread of the return to lowland life?

Walking along the Bheri hills this afternoon, I remembered how careful one must be not to talk too much, or move abruptly,

107

after a silent week of Zen retreat, and also the precarious coming down from highs on the hallucinogens. It is crucial to emerge gradually from such a chrysalis, drying new wings in the sun's quiet, like a butterfly, to avoid a sudden tearing of the spirit. Certainly this has been a silent time, and a hallucinatory inner journey, too, and now there is this sudden loss of altitude. Whatever the reason, I am coming down too fast—too fast for what? And if I am coming down too fast, why do I hurry? Far from celebrating my great journey, I feel mutilated, murderous: I am in a fury of dark energies, with no control at all on my short temper.

Thus, when a Hindu of Roman, knocking small children aside, pushes his scabby head into my tent and glares about in stupid incredulity, yelling inchoate questions at my face out of a bad mouth with a rotting lip, I lunge at him and shove him bodily out of my sight, lashing the tent flap and yelling incomprehensibly myself. I do not have the medicine he needs, and anyway there is no cure for him, no cure for me. How can he know, poor stinking bastard, that it is not his offensiveness that offends me, the pus and the bad breath of him—no, it is his very flesh, no different from my own. In his damnable need, he returns me to our common plight, this pit of longing into which, having failed in my poor leap, I sink again.

"Expect nothing," Eido-roshi had warned me on the day I left. And I had meant to go lightly into the light and silence of the Himalaya, without ambition of attainment. Now I am spent. The path I followed breathlessly has faded among stones; in spiritual ambition, I have neglected my children and done myself harm, and there is no way back. Nor has anything changed. I am still beset by the same old lusts and ego and emotions, the endless nagging details and irritations. I have lost the flow of things and gone awry, sticking out from the unwinding spiral of my life like a bent spring. For all the exhilaration, splendor, and "success" of the journey to the Crystal Mountain, a great chance has been missed and I have failed. I will perform the motions of parenthood, my work, my friendships, my Zen practice, but all hopes, acts, and travels have been blighted. I look forward to nothing.

November 25

Remembering the depression of my first descent from Tarakot into the Bheri Canyon, I have convinced myself that sudden loss of altitude is the main clue to my veering moods. A change is taking place, some painful growth, as in a snake during the shedding of its skin—dull, irritable, without appetite, dragging about the stale shreds of a former life, near-blinded by the old dead scale on the new eye. It is difficult to adjust because I do not know who is adjusting; I am no longer that old person and not yet the new.

Already the not-looking-forward, the without-hope-ness takes on a subtle attraction, as if I had glimpsed the secret of these mountains, still half understood. With the past evaporated, the future pointless, and all expectation worn away, I begin to experience that *now* that is spoken of by the great teachers.

To the repentant thief upon the cross, the gentle Jesus of the modern Bible holds out hope of Heaven: "Today thou art with me in Paradise." But in older translations, as Soen-roshi points out, there is no "today," no suggestion of the future. In the Russian Orthodox translation, for example, the meaning is "right here now." Thus, Jesus declares, "You are in Paradise *right now*"—how much more vital! There is no hope anywhere but in this moment, in the karmic terms laid down by one's own life. This very day is an aspect of nirvana, which is not different from samsara but, rather, a subtle alchemy, the manifestation of dark mud in the pure, white blossom of the lotus.

"Of course I enjoy this life! It's wonderful! *Especially* when I have no choice!"

And perhaps this is what Tukten knows—that the journey

to Dolpo, step by step and day by day, is the Jewel in the Heart of the Lotus, the Tao, the Way, the Path, but no more so than small events of days at home. The teaching offered us by Lama Tupjuk, with the snow leopard watching from the rocks and the Crystal Mountain flying on the sky, was not, as I had thought that day, the enlightened wisdom of one man but a splendid utterance of the divine in all mankind.

We climb onward, toward the sky, and with every step my spirits rise. As I walk along, my stave striking the ground, I leave the tragic sense of things behind; I begin to smile, infused with a sense of my own foolishness, with an acceptance of the failures of this journey as well as of its wonders, acceptance of all that I might meet upon my path. I know that this transcendence will be fleeting, but while it lasts, I spring along the path as if set free. So light do I feel that I might be back in the celestial snows.

This clear and silent light of the Himalaya is intensified by the lack of smoke and noise. The myriad high peaks, piercing the atmosphere, let pass a light of heaven—the light on stones that makes them ring, the sun roaring and the silverness that flows in lichens and the wings of crows, the silverness in the round tinkle of a pony's bell, and in the scent of snows.

The world turns, and the silver light takes on an unholy shine. It pierces small figures high up on the slopes, the peasants of fateful, demon-ridden ages, stiff two-legged effigies of men, harassing the accursed brutes that drag the dull wood blade. *E-ughaa!* Grunting and bellowing, man turns beast with the cruel ring through the nostrils, back again, turn again, back again, century upon century, in the grim plod that drags the harrow through the stony soil. And the lump woman, bent to earth one row ahead, hacking at stones with the crude mattock—step, hoe, step, hoe—*whut!* She flinches as the twig goad stings the hard flanks of the beasts. *Whut! E-ughaa!*

Whut!

Below the track, an old woman in wild black rags flails barley heaps on the flat roof of her hut; the wood blade cuts the

110

mountain sky as she rears to strike. Under a walnut tree, a hangman's limb, a black cow awaits the dusk. Its bell is still.

At the trekking company, where we return our pots and tents, all praise of Tukten is in vain: he is known by bad reputation to the manager, who will have no part of him. Tukten, he says, is a loner who does not get on with the clannish sherpa groups who make up the best expedition teams. Unlike most sherpas, he is an aggressive drinker, and his foul barracks language offends them. No doubt he is intelligent and able, no doubt he is excellent day by day, but sooner or later—the manager points sternly at the door, outside of which my friend awaits—that fellow will let you down when you most need him.

And Tukten has known the answer all along, having only assented to my great plans to be polite, for he smiles as I come out—not to make light of things, far less to save face, but to console me. "Plenty job, sah," Tukten says. He accepts his life, and will go on wandering until it ends.

Suddenly it is twilight, and our ways are parting. Tukten insists on escorting me to the door of my hotel, and is sorry that I will not let him pay the taxi. He wishes that I meet him three days hence at the great stupa at Bodhinath, four miles away, where he will stay briefly with his father's sister and renew himself as a good Buddhist before returning to Khundu, near Namche Bazaar, to pass the winter.

With hotel staff hissing at my elbow, I shake Tukten's hand under the portico, and it occurs to me to invite him in to supper. I know that this is sentimental, a show of democratic principles at his expense, for the caste-crazy staff will make things miserable for this soiled sherpa in the jersey much too big for him. Even if they restrain themselves for the sake of their baksheesh, a friendship formed in mountain sun might be damaged in the

111

sour light of the hotel. All true, all true, and yet that I feel too tired to transcend these difficulties upsets me very much. I let him go.

In the rear window of the cab, Tukten is ghostly; I stare after him as he withdraws into the dusk. It is not so much that this man and I are friends. Rather, there is a thread between us, like the black thread of live nerve; there is something unfinished, and he knows it, too. Without ever attempting to speak about it, we perceive life in the same way, or rather, I perceive it in the way that Tukten lives it. In his life in the moment, in his freedom from attachments, in the simplicity of his everyday example, Tukten has taught me over and over, he is the teacher that I hoped to find: I used to say this to myself as a kind of instinctive joke, but now I wonder if it is not true. "When you are ready," Buddhists say, "the teacher will appear." In the way he watched over me, in the way he smiled, he was awaiting me. Had I been ready, he might have led me far enough along the path "to see the snow leopard."

Out of respect, I stand in the same place until Tukten is out of sight. The Hindus dart off with my backpack, sleeping bag, and rucksack, and for a moment I am all alone on the hotel steps. Off to the north, black clouds are shrouding the black mountains; it is snowing. Here I am, safely returned over those peaks from a journey far more beautiful and strange than anything I had hoped for or imagined—how is it that this safe return brings such regret?

By mistake, all my November mail has been sent to Jumla: I stood right next to it this morning at the airstrip. India Airlines is on strike, and no one will say when a flight out of Nepal will be available. In my room with bath, anticipated for two months, the room is wintry and the bath has no hot water; for an hour, the unqualified crowd in and out while I stand fuming in my grimy long johns. Four or five line up at last for their baksheesh, and the plumber, whichever one is he, departs—gone until tomorrow, as I learn when it turns out that there is no more hot water than before. I force the door of the next room, usurp

112

the bath: the hot water runs out as I soap. Stomping back to my own room, I discover that the hot water has turned up magically of its own accord. Feeling silly and quite suddenly exhausted, I sit down on the bed and begin to laugh, but I might just as easily weep. In the gaunt, brown face in the mirror—unseen since late September—the blue eyes in a monkish skull seem eerily clear, but this is the face of a man I do not know.

December 1

On the day appointed to meet Tukten, I pedal across the late-autumn landscapes of the Kathmandu Valley to the ancient shrine at Bodhinath. The painted eyes above the white dome of its stupa, peering over the brown rooftops, watch me come. Tradition says that Bodhinath's creation was blessed by Ava-lokiteshvara, and that it contains relics of Kasapa, he who smiled a Tukten smile when the Buddha held up the lotus flower in silent teaching. In former years the shrine was visited by throngs of pilgrims from Tibet, and the colorful stupa is surrounded by a square of dwellings and small shops that sell brass Buddhas, icons, urns, and ritual daggers, beads of bone, stone, wood, and turquoise, incense, prayer wheels, cymbals, drums, and bells.

In one of these houses, Tukten said, he would be staying with his father's sister. Accosting inhabitants, calling his name, I walk my bicycle round and round the square, under the huge painted eyes, the nose like a great question mark, the wind-snapped pennants—Tukten? Tukten? But there is no answer, no one knows of Tukten Sherpa. Under the Bodhi Eye, I get on my bicycle again and return along gray December roads to Kathmandu.

JAPAN

SOTO JOURNALS 1976–1982

Now, mountains, rivers, earth, the sun, moon, and stars are mind. At just this moment, what is it that appears directly in front of you? The sun, moon, and stars as seen by humans are not the same, and the views of various beings differ widely. Likewise the views about one mind differ. Yet these views are nothing but mind. Is it inside or outside? Does it come or go? Does it increase one bit at birth or not? Does it decrease one particle at death or not? . . . All this is merely a moment or two of mind. A moment or two of mind is a moment of mountains, rivers, and earth, or two moments of mountains, rivers and earth. . . .

"Everyday mind" means to maintain an everyday mind in the world of life and the world of death. Yesterday goes forth from this moment, and today comes forth from this place. When it goes the boundless sky goes, when it comes the entire earth comes. . . . This boundless sky and entire earth are like unrecognized words, or the one voice that gushes out of the earth.

Body and Mind Study of the Way
—EIHEI DOGEN

CHAPTER NINE

ON the day that ended the great inaugural sesshin at Dai Bosatsu, a group of Zen priests led by Sochu-roshi wished to visit the large bronze statue of the Buddha on the farther shore of Beecher Lake, perhaps two hundred yards across the water from the monastery. Instructed to ferry them across, I watched in alarm as buddha after buddha stepped blithely from the little dock into the leaky flat-bottomed rowboat, then remained standing, not simply because of inexperience with boats but because there was no room to sit down. Speaking not a word of Japanese, I waved and motioned with respectful gestures, trying to convey the impossibility of the whole plan.

Cheerfully the roshis waved and motioned back. Being innocent of nautical experience (or privy to miraculous information), they saw no reason why arm-waving, enthusiastic groups of upright and robust Zen masters should not travel in confidence across dark waters in a small, overloaded boat. Impatient with this indecisive student, one waved me on while another attempted to join me on the oarsman's seat; a third leaned far overboard in a strenuous effort to push the boat free from the dock, to which I clung with straining arms until all at last were squashed onto the seats. At this point the boat was so low in the water that even if some ill-considered motion did not capsize it, the first zephyr of ill wind would bring the lake pouring in over the gunwales. I groaned as yet another buddha, coming down the slope, was greeted with shouts of welcome from the boating party.

This roshi, a handsome man in his early forties, was the Soto teacher from Los Angeles who had participated in Eido-roshi's *shin-san-shiki*, or abbot installation, in 1972. Taizan Mae-zumi-roshi[1] made no effort to get in the boat, nor did he caution the other roshis to abandon the doomed craft while there was time. Ignoring my signals of distress, he smiled like a sad angel, as if this group was already beyond saving, and nodded his head in the direction of the Buddha statue across the lake. Still I hesitated, and he murmured quietly, "It is all right." Either he knew something that I did not, or he refused to intervene in the imminent destruction of his Rinzai brothers. "It is all right," he repeated with implacable serenity, still smiling that sad, beatific smile, as if giving me the Zen instruction, "Do not cling!"

His conviction was impressive, and fired my spirit. Letting go, I set off with small and mindful strokes across the water. Maezumi-roshi stood unmoving on the dock, a guardian spirit, as I transported those buddha-beings to the other shore, then steadied the boat in the mad thrash for camera angles that took place beneath the bronze eye of the Buddha (for even Zen masters, in camera-crazed Japan, are equipped to record the illusory nature of existence). Returned to the dock, they cried out, *"Kino doku!"* ("Oh, this poisonous feeling!" [of being in your debt]) and *"Arigato!"* (*"Such* a difficult matter!").[2] Maezumi-roshi, with a minute bow, turned away and walked back up the hill.

Maezumi-roshi had been preceded to Dai Bosatsu by his two senior monks, Tetsugen and Gempo, who urged me to come and study with him in Los Angeles. The timing was auspicious since I was frequently in California on research related to American Indians. American Indian spirituality seemed so akin to Zen (as well as to Tibetan Buddhism) that in my Himalayan journals I was speculating about ancient common origins, an archaic religion, perhaps, in some formerly fertile heartland such as Soen-roshi's old haunt in the Gobi Desert.

In mid-January of 1977, on a two-day visit to the Zen Center of Los Angeles, I received a warm welcome from Maezumi-roshi, Tetsugen, and Gempo. The following week I returned to ZCLA for January sesshin. Maezumi-roshi was extremely hospitable, putting me up in his own house, but sesshin itself was disconcerting. Although I enjoyed my outdoor work on the center's buildings, the long work-practice periods that are customary in Soto temples weakened the intensity of relentless zazen that I had come to depend on in Rinzai practice. And Soto Zen, which traditionally emphasizes shikan-taza, or "just sitting,"[3] over the use of koan study, lacks the rigor and precision, the shouting and strong use of the keisaku or "warning stick" that characterizes the more spartan Rinzai tradition. (In Soto, the same word is pronounced *kyosaku* and is translated as "encouragement stick.") Maezumi's undramatic teisho, delivered in a murmur so soft that one could scarcely make out his words, was a gentle teaching very different from the vivid, often startling performances of the Rinzai masters.

Nevertheless, Maezumi emphasized strong koan study, which has rarely been associated with Soto Zen. Koan study seems to have evolved out of a split between Zen schools which occurred as early as the Golden Age of Zen in China, among the Dharma heirs of the Sixth Patriarch, Daikan Eno (Hui Neng, 638–713).[4] One faction put special emphasis on Bodhidharma's teaching of a "special transmission outside the scriptures . . . pointing directly to man's own mind." This was later identified with "sudden" illumination or enlightenment born of koan study—the profound contemplation, in zazen, of the cryptic acts, sayings, and responses of the old masters, such as the First Patriarch's exchange with the Emperor Wu. A second faction, founded by Hui Neng's foremost disciple, Seigen Gyoshi, is identified with "gradual" or "silent" illumination based on "just sitting," citing the tradition that, after his encounter with Emperor Wu, the First Patriarch, Bodhidharma, crossed the Yangtze River, retired to Shorin Temple on Mount Su, and spent nine years "just sitting" in shikan-taza, "facing the wall."

The sudden flourishing of the Zen schools is credited to Masters Sekito and Baso, "the two gates of elixir," whose many disciples would travel all over China. Sekito Kisen, the remarkable "Monk on the Rock," had studied with Daikan Eno in the Sixth Patriarch's last years before receiving Dharma transmission from Seigen Gyoshi, and he tried in vain to heal the dissension between Daikan Eno's forty disciples that would harden eventually into rival schools. Meanwhile Sekito composed the *Sandokai*, or "Identity of Relative and Absolute," a seminal Zen document which laid the foundation for the *Hokyo Zammai* (Jeweled-Mirror Samadhi) teaching set down by his Dharma heirs. Sekito's "gradual" lineages, distinguished by such eminent masters as Tozan, Sozan, and Tokusan, were eventually consolidated in the T'sao-t'ung school, called Soto (from Sozan and Tozan) in Japan.

> Once Tozan asked Sozan, "Where are you going?"
> Sozan said, "To an unchanging place."
> Tozan said, "If it's unchanging, how could there be any going?"
> Sozan said, "Going, too, is unchanging."[5]

Over the centuries the schism deepened as the "sudden" faction gained the ascendancy. A Baso lineage descending through

Hyakujo (Po Chang) and Obaku (Huang Po) eventually produced Rinzai (Lin Chi), whose name is attached to what was to become the strongest school in the Land of T'ang. Another Baso lineage that included Nansen and Joshu would die out, as would the line that ended with Gutei. Soto lines were also disappearing for want of qualified Dharma successors. When Unmon's line came to an end not long after his death in 949, the prestige and power of the Zen schools was already waning, and the Golden Age was at an end, yet the rivalry between T'sao-t'ung and Lin Chi continued fiercely.[6]

In the koan collections of both schools, there are wonderful "Dharma combats" between monks and masters, but the spare exchanges lack descriptive details, and only a few teachers such as Joshu and Unmon emerge from the records with distinct and idiosyncratic qualities. No teacher, not Daikan Eno (nor even Shakyamuni), comes to life so insistently as that hard-looking 110-year-old called Bodhidharma, who favored dispensing with abstractions, idle words in order to point directly at "the fact itself."

> Rinzai was washing his feet. Joshu came along and asked, "Why did Bodhidharma come from India to China? [What is this "Zen"? What is the essence of the Buddha Dharma?]
> Rinzai continued washing his feet.
> Joshu came closer, pretending he had not heard Rinzai's response.
> Master Rinzai poured away the dirty water.

If koan are teaching devices designed to break down intellectual concepts of reality and open the way for a profound apprehension of the universal reality beneath, they are also pure expressions of enlightened mind. "The koan," Maezumi-roshi says, "is quite literally a touch-stone of reality . . . in which a key issue of practice and realization is presented and examined by experience rather than by discursive or linear logic . . . to help us penetrate more deeply into the significance of life and death." The student's understanding is repeatedly fired in dokusan—face-to-face confrontation with a living buddha, as a Zen master of authentic lineage must be regarded—and tempered by the master's teisho,[7] which are not lectures but vivid manifestations of the Dharma.

The split between the "sudden" and "gradual" schools carried over to Japan, but from the start, in both China and Japan, the more interesting masters tended to ignore it. Maezumi-roshi's teachers (both Rinzai and Soto) considered koan study important, and during sesshin he tested my understanding with the Sound of One Hand and its fourteen "checkpoints"—each one a separate koan—which are progressively more difficult. At one point he asked if I had ever had a kensho, and I related my premature experience of November 1971 and the few small "openings" or glimpses since that time. He murmured, "Just keep practicing and you will have another clear experience." Of my "flat" sesshins he said, "They should not be flat—deep and quiet, yes. And when you get to this deep place, it is very comfortable, but you must not stay there—go beyond!"

Maezumi-roshi's koan study mainly derives from a system transmitted by Hakuun Yasutani-roshi, who led sesshin in America almost every year between 1962 and 1969. His Los Angeles sesshin in 1967 was attended by a young aeronautics engineer named Bernard Glassman, born in Brooklyn, New York, in 1939. Glassman had been attracted to Zen writings in the late fifties, while still in college, but had no idea where he might find a teacher. About 1965, he heard about a weekly sitting, or *zazenkai*, mostly for Caucasians, that was being held at the Soto temple in Los Angeles. After zazen there was tea and talk, and Glassman asked about the purpose of the slow walking between sittings. The head priest, Sumi-roshi, told a young Japanese monk to explain, and this monk said, "When you walk, just walk."

"I guess that was my first Zen instruction," says Bernie Glassman, better known today by his Dharma name, Tetsugen. "Not long afterwards, this monk left the Soto temple, and I did, too, because Sumi-roshi did not really speak English, and I was making no progress at all. Then, in 1966 or 1967, I heard that a Zen master was to give a talk at the Theosophical Society. The master was Yasutani-roshi and his translator was this same young monk, Maezumi-sensei, who had opened his own 'Los Angeles Zendo' on Serrano Avenue. I was very impressed by Maezumi's translations, and I knew that he was someone I could study with."

In 1968, young Bernie Glassman practiced zazen at the L.A. Zendo, and that year Yasutani came again and led a one-day sesshin. At dokusan, he gave Glassman the koan Mu. Afterward, Glassman had a lot of questions about Mu, but Maezumi-sensei, who had not completed koan study, would not answer them. Maezumi told his student to do shikan-taza until Yasutani came back the following year. By that time, all Glassman wished to talk about was shikan-taza.

"He had a dirty beard!" Maezumi recalls, remembering his first impression of young Glassman. "But he also had a flashing light in the eyes, and naiveté in the good sense of the word, open and ready to receive anything he could get. He became an exceptional Zen student because of his devotion to his practice, an ability to hurl himself into whatever he had to do. Very early, he knew how to throw the self away, to become selfless; that's why he could do so well under hard circumstances. He *knew* what was important and what was unimportant, and he did not waste his time." From the start, Maezumi-sensei gave this unusual student unusual responsibilities, and for fifteen months, beginning in September 1969, when Maezumi accompanied Yasutani back to Japan, Glassman was in charge at ZCLA.

In 1970, when Bernie Glassman received a Ph.D. in applied mathematics from UCLA, he was already employed as an aeronautical engineer and administrator for McDonnell-Douglas. He was also a fervent practitioner of Zen. In the year of his doctorate, he shaved his head and was ordained by Maezumi as a Zen monk or priest—neither term is accurate—in the *tokudo*, or "home-leaving," ceremony, which almost persuaded his wife Helen to pack up their two infant children and leave home. Meanwhile he was contributing his salary to the new Zen Community of Los Angeles, which otherwise depended for support on the savings earned in a poor neighborhood by the gardening efforts of his new friend and teacher.

In December 1970, Maezumi completed his studies with Yasutani and received his Dharma seal. Yasutani-roshi never returned to the United States; he died in March, 1973, just prior to a planned journey to the United States for his ninetieth birthday. His friend Soen, concluding a long poem of commemoration, said:

> Eighty-nine years, just-as-it-is!
> How can I express, right now,
> The grave importance of this very thing?

In May 1970, Maezumi's Rinzai teacher, Osaka Koryu-roshi, asked if he might come to America to complete Maezumi's koan training and give sesshin in Los Angeles. "Because I was at the Zen Center all the time," Tetsugen says, "I got to know both Yasutani-roshi and Koryu-roshi very well. Maezumi was close to finishing his own koan study and I had decided to put off my own, so that I could begin properly with my own teacher when he came back from Japan. But Koryu's first teisho at that May sesshin was so powerful that I changed my mind. I went to work again on the koan Mu as soon as I sat down in the zendo that first day. I really got into it, and by the second day, both Koryu and Maezumi knew that, essentially, I was already there. I wasn't asking any questions, I was just totally immersed. By the third evening, I had passed through it, but Koryu wanted something more from me, wanted me to go deeper, and when I went to dokusan on the fourth morning, I must have been right at the edge of something very powerful. I was still concentrating when I returned to the zendo, and right away I entered a different space, really beautiful, exquisite, very deep.

"All of a sudden, Maezumi-sensei shook me out of that

space by really blasting me with MU! He had seen me come out of dokusan, and he knew that I was right on the point of explosion. So after I sat down, he stood right behind me, I don't know how long he stood there, but when he saw that I was really settled in, he yelled MU! very loud, right there in the zendo! It broke the logjam; the world just fell apart! So Maezumi took me immediately to the dokusan room and Koryu-roshi confirmed the passing of Mu-ji, and Koryu and I spent about half an hour just hugging and crying—I was overwhelmed. At the next meal—I was head server—tears were pouring down my face as I served Koryu-roshi, and afterwards, when I went out of the zendo—well, there was a tree there, and looking at the tree, I didn't feel I was the tree, it went deeper than that. I felt the wind on me, I felt the birds on me, all separation was completely gone."

Relating this experience, Tetsugen looked slightly uncomfortable, and a bit awed, as if speaking of someone else. His kensho had been a classic one, not only because it came from a classic koan but because it occurred in the middle of sesshin, with two or three days left in which to deepen his insight. Koryu-roshi would later refer to it as one of the most powerful enlightenment experiences he ever witnessed.

"Maezumi-roshi had passed through Mu-ji in his first kensho, after three years of study with Koryu-roshi in Tokyo. He had his second major opening about a year later, while studying at Soji-ji, in Yokohama. I followed a very similar pattern. After that first kensho, I still had doubts about certain things, in particular reincarnation. When I asked Maezumi about it, he would not comment on my questions: he told me to reread the letters on the subject in *The Three Pillars of Zen*, then work on the question myself. And one day I was reading one of these letters in a car going to work—I was in a car pool, and my office was about an hour from the Zen Center—and a powerful opening occurred right in the car, much more powerful than the first. One phrase triggered it, and all my questions were resolved. I couldn't stop laughing or crying, both at once, and the people in the car were very upset and concerned, they didn't have any idea what was happening, and I kept telling them there was nothing to worry about!" Tetsugen laughed. "Luckily I was an executive and had my own office, but I just couldn't stop laughing and crying, and finally I had to go home.

"That opening brought with it a tremendous feeling about the suffering in the world; it was a much more compassionate opening than the first. I saw the importance of spreading the Dharma, the necessity to develop a Dharma training in America that would help many people. Until then, I had believed in strong zazen, in 'forcing' people, using the kyosaku. That method encourages kensho, but the effects are not so deep and lasting, and anyway, it doesn't work for everybody. I wanted to work with greater numbers because I saw the 'crying out' of all of us, even those who do not feel they are crying out. And that second opening had nothing to do with the zendo atmosphere, or working on a koan. The major opening can occur anywhere, we never know when it's going to happen."

In the early days of American Zen practice, much was made of kensho. Yasutani, for example, would announce who had had an "opening" at the end of each sesshin. Maezumi does not do this, and neither did Tetsugen when he began to teach. "Personally, I don't stress openings, or talk about them, because I don't want people to get caught up in that. Yet I think kensho is essential—*it has to happen*. And so long as the practice is constant and steady, so long as the student continues to practice without being intent on *achieving* some 'special' state, something that he or she has heard about, it will. When that idea of gain falls away, people open up. That's why a teacher is so important—to keep the student from getting caught up in some incomplete idea of what it's all about, and forcing his zazen in that direction."

While in Japan, Maezumi had also resumed koan study with Koryu-roshi, who gave him Dharma transmission in 1972. "Like Yasutani, Koryu gave him inka right after he finished koan study, which is very unusual," Tetsugen says. "For example, Harada-roshi waited three years before giving inka to Yasutani, who was already fifty-eight. Until 1972, Koryu had never given inka to anybody. In December of that year, he finally gave it to five people, all of whom except Maezumi had finished koan study at least five years earlier. Anyway, the speed with which Maezumi finished Koryu-roshi's koan system was amazing. He started all over again from the beginning, and there are about four hundred koans, and he did the whole thing in three years, even though Koryu was only in the United States for three months each year! Before Koryu and Yasutani, his teacher had been his father. In a very unusual accomplishment, he received Dharma transmission from all three."

In 1973, after Maezumi was formally approved by his own teachers as a roshi, Tetsugen was installed as his first *shuso*, or head monk, and three years later, with ZCLA well founded, Tetsugen left the aerospace industry for good. That summer he participated in the great opening sesshin at Dai Bosatsu, where our journeys crossed for the first time.

In early autumn of 1977, returning to ZCLA for a second sesshin, I applied for ordination as a monk. The impulse was vague (and no doubt tainted by spiritual ambition), but I had an idea that shaving my head would renew my practice. Maezumi-roshi, nodding politely, making his soft murmuring sounds, remained studiously noncommittal. Meanwhile, I continued intense study of the Sound of One Hand, not only with Maezumi but with Tetsugen-sensei, who had recently received *shiho*, or Dharma transmission, becoming the first Dharma successor in Maezumi-roshi's apostolic line.[8] I passed thirteen of the fourteen checkpoints but on the last, instead of a vital expression of the inexpressible, I could only come up with a weak intellectual "answer," which was refused.

Roshi wished to give me the Dharma name Mukaku, which he said should accompany the name given me by Soen-roshi: Mukaku Isshin. This Mu is not the Mu of the koan Mu: it signifies "dream" in the sense of the illusory nature of the relative world, of everyday existence. *Kaku* is the awakening from that dream through realization. The final written and spoken word of Soen-roshi's teacher, Yamamoto Gempo-roshi, was "dream," Maezumi says. He presents me with his calligraphy of "Dream-awakening," saying that Soen-roshi would approve this name.

At the end of sesshin, Tetsugen and I went over to Roshi's house, where we celebrated with a good deal of sake. At one point Roshi, wonderfully drunk, put his arm around me with a beatific smile. "*Mu-kaku!* Do you see how greedy you are?" Disconcerted (since I know that I *am* greedy), I asked if he meant that I was pushing too hard in my practice, and he laughed, saying, "No, not hard enough!" Not understanding, I was bothered. Later, Tetsugen assured me it was simply a teaching, intended to "push all my buttons," keep me off balance and alert. Roshi gave me a great hug when he said goodbye.

I had not made my peace with leaving Eido-roshi, and in September 1978 I telephoned Dai Bosatsu and was admitted for October sesshin. Arriving, I was sad to find how very few of the old faces were left, but Maurine F., accompanying me on a walk to Ho Ko's grave, reported that Eido-roshi had recently said, "It is wonderful that some of you can lead strict moral lives. But for others, including me, this is very difficult." Everyone interpreted these remarks as a strong sign that he was confronting his frailties at last. By this time, in apparent rejection of Soen-roshi, he had announced a formal separation of Dai Bosatsu from its parent monastery in Japan.

I found myself very glad to see him. I had missed him, and after three years, my righteous indignation had burned away. Having weathered his crisis, Eido-shi seemed very well, and his teisho were as lively as before. The new monastery, now completely furnished, still struck me as rather opulent, but otherwise the Dai Bosatsu atmosphere was exhilarating. Strong sesshin atmosphere was quickly induced by the strict, precise gongs, clappers, bells, the quiet click of the *jihatsu* bowls at table, the incense smell and smell of new tatamis, the fierce cleanliness, bare humble feet, dark mountain silence, which I remembered so well from other days.

In teisho, Eido-roshi recited a poem by Soen:

> I went to the mountain seeking enlightenment
> There was no enlightenment on the mountainside.
> In desolation
> I cried out and there came an echo.
> I shouted again.
> The echo came again.

"What more Mu could we ask for than that echo?" Eido-shi demanded.

Late in sesshin, after six long days of pain, hurling myself to no avail against iron cliffs, I began to wonder why I had come, why I persisted year after year in this frustrating practice. A spider hanging from the zendo ceiling, spinning its Mu out of its belly, was my echo. I gave up struggling and settled calmly into moment-by-moment quiet Mu-spinning, breath after breath. Soon I was light and taut, at one with my pain in the same way that I was one with breathing, incense, far crows, and the autumn wind. *Caw, caw* was not different from *Peter, Peter*. Small silver breaths, farther and farther apart, scoured the last tatters of thought and emotion from the inside of my skull, now a silent bell. And very suddenly, on an inhaled breath, this earthbound body-mind, in a great hush, began to swell and fragment and dissolve in light, expanding outward into a fresh universe in the very process of creation.

At the bell ending the period, I fell back into my body. Yet those clear moments had been an *experience* that everything-was-right-here-now, contained in "me." I mourned that bell that had come so swiftly, and tried to cheer myself during kinhin— "Who, *me*?" I murmured, right out loud, and began to laugh. The laughter quickly turned to weeping, and with the tears came a spontaneous rush of love for friends, family, and children, for all the beings striving in this room, for every one and every thing, without distinction. This feeling was followed instantly by a rush of doubt—had I *really* perceived something? All this damned soggy weeping—had my mind gone soft? Was I still too greedy for attainment?

At dokusan, describing what had happened, I burst into tears twice, as Eido-roshi beamed. As I did my bows, he struck me six times with the keisaku: "Very *good!* Good! Very *good!*"

On my evening walk I visited Ho Ko's rock, and in her absence related to the rock just what had happened. "Out of my mind," so to speak, I laughed and spoke aloud, as if the entire universe had come to attention. For want of any better plan, I burst out with a yell of joy, and yelled again, delighted by such freedom from my self.

And again the doubt came sweeping back. Perhaps I wanted such experiences too badly, perhaps I was exaggerating everything. I was filled with gratitude, and also I felt frustrated, aborted. Seven years had passed since that first opening of November 1971, which I now dismissed as premature and shallow, and this one, valid or otherwise, had scarcely started before being cut off by that bell, which—had it come even a few minutes later—might have rung those cliffs of iron down around my head.

I expressed my doubts and bitterness to Eido-shi, who made light of both, assuring me that more complete kensho experiences were still to come. By next morning I had mainly recovered, sitting calmly and strongly most of the day. In the evening, however, "forcing" again, sitting through kinhin with worn-out legs, I brought down on myself excruciating pain, and went reeling to bed with my teeth chattering, none the wiser for my joy, doubts, and ambitions. And it was now that I resolved, once and for all, to drop the practice of these sesshin notes, with their hoarding of miraculous states and "spiritual attainments," with their contaminating clinging, their insidious fortification of the ego. I never kept a journal of sesshin again.

When I left next morning directly after breakfast, Maurine in her black cape stood smiling by the road. She has moved to Cambridge, Massachusetts, and founded her own Zen group, and I have scarcely seen her since the weekend sesshin, just before Deborah's death, when she came to see Ho Ko at the hospital. Yet in some way we know each other, we shall always be close. In parting, she said, "I love you," with complete simplicity.

At the bridge, in rain, I stopped to peer into the black stream, thick as mercury with its tumbling yellow leaves. Here Beecher Lake began its long journey to rejoin the sea. I walked up to the boulder in the field to bid Ho Ko goodbye; I gathered tart apples from the ancient orchard by the gate. Then I drove to New England on a wild wet windy day, pursuing a wild wet windy sun that later opened out and softened a golden autumn afternoon. At his school, I had a good visit with Alex, his boy's head so small in football shoulder pads too big for him, and later a warm evening with friends in northwestern Connecticut, with much wine and laughter and good conversation.

That evening I could not sit still. Leaving the dinner table rudely, I rushed out after supper, in a blue-black night with a wild moon spinning through the clouds. A little drunk, not knowing what was up, I strode down winding country roads by the light of the moon on the white birches, embracing the compliant trees, pressing my face to soft, thigh-smooth trunks, whispering and laughing with the silent company gathering around me, and otherwise playing the cosmic fool. Then I walked back to that white New England house, at peace, tears of happiness cool on my face in the black autumn wind down out of Canada. The feeling of being "blown out," clear, would stay with me for another fortnight.

The following month, at sesshin in Los Angeles, I described my Dai Bosatsu sesshin to Maezumi-roshi. In regard to my aborted experience, he observed that it was not dai kensho, that is, great or "true" kensho, which wipes away the last traces of doubt. Later he said, "I did not say this was *not* kensho. You glimpsed

131

the ox, but you did not see what color it was, whether male or female, fat or thin, poor or healthy. Work very hard on your koan, and then you will see the ox up close."[9]

In koan study, I pass through the last checkpoint of One Hand, but Roshi, keeping me off balance, returns me to a previous point, although I protest that my presentation of it had been accepted the year before. I present it a different way and am refused. "What is the true state of one hand? In other words, what is the true state of your *self*? That will be good for you to work on until we meet again."

All-inclusive study is just single-minded sitting, dropping off body and mind. At the moment of going there, you go there; at the moment of coming here, you come here. There is no gap. Just in this way, the entire body studies all-inclusively the great road's entire body. . . . Gourd studies gourd all-inclusively. In this way a blade of grass is realized.

Pilgrimage
—EIHEI DOGEN

CHAPTER TEN

THE previous year, Maezumi-roshi had asked me to help Tetsugen-sensei establish a Zen community somewhere in the New York region. In June of 1979, Tetsugen held a sesshin at the Catholic retreat house in Litchfield, Connecticut, that I knew so well from Rinzai sesshins of other years.

Tetsugen-sensei calls his teisho "Dharma talks," partly in deference to American Zen and partly because teisho are traditionally reserved for roshis. (In Japan, *roshi* signifies an elderly abbot of a training center, and is never used for a Zen master less than a half century old, but in America, where not a few "roshis" have never completed formal study nor received an authentic Dharma transmission in a recognized lineage, the term is used a lot more freely, often at the insistence of the students, for whom nothing less than a roshi will suffice.) Tetsugen speaks as easily as other people yawn, and his talks are a strong combination of beginners' instruction and preliminary inspection of such classic koans as Joshu's Mu ("Joshu's way of expressing Buddha-nature, our true nature, the Absolute") and "Where do you go from the top of a hundred-foot pole?" ("This is my favorite koan: Zen as a never-ending practice, Zen as our life"). He urges us to let go of all prior zazen experiences and expectations, including kenshos—they are just "stinks" to be aired out, since they taint the freshness of this present moment. At dokusan, he refuses my presentation of the last checkpoint of One Hand, even though Maezumi-roshi had accepted it. You understand more now, said he, and last year's answer is no longer good enough.

In Rinzai study, in which one strives to present the "spirit" of the koan, there were many koans I had "passed" rather than passed *through*, as Soto teachers say, that is, thoroughly experienced and made a part of me. Knowing that my grasp was weak, I was almost as pleased as I was annoyed by Tetsugen's rejection. Until now I had wondered how we would fare in a teacher–student relationship, since in Los Angeles this amiable fellow had mainly been my friend and fellow student. His rejection was appropriate, clearing the way for his own standards for koan study, and I admired that. To encourage me, he says that Harada-roshi, Yasutani's teacher, had given seventy answers to this checkpoint before one was accepted, and that he, Tetsugen, had also been passed and then rejected on the same point. "Go deeper," he said. "Come to dokusan as often as possible."

I saw at once how much this man could teach me, and how exciting it would be to study with him in a formal, yet free-wheeling way, unhampered by subtle language barriers and the strict and brittle protocol of Japanese Zen. Without effort we maintain an easy balance between friendship and strict deference, which I gladly award him on ceremonial occasions and in dokusan.

The insects are helping me again, a small white moth and also a wandering caterpillar on the carpet, lifting its weird head to inspect my presence: *Who are* you? A fly draws me taut with a *buzz-z* of warning, and I stop a mosquito with accumulated Mu power, closing my skin; off it goes with a loud whine of frustration. A bumblebee met with out of doors set me an example of precision, tending more than one blossom each second from flowers lilting in the wind.

My sitting is steady, uneventful. In six days of sesshin, I fail to pass through that final checkpoint, yet I am content. I've dropped some aggressiveness and haste, I am more patient, and content to do my best. Driving Sensei to his sister's house on Long Island, I speak again about becoming a monk as soon as Roshi thinks me qualified. "Roshi just wants to be sure that you are serious. You're qualified right now," Tetsugen says.

I like and respect this round-eyed man of round-shouldered and compact construction whose easy smile and unlined forehead are held in balance by the intelligence that shines from beneath his fierce black brows. Like most American students, I have been attracted to the flavor of Asian Zen, so removed in its enigmatic self-containment from the wasteful sprawl of Western life, but I adjust more quickly than I had expected to the idea of a non-Japanese Zen teacher—Bernie Roshi! How different this man is, in style, manner, and appearance, from a quixotic "classical" Zen master such as Soen, a samurai-style master such as Eido, an elegant, autocratic scholar such as Maezumi, and no doubt other teachers from the East whom I do not know.

Those Asian teachers are here now, they have been here since the beginning, and in their teachings they will always be here; once American Zen is under way, it might be said, they will have truly arrived. But looked at from the relative point of view, no more will come; that first great wave of Japanese masters in America is also the last. Therefore it is crucial to develop our own teachers with training and standards at least as exacting as those of the best teachers in Japan.

Tetsugen-sensei is the first American Zen master to complete koan study as well as priestly training. He has been recognized as a Dharma-holder in formal ceremonies at the great Soto temples of Eihei-ji and Soji-ji in Japan. More important still, he is truly enlightened, having experienced two classical dai kensho. Despite his youthfulness—he was born in 1939—

135

he is already a major influence on the future course of American Zen. He is also very ordinary, in the best Zen sense, without idiosyncratic airs or quirks that draw attention to him. He is— and also he is not—plain Bernie Glassman, with a passion for pizza, innovative ideas, and mechanical gadgetry of all descriptions.

In 1980, in Riverdale-on-Hudson, Tetsugen founded the Zen Community of New York. He also officiated at my marriage in Sagaponack to Maria Eckhart. The following year, in a tokudo or "home-leaving" ceremony conducted by Maezumi-roshi, my head was shaved and I was ordained a Zen monk. (To Maria's alarm, Maezumi stated that tokudo was a more important ceremony than marriage.) Maezumi gave me a new Dharma name, Muryo,[1] and also his splendid calligraphy of Master Hyakujo's "Sitting Alone on Daiyu Mountain."[2] The ceremony was attended by a few friends and by my older children, Luke and Sara, and also by old associates from my Rinzai days, two of whom, Lou Nordstrom and Lillian Friedman, had already joined ZCNY and would later receive tokudo from Tetsugen-sensei. Sheila offered this poem by the eleventh-century poet Narihara:

I have always known that at last I would take this road
But yesterday I did not know
It would be today.

Tetsugen's formal installation as abbot of ZCNY's Zen temple, Zenshin-ji, had now been scheduled for June 1982. In the fall he would preside over his first three-month *ango*, or training period, to be led by his first shuso, or head monk. This training period would complete his studies as a Zen priest, after which his certification in this Soto lineage as a roshi or Zen master would become a formality.

Before his abbot installation, Tetsugen wished to make a pilgrimage to Japan in order to pay formal respects to those teachers, alive and dead, who are associated with his lineage and with his training. Since I am to be his first head monk, I shall travel with him as his jisha, or attendant. "After being shuso, you are a senior monk," he says, "and your training enters a new phase. Your knowledge and understanding should be developing into prajna wisdom. Without prajna, you don't really know what you are talking about." Tetsugen feels that, in America, there are too many self-described "Zen teachers" who really don't know what they are talking about, and it is very plain that they embarrass him.

"After I became Roshi's first shuso," he says, "I considered myself very lucky to go with him to Japan, but I think it is better that you go beforehand, since being shuso will mean much more to you that way." We would go to the historic Buddhist cities of Kamakura, Nara, and Kyoto; we would visit Maezumi's last living teacher, Osaka Koryu-roshi, who had been one of Tetsugen's teachers, too; and whether or not he chose to see us, we would pay our respects to Nakagawa Soen-roshi at the "Dragon-Swamp Temple," under Mount Fuji.

The underlying purpose of our journey to Japan was a pilgrimage to those ancient places associated with Dogen Zenji, the thirteenth-century Soto Zen master who has emerged in recent years as one of the most exciting minds in the history of thought.

"One thing that first attracted me to Zen," Tetsugen says, "was an essay by Dogen called 'Being-Time,' translated by Yasutani-roshi. I was studying quantum mechanics in those days, and it read like a twentieth-century treatise on relativity, on the interpenetration of space and time."

The traces of the ebb and flow of time are so evident that we do not doubt them; yet, though we do not doubt them, we ought not to conclude that we understand them. . . . Man disposes himself and construes this disposition as the world. You must recognize that every thing, every being in this entire world is time. . . . One has to accept that in this world there are millions

137

of objects and that each one is, respectively, the entire world—this is where the study of Buddhism commences. . . .

At one time I waded through the river and at one time crossed the mountain. You may think that that mountain and that river are things of the past, that I have left them behind. . . . However, the truth has another side. When I climbed the mountain and crossed the river, I was time. Time must needs be with me. I have always been; time cannot leave me. . . .

Because you imagine that time only passes, you do not learn the truth of being-time. In a word, every being in the entire world is a separate time in one continuum. And since being is time, I am my being-time. Time has the quality of passing, so to speak, from today to tomorrow, from today to yesterday, from yesterday to today, from today to today, from tomorrow to tomorrow.[3]

This passage is from *Shobogenzo* (Treasury of the True Dharma Eye), an extraordinary work of metaphysical exploration that few of Dogen's contemporaries in the early Zen priesthood of Japan would have been able to appreciate even if they had had access to a copy. Within a century of Dogen's death in 1253, *Shobogenzo* became an unread temple relic, and not until recent decades has it been perceived as a unique and shining vision that far transcends its original purpose as a synthesis of thirteenth-century Buddhist thought. Yet Dogen continues to receive more praise than real appraisal, and he remains all but unknown in the West, not because his language is opaque—it is brilliant, lucid, and poetic—but because he has attempted to convey a set of concepts—not concepts or even perceptions, but intuitions, *apprehensions*—for which no suitable vocabulary exists. To approach his formidable masterwork is to seek an ascent to a shining peak, glimpsed here and there against the blue through the wild tumult of delusion. With each step forward, the more certain one becomes that a sure path toward the summit can be found.

Maezumi-roshi is an inspired interpreter of Dogen's thought. In his opinion, Dogen's writings are "among the highest achievements not only of Japanese but even of world literature. His work . . . displays true poetic mastery. . . . Viewed philosophically, it is a near-perfect expression of truth. . . . Dogen Zenji's expression is like an inexhaustible spring which gushes out of the ground naturally and without impediment. . . ."⁴ Maezumi-roshi has done a superb translation of Dogen's *Genjo-Koan* (*Actualization of the Koan*), which one Western scholar has referred to as "surely one of the most brilliant, profound, and moving documents in world religious literature."⁵

"What most impresses and attracts me about Dogen," Tetsugen says, "is his ability and willingness to articulate his understanding of the universal nature of existence. He refuses to make any distinction between the absolute and relative realities. Many teachers will say that 'you cannot express the inexpressible,' and they do not try. But teachers like Yasutani and Maezumi don't agree, and I feel as they do: *if you perceive deeply enough*, a clear and simple way to express it can be found. Dogen tried to set down in words a very profound understanding, and I think he succeeded. His actions, his practice, and his words —he puts it all together."

Dogen is many centuries in advance of his pre-medieval epoch, and his vibrant efforts to transcend the old limits of language, like his insistence on the identity of space and time, would not be appreciated until seven centuries later. Like all born writers, he wrote for the sheer exhilaration of the writing, in a manner unmistakably fresh and poetic, reckless and profound. Though the risks he takes make the prose difficult, one is struck at once by an intense love of language, a mastery of paradox and repetition, meticulous nuance and startling image, swept along by a strong lyric sensibility in a mighty effort to express the inexpressible, the universal or absolute, that is manifest in the simplest objects and events of everyday life.

When we view the four directions from a boat on the ocean where no land is in sight, it looks circular and nothing else. However, this ocean is neither round nor square,

and its qualities are infinite in variety. It is like a palace;
it is like a jewel. . . .
When a fish swims in the ocean, there is no limit to the water,
no matter how far it swims.
When a bird flies in the sky, there is no limit to the air,
no matter how far it flies.
However, no fish or bird has ever left its element
since the beginning. . . .[6]

You should entreat trees and rocks to preach the Dharma, and you should ask rice fields and gardens for the truth. Ask pillars for the Dharma and learn from hedges and walls. Long ago the great god Indra honored a wild fox as his own master and sought the Dharma from him, calling him "Great Bodhisattva."

Bowing, Prostrating the Marrow
—Eihei Dogen

CHAPTER ELEVEN

THE ancient town of Kamakura on the Pacific sea coast of Japan is celebrated for its huge bronze Buddha, which rises forty-one feet from the gardens of Kotoku-in Temple against a background of steep, forested hills and island sky. According to a postcard sold on these flowered premises, this primordial "Buddha of Boundless Light," was cast in A.D. 1252 "at the request of Miss Idano-no-Tsubone and Priest Joko." The hall which enclosed it was borne away by a tidal wave of 1495—and doubtless the dust of Miss Idano danced in the great dun flood—but the Daibutsu or Great Buddha sat unperturbed, turning green in long, calm centuries in the open weather. On this April Sunday, in cherry-blossom festival, the travel-mad Japanese have hurried in orderly thousands to the town, and flocks of pretty schoolchildren in navy-blue uniforms and bright yellow caps dart and flutter through the gardens. Cheeping, they peer around the door in the Buddha's platform, and an emanation of sweet voices pours from the vast emptiness within.

On wayside shrines, stone Jizo Bodhisattvas, protectors of wayfarers and children, are decked out in red caps and smocks and honored by tossed blossoms. Bright fresh flowers, fruit, and flags bring the avenues to life, and even the Pacific fish in the open markets—mackerel, silver mullet, sole, squid, salmon, red-fish, and bonita—are starry-eyed and sparkling if not entirely cheerful in appearance. Pink-white paper lanterns in the pink-white-blossomed trees sway in the breeze, and altars of gold are carried on stout poles by teams of youths in archaic dress who shout and jump as they lurch their burden up the street, for today there is a celebration at Hachiman-gu, the huge shrine of the old Shinto god of war on the north side of the city. From the sidewalks the celebrants are cheered by young friends in American-style jeans and sweatshirts emblazoned with Ameri-can-style legends: *Fascination Ski, Shooting 4 Fomation, Apricot Sports, Rude Boys, Peppermint Gal.*

At Hachiman-gu, the red-bridged canal is speckled with fallen blossoms, and flocks of white pigeons snap wings on the blue sky as they wheel over the crowds. An officiant in a high black, shiny Shinto hat strikes the big drum, the pigeons fall. Long horns resound, the red flags flutter, and a florid householder who presides over the family picnic lifts his bottle of rice wine to the big *gaijin* ("outsiders" or foreigners) and shouts in cele-bration. As in many country Japanese, his face is open and his eyes round in unfeigned innocence and acceptance of his life. Surely this ruddy and befuddled face was here at the dedication of Hachiman-gu in 1063, when the shogun Yoshiye, at the ocean gate, set free a multitude of Japanese cranes with silver and gold prayer strips attached to their legs, and lent an intoxicated shout to the wind of awe that rose at the spectacle of the great white birds, trailing the streamers down the Pacific sky.

Among Kamakura's many temples, the most celebrated is Engaku-ji, a "mountain" or head monastery of Rinzai Zen built into the evergreens in a ravine on a high hill north of the town. "Even when he reached Kamakura and the Engaku-ji Temple, Kikuji did not know whether or not he would go to the tea ceremony"—so begins *One Thousand Cranes*, a novel by the 1958 Nobel Prize winner Yasunari Kawabata. The immense peaked

142

entrance gate stands at the mouth of the ravine in a company of guardian pines and cedars, and behind this portal, tiled rooves with their dull pewter shine climb between heavy forest walls, straight to the throat of the ravine. In spring, the weather-darkened walls are half hidden in cherry blossom clouds and pale bamboo; delicate light-filled red-bronze leaves of a Japanese maple flutter and point at the might and weight of the old buildings. Here at Engaku, one moonlit night, the nun Chiyono, hauling water, attained enlightenment when her wood bucket collapsed and the water splashed onto the ground. In gratitude, she wrote a poem:

> In this way and that I tried to save the old pail
> Since the bamboo strip was weakening, about to break
> Until at last the bottom fell out.
> No more water in the pail!
> No more moon in the water![1]

We ascend the steep hill by leafy walks that pass beneath the bursts of sun-filled blossoms. Two monks in black work tunics, pates tight-bound in white cloths, pad past, incurious; they are hauling firewood slung from a pole. When Tetsugen, who speaks some Japanese, asks to be shown the former dwelling of Soyen Shaku, first Zen teacher in America, another monk points doubtfully at a cloistered cottage. He seems not to have heard this name before.

Bronze pigeons cross the trees where the ravine vanishes into the forest. In a pond beneath a moss-green wall, the sun glints on the raised red-and-yellow head of an old turtle on an ancient rock, drawing its slow eyelid closed as it stares and listens, winking out the world, then letting the world in slowly, slowly once again.

In June of 1973, on the way to sesshin at Ryutaku-ji, Soen-roshi's students descended from the coast train here at Kamakura to visit Engaku-ji, the immense Daibutsu, and the house and library of D. T. Suzuki, now a museum. We also chanted and sat in zazen at the San-un zendo established here by Yasutani-roshi and administered by his disciple, Koun Yamada-roshi.[2] Many years ago, at high school and at Imperial University in Tokyo, Yamada's roommate and close friend had been Soen Nakagawa, a student of Japanese literature whose hero was the Zen hermit-poet Basho. Much influenced by Basho's style of life, this young poet was ordained a Zen monk[3] not long after his graduation in 1930. Inspired by Soen, Koun Yamada took up Zen studies under Yasutani-roshi fifteen years later, and his profound enlightenment experience in 1953, following a stay at Ryutaku-ji, is described in a wonderful letter to his old friend (addressed here formally as "Nakagawa-roshi"):

> The day after I called on you . . . riding home on the train with my wife . . . I ran across this line: "I came to realize clearly that Mind is no other than mountains and rivers and the great wide earth, the sun and the moon and the stars." I had read this before, but this time it impressed itself upon me so vividly that I was startled. I said to myself, "After seven or eight years of zazen I have finally perceived the essence of this statement," and couldn't suppress the tears that began to well up. . . .
>
> Meanwhile the train had arrived at Kamakura station and my wife and I got off. On the way home I said to her, "In my present exhilarated state of mind I could rise to the greatest heights." Laughingly she replied, "Then where would I be?" All the while I kept repeating the quotation to myself. . . .
>
> At midnight I abruptly awakened. At first my mind was foggy, then suddenly that quotation flashed into my consciousness, and I repeated it. Then all at once I was struck as though by lightning, and the next instant heaven and earth crumbled and disappeared. Instantaneously, like surging waves, a tremendous delight welled up in me, a veritable hurricane of delight, as I laughed loudly and wildly, "There's no reasoning here, no reasoning at all! Ha! Ha! Ha!" The empty sky split in two, then opened its enormous mouth and began to laugh uproariously: "Ha! Ha! Ha!"
>
> I was now lying on my back. Suddenly I sat up and . . . beat the floor with my feet, as if trying to smash it, all the while laughing riotously. My wife and youngest son, sleeping near me,

144

were now awake and frightened. Covering my mouth with her hand, my wife exclaimed, "What's the matter with you? What's the matter with you?" But I wasn't aware of this until told about it afterwards. My son told me later he thought I had gone mad. "I've come to enlightenment! Shakyamuni and the Patriarchs haven't deceived me! They haven't deceived me!" I remember crying out. When I calmed down I apologized to the rest of the family. . . .

That morning I went to see Yasutani-roshi and tried to describe to him my experience of the sudden disintegration of heaven and earth. "I am overjoyed, I am overjoyed!" I kept repeating. . . . Tears came which I couldn't stop. I tried to relate to him the experience of that night, but my mouth trembled and words wouln't form themselves. In the end I just put my face in his lap. Patting me on the back, he said, "Well, well, it is rare indeed to experience such a wonderful degree. It is termed 'Attainment of the emptiness of Mind.' You are to be congratulated!" . . .

Although twenty-four hours have elapsed, I still feel the aftermath of that earthquake. My entire body is still shaking. I spent all of today laughing and weeping by myself. I am writing to report my experience in the hope that it will be of value to your monks and because Yasutani-roshi urged me to. . . . That American [Philip Kapleau] was asking us whether it is possible for him to attain enlightenment in one week of sesshin. Tell him this for me: don't say days, weeks, years, or even lifetimes. Tell him to vow to attain enlightenment though it take the infinite, the boundless, the incalculable future.[4]

Yamada-roshi had been absent on the day of our visit in 1973 (he administers a small Tokyo hospital where his wife is head surgeon), but on this April Sunday, nine years later, a zazen kai—a day of sitting meditation—was just coming to an end when Tetsugen and I arrived in the late afternoon.

Although Yamada was ordained a monk and became Yasutani's first Dharma successor, he had no training as a priest and no longer shaves his head. At seventy-five, he is a big man of strong presence, with silvering dark hair, dark pouches like shadows beneath watchful eyes, and an expression of wry humor tinged with regret. In the past century (as Soyen Shaku had anticipated), a number of Zen monasteries had closed down or sold off their lands for lack of interest among modern Japanese. "It is no exaggeration to say that Zen is on the verge of completely dying out here in Japan," Yamada has written. "Some people may think I am stretching the point, but sad to say, this is the actual state of affairs."[5] Yasutani had also been of this opinion, and both teachers blamed it on the decline of zazen practice and of hard training directed toward "Attainment of the Emptiness of Mind."

At tea in his house after the zazen kai, Yamada-roshi was joined by three old friends[6] who had also received Dharma transmission from Yasutani. A little earlier, introducing the American visitors to Yamada's students, one of these teachers had mentioned that Tetsugen-sensei had attained "a complete enlightenment," and Yamada had nodded in confirmation, saying, "I have met him in dokusan and it is so."

Tetsugen had been bothered by that word "complete." "I don't think it is *ever* complete," he told me later. "That's why my favorite koan is, 'Where do you step from the top of a hundred-foot pole?' Zen is your life—it is life itself!—and you must always go further and deeper."

Since returning from America in 1975, Soen-roshi had become a hermit, Yamada told us; these days he saw nobody at all. Learning that I had once been Soen's student, he fetched a published volume of his old friend's haiku. "There is also a much fatter one," he said. Of Soen Nakagawa the American poet Gary Snyder has remarked that "In Japan he had a tremendous stature as a haiku poet; he is considered the Basho of the Twentieth Century."[7] Yamada-roshi confirms this opinion. "Soen-roshi is one of the great haiku poets, one of the very best in Japan. But he does not write haiku anymore. He is in pain from an old head injury, and from other reasons"—here he paused and cocked his head, peering out from beneath dark, heavy lids. He wished to see if I was aware of Soen's rupture with Eido-roshi, and perceiving that I was, said, "A great tragedy. Also, he is suspicious of Western medicines, so he deals with the pain by taking too much sake." Yamada-roshi shrugged. We could visit Ryutaku-ji if we liked, but there was no hope that Soen-roshi would see us.

In June 1973, Soen-roshi's students had traveled from Kamakura to Mishima, under Mount Fuji, arriving at Ryutaku temple, in the foothills, in time for a late supper with our teacher. Next day, the roshi awoke us at 3:30 A.M. for morning service, after which we visited the graves of Hakuin Zenji, founder of this temple, and Torei Zenji, who had seen to its construction. On the moss-covered hillsides we paused to admire bright green frogs and huge multicolored carp in the temple's goldfish pond, and the rice paddies and pines on the slopes below. Pointing at swallows, the roshi instructed us on *tatha*, or "suchness," the awareness of everything just as it is: "The swallows come back to Ryutaku by just-coming, no thought of migration, navigation—they are *just-coming!*"

Ryutaku's new abbot, Sochu-roshi (who would attend the opening of Dai Bosatsu three years later), had made us welcome in a greeting ceremony, after which a ceremony was held for the opening of "International Ryutaku Zendo." With these priestly formalities at an end, Soen-roshi had immediately brightened, whisking up thick green *koicha* tea, then serving sake and lemon wine in his snug quarters at the top of the long stair up the steep hillside. Uproarious, we blew bamboo whistles and triton horns. Then a red demon mask appeard from behind a sliding screen; the mask looked us over one by one, and the laughter died. When Soen dropped the mask, his face was serious. "I have taken off my mask," he said. "Now take off yours."

Soen-roshi led us down the stairwell to the entrance, where he sent us off with his kind monk Ho-san to Nara and Kyoto; we were to return here for sesshin the following week. Standing beneath a tattered old umbrella, in spring rain, he spoke of the great "weightless Buddha" at Nara. "See everything with *hara*," he said, slapping his stomach two inches below the navel, "not just with eyes."

When we look at human life, we see that often the compassionate person suffers and dies, while the wicked person who gets along in the world by means of violence is happy and lives a long life. Also, the decent person is unhappy and wretched, while the wicked person who commits offenses without ever thinking twice about it is happy. This is the way it seems, and we may wonder why it is this way. When we study the situation, we see that the person who trains in a superficial way thinks that cause and effect have nothing to do with this life and that misery and unhappiness have nothing to do with cause and effect. This person does not understand that the law of cause and effect never deviates, any more than a shadow or echo deviates from its source.

Deep Faith in Cause and Effect
—EIHEI DOGEN

CHAPTER TWELVE

NOW a decade has passed, and once again I travel southeast toward Nara and Kyoto. Today I am a Soto monk, not yet white-haired nor sparse of tooth but older and more scarred than my fresh-faced teacher. Isshin-Mugaku-Muryo stares out the window. I have never cared much for Dharma names, which strike me as "extra" in the context of American Zen, and which reproach me for my stubborn flaws of character. Yet they serve as a reminder (I suppose) not to cling to the badge of identity in my given name—the illusion of separation, which is ego—but to aspire as best I can to One Mind, Dream Awakening, Without Boundaries. Sometimes in zazen on my black cushion I approach these states, but in the much more difficult zazen of daily life, there remains a dismaying separation between what I know and what I am.

Near Ise, the train turns inland toward Mount Yoshino, a shrine of poets for more than a thousand years. ("I could no longer suppress the desire to leave for Yoshino," wrote Basho, "for in my mind the cherry blossoms were already in full bloom.")[1] The mountains rise under the sun to westward. The iron track threads dark, steep valleys gouged by swift gray torrents; bursts of lavender azalea blossoms near the higher forest of tall pines are the only light. Some of the perched villages are modern, flat, of raw chemical colors, while others are somber assemblies of high-peaked old dwellings with pale *shoji* windows and pewter-colored rooves, the tiles long weathered to dark mountain hues.

Emerging onto a broad valley floor, the train approaches the ancient capital at Nara from the south and east. I point out to Tetsugen-sensei a wild duck, setting its wings in swift descent through the spring twilight toward the cold gleam of a sedentary river. Wild things are sparse on this central island of Japan, and the duck stirs me.

Tetsugen is less interested in wild ducks and ancient landscapes than amused by my reactions to them. Art and literature (and landscape) don't attract him much, though he delights in opera. His leanings toward engineering and mathematics are still strong, he loves computers, and anyway he is an unabashed fanatic who thinks mostly about how best to transmit the Buddha Dharma to American students, a task for which he is admirably suited even in appearance. With his big head, round-shouldered slouch, and prominent, piercing eyes, Tetsugen reminds Japanese teachers of Zen's first great spiritual messenger, Bodhidharma, who carried the Dharma from India to China.

In the distance, as Nara draws near, rise the jutting roofs of the great outlying temples that came into existence thirteen centuries ago, with the arrival of the Mahayana teachings in the backward islands known to the Chinese as "the Land of Wa." Half hidden in an isolated grove west of the city stands a huge compound of white-walled dark brown wooden buildings with high gray-tiled rooves. Horyu-ji is the first seat of Japanese Buddhism, established in 607 as a seminary or "learning temple" of the Hossu sect. Farther east, at Yakushi-ji (where we spent the night in 1973), in a wonderful airy open court of golden and red buildings, stands the famous East Pagoda, last surviving example of the mighty architecture of this period.[2] This early Buddhism in Japan was not yet "Zen," although Zen traces may have been apparent: Japanese visitors to China, staying close to the cities and old monastic centers, had little exposure to the new "Zen" school which was developing in China's southern mountains.

By the middle of the sixth century, the first sutra books and Buddhist relics had turned up in Japan. Unlike India, where the teachings of Shakyamuni had to compete with Hinduism and Vedanta—and unlike China with its Taoism and Confucian law—Japan had no philosophical religion or literate priesthood, no body of teachings, nor a written language. The early peoples who had arrived over long ages from the mainland coasts lived in shifting settlements along the rivers and practiced an indigenous form of sun and nature worship (later called Shinto, "the Way of the Gods"). Therefore these first holy objects, accompanied by a written language, made a great stir in the rude assemblies that history books refer to as the imperial courts, and were used to political advantage by the enterprising Soga family, which soon came to dominate the more traditional clans. In 593, Umako no Soga took the precaution of murdering the emperor to ensure the accession of a crown prince who would proclaim Buddhism as the state religion.

Despite the bloody circumstances of his ascendancy, Shotoku Taishi, the "father of Buddhism" in Japan (d. 622), was a sincere practitioner who propagated the moral and philosophical precepts of the new religion and issued a list of behavioral edicts in an effort to bring unity and harmony to his backward country. Soon there were more than forty Buddhist temples in this region, complete with relics, priestly vestments, and colorful ceremonies to attract the people. Most of these ceremonies, as in Shinto, were devoted to curing, summoning rain for crops, and other practical considerations.[3]

Enthusiasm in imperial court circles for the new culture

from "the Land of T'ang" was evident in the foolhardy adoption of the complicated Chinese ideographs for the relatively simple Japanese language, and a somewhat less disastrous decision to replicate a Chinese city in Japan. Until now there had been no capital town in the islands; the imperial court had moved with each new reign, not only to invite good fortune and evade epidemics but because it was easier to replace than to rebuild the frail wood buildings. With the advent of a more sophisticated culture, this makeshift situation was no longer tolerable, and in 646 a reform edict authorized the construction of a capital city on the model of the Chinese capital at Ch'ang-an. The new "Central City" of Nara, some forty miles inland from the present Osaka, was eventually laid out in A.D. 710, and remains a Buddhist shrine twelve centuries later.

In this period, the emperor Shomu, inspired by reports of an eighty-five-foot "Universal Buddha" installed by T'ang dynasty rulers at Lo-yang, proposed to erect a local version here at Nara. In traditional circles, his grandiose plan was widely denounced as a threat and insult to Shinto deities, and the Buddhists perceived that the Way of the Gods, still strong in the outlying districts, would have to be placated. In 742 the energetic monk Gyogi, a leader of the Hossu sect, carried a holy relic to the Sun Goddess at the great Shinto shrine at Ise, inquiring respectfully as to her views on the proposed Buddha, who was, he explained, her spiritual descendant as well as her own emissary on earth. In a loud voice, the oracle proclaimed in Chinese verse that news of this enterprise was very welcome to her. Not long thereafter, the Sun Goddess, appearing as a disc in the emperor's dreams, revealed to him that the Sun was none other than this supreme Buddha. And since Buddhism has ever made room for the indigenous faiths it has displaced, adopting their deities as Dharma guardians and even Buddha manifestations, the Shinto war god Hachiman confided in the oracle that he wished to serve as a protector of the Dharma, and was speedily pressed into service by the Hossu sect at Yakushi-ji, where he appears in the plain garb of a Buddhist priest.[4]

And so the emperor commissioned the Dai Butsu or Great

Buddha at Nara, which rises fifty-three feet from the bronze lotus of its throne. Though less than two-thirds the height of the Lo-yang figure and entirely innocent of artistic distinction, it was the greatest technical accomplishment ever beheld in the Land of Wa. The great hall that replaced the original Daibutsu Hall after a twelfth-century fire is 284 feet long, 166 feet wide, and 152 feet high—by far the largest wooden building in the world—and the statue itself is a conglomerate of 500 tons of copper, tin, and lead, heaped up in sections, supporting a twelve-foot head cast in a single mold—"the weightless Buddha at Nara," Soen-roshi had called it in 1973, sending his students off to have a look at it.

Todai-ji, which grew up around the black Daibutsu, is located at the base of the eastern mountains that surround this flat, rich valley. The huge red Buddha Hall is fronted by an enclosed court perhaps one hundred yards long by one hundred wide, the whole surrounded by a deer park of old pines. More people, perhaps, than existed in all the Land of Wa when Buddhism arrived in the sixth century were visiting the Dai Butsu on the fine spring day of our own visit. However, we are the only visitors at Monk Gyogi's small, forgotten temple[5] awaiting fire and decay in a little park of flowering trees and untended graves among the hard-edged structures of the modern city. Reputedly it was inside these brown, worn, shuttered buildings that zazen was first practiced in Japan.

Kohuku-ji, a mile away across the deer park, is noted for the five-story golden pagoda paid for originally by the powerful Fujiwara clan; other eighth-century Buddhist temples were also dependent on their wealthy patrons. Awarded large tracts of tax-free land by the imperial court, and generously endowed by gifts from aspirant Buddhists, the rich monasteries became centers of learning and culture, sharing their prosperity to a certain degree through the creation of charitable institutions. But as in China, the priesthood's dependence on aristocratic influence soon led to corruption and decline. Few of the new Buddhists understood the profound nonmaterial nature of the teaching, and no true teachers seem to have developed, even though the great classical period Ch'an Buddhism in China was well under way.

In the Nara period, Kegon (Hua Yen) Buddhism also became established in Japan, but throughout the T'ang dynasty, when Chinese Zen was at its height, Japanese Buddhism remained primitive. By 779, hordes of parasitic monks and nuns from new temples in the remote districts had gathered to the feast at Nara, where the power of the priests in court had encouraged political ambitions as well as excess and dissolution of every kind. Possibly this rampant corruption encouraged the decision, three years later, to remove the court to Nagaoka, a few miles to the northward, despite the great inconvenience and expense, but it seems more likely that the hasty departure reflected obscure maneuvers of the Fujiwara clan, in particular Tanetsugu, a favorite of the emperor Kwammu, who was allowed "to decide all matters, within and without." In 785, Tanetsugu was assassinated by the emperor's brother, Prince Saware, who paid for this deed with his own life, and these dark events discouraged the completion of Tanetsugu's plans for the new capital, which was moved again in 793 to a plain perhaps twenty miles to the northeast, called Heian-kyo.

The new capital, later called Kyoto, was to become one of the largest cities in the world, with a population that may well have approached a half-million people, but as at Nara, there was little about it that could be called Japanese. Every aspect of its culture, from its architecture to its etiquette, was a painstaking imitation of T'ang dynasty culture in China. For the next two centuries, the Heian aristocracy preoccupied itself with art and poetry in the Chinese style, infused by *mujo*, a rarefied, romantic sense of life's impermanence, often symbolized in the fall of cherry blossoms in spring.[6]

The founding of Kyoto coincided with ominous invasions of the main island of Honshu by a wild blue-eyed people called Emishi (the "Hairy Ainu") from the northern island of Hokkaido, who "gathered together like ants but dispersed like birds," and in 794, the first shogun or "General for Subduing the Barbarians" was appointed. Meanwhile, the Buddhist monasteries were controlled by the imperial court and the Fujiwara clan, which endowed the tax-free lands and built the temples. After 877, when a Fujiwara was named the first minister or regent, the power of the emperor himself was usurped by this aggressive family; its daughters were married regularly to the emperors and princes, and none but Fujiwara consorts reached the throne. Lacking true teachers, the corrupt monasteries, seeking special privilege and tax-free lands, competed for the favors of the aristocracy (which held almost all the important monastery posts). At the same time, the priests resorted to occult ceremonies and tantric practices of the Shingon sect to win the interest and allegiance of a populace which understood almost nothing at all about the true nature of the Buddhist teachings.

In 788, an inspired eighteen-year-old monk named Saicho, after ordination at Todai-ji, withdrew from Nara to the high forests on Mount Hiei west of Kyoto to escape the rigid structures and corruption of the priesthood and to renew Shakyamuni's emphasis on meditation. In 804 he spent a year in China at the monastery at Mount T'ien-tai, adding Zen precepts and esoteric teachings to the Tendai (T'ien-tai) teachings he brought back to the Land of Wa. Saicho established a twelve-year course in religious studies that would make Mount Hiei the greatest school of religion in the nation, and it was in his Tendai temple, known today as Enryaku-ji, that most of the later schools of Buddhism would have their start.

But Japanese Buddhism remained a pale, priest-ridden imitation of the Chinese schools, since the great teaching lineages that ensured the continuity of the true Dharma had not yet made their way across the China Sea. By the tenth century, in open contravention of the Buddhist precepts, Enryaku-ji (and the large Nara temples) maintained standing armies, since the strength of their temples depended, not on the power of the Buddha Dharma, but on the armed monks who battled in Kyoto's streets with monks of other monasteries. In one such battle, early in the eleventh century, about 40,000 monks, backed by mercenaries, are thought to have taken part.

The pollution of the Buddha Dharma, already under way by the end of the Nara Period, would culminate about 1050 in what the faithful themselves called the Age of Degenerate Law, a dark epoch of epidemic, earthquake, fire, famine, banditry, and murder. The Fujiwara, to whom the imperial government had long since ceded its prestige, had been infected by their own decadence even as they attained the summit of their power. Their armed monks were now a threat to their own masters, and the soldiery of feudal lords in the outlying provinces was finally called upon to bring the anarchy under control. These lords—descendants of outcast emperors—detested the decadent despotism at Kyoto. Over the course of the next century, the Fujiwara were challenged and defeated by the strong provincial clans, notably the Taira or Heike, descendants of that Emperor Kwammu who had done so much to bring the Fujiwara into power.[7] The Heike were challenged in their turn by other claimants, notably an alliance of strong clans that was grouped around the family Minamoto. In five bloody years between 1156 and 1160, when the Fujiwara were already in retreat, the Heike gained a brief ascendancy over the Minamoto and established their own emperors in court, but within a few years, they were overthrown by Yoritomo Minamoto in a series of epic battles that culminated in 1185 in the great sea coast battle at Dannoura. Within four years Yoritomo had eliminated the last resistance of the Fujiwara in the eastern provinces.

As shogun, or administrator general, Yoritomo established his own headquarters at Kamakura, three hundred miles east of Kyoto. A feeble court persisted in that city, but the Heian period was at an end. For the next seven hundred years Japan would be governed by military shoguns, mostly of Minamoto origin, who paid mere ceremonial homage to the emperors.

Toward the end of the twelfth century, on a second pilgrimage to China, a Tendai priest called Eisai received Dharma transmission in the Oryu branch of Rinzai Zen. In *The Propa-*

gation of Zen for the Protection of the Country, Eisai deplored what had become of the old Buddhism on Mount Hiei. His proposed reforms won the approval of the second Minamoto shogun, who sponsored the construction of Kennin Temple, in Kyoto.

Kennin-ji deferred to the older sects by including Tendai and Shingon subtemples, but Master Eisai, nonetheless, might be called the first Zen teacher in Japan. Not until a century later would Master Daio institute the first Rinzai teaching that did not have to take the older sects into account. Daio's "poem" "On Zen" is still recited by Rinzai students in America:

> There is a reality even prior to heaven and earth;
> Indeed, it has no form, much less a name;
> Eyes fail to see it; it has no voice for ears to detect.
> To call it Mind or Buddha violates its nature. . . .[8]

His successor, Daito, after living with beggars for twenty years under the bridges of Kyoto, founded the great Rinzai temple called Daitoku-ji. A celebrated poet and calligrapher, Daito was challenged by Emperor Hanazomo: "Is it not unthinkable that the Buddha Dharma should come face to face with the emperor of the state?" Master Daito retorted, "Is it not unthinkable that the emperor of the state should come face to face with the Buddha Dharma?" In fact, the two came face to face quite often, at least in the "five mountains" of Rinzai in Kyoto, which remained close to the imperial family. Like Daio before him, Daito was made a *kokushi*, or national teacher, by the emperor, and these two, together with Daito's successor Kanzan Egen, developed Japanese Rinzai Zen as it is known today.

Daito emphasized that there was no real existence outside of this "moment-to-moment freshening of the mind," and in his last exhortation to his monks, he did his best to emphasize the importance of kensho: "Some of you may preside over large and flourishing temples with Buddha-shrines and rolls of scripture gorgeously decorated with gold and silver. You may recite the sutras, practice meditation, and even lead your daily lives in strict accordance with the precepts. But if you carry on these activities without having the eye of kensho, every one of you belongs to the tribe of evil spirits. On the other hand, if you carry on your activities with the eye of kensho, though you pass your days living in a solitary hut in the wilderness, wear a tattered robe, and eat only boiled roots, you are the man who meets me face to face every day and requites my kindness."[9] A poem by Daito describes existence after the Dharma eye is opened and "eyes, ears, nose, tongue, body, mind" have dropped away:

> If your ears see and your eyes hear,
> Not a doubt you'll cherish.
> How naturally the rain drips from the eaves!

In Zen tradition, there is a saying, "Only be ready, and the teacher will appear." Apparently the Land of Wa was ready, for the first true teachers and strong teaching lineages were emerging, even as Zen in China was on the wane.

When you prepare food, do not see with ordinary eyes and do not think with ordinary mind. . . . Do not arouse disdainful mind when you prepare a broth of wild grasses; do not arouse joyful mind when you prepare a fine cream soup. Where there is no discrimination, how can there be distaste? Thus, do not be careless even when you work with poor materials, and sustain your effort even when you have excellent materials. Never change your attitude according to the materials; if you do, it is like varying your choice of words for different people. Then you are not a practitioner of the Way. . . .

A refined cream soup is not necessarily better than a broth of wild grasses. When you gather and prepare wild grasses, make it equal to a fine cream soup with your true mind, sincere mind, and pure mind. This is because when you serve the assembly—the pure ocean of Buddha Dharma—you do not notice the taste of fine cream or the taste of wild grasses. The great ocean has only one taste. How much more so when you bring forth the buds of the Way and nourish the sacred body. Fine cream and wild grasses are equal and not two.

Precautions for the Tenzo
—EIHEI DOGEN

CHAPTER THIRTEEN

THE city of Kyoto—which was spared from bombing during World War II—is one of the most precious in the world. When I came here first as a Rinzai student in June 1973, I stayed at a student boarding house near high-peaked, dark Daitoku-ji, perhaps the mightiest in aspect of all Zen temples in Japan. Wandering the city day after day, I paid my respects at Myoshin-ji (the mother temple of Ryutaku-ji, with its Taizo-in temple rock garden and waterfall, its magnificent bird screen portraits of geese and falcons) and at Tofuku-ji (which became the seat of Rinzai

Zen a few years after Eisai's death, and remains the largest Rinzai monastery in Japan).[1] One morning I had the marvelous luck to find myself alone for fifteen minutes on the wood platform that overlooks the austere, disturbing stone garden at Ryoan-ji, where the old earth wall is as beautiful as the composition of large stones. (A simple wash basin bears the legend "I learn only to be contented.")[2] From Ryoan-ji, two Japanese students who wished to try their English escorted me to Koryu-ji and its lovely Miroku Bodhisattva,[3] a reproduction of which still hangs upon my wall. I admired Nanzen-ji, with its vivid tiger screens, and Kinkaku-ji, the "Gold Pavilion," with its sculpted woods and ponds. But at none of these Rinzai temples was zazen permitted to the public. The small woodland *dojo*, or meditation hall, known as Antai-ji, where we went for daybreak zazen every morning, was the one Soto temple I visited in Kyoto, which has always been a stronghold of Rinzai Zen.

Every day for ten years, it is said, one may see a different temple without exhausting the temples of Kyoto. Few of these are half as interesting as the public baths, antique shops, and bazaars, and the chaos of the downtown modern city, not to speak of such harmonious places as the ancient Tawaraya Inn, the romantic country retreat at Shisen-do Hermitage in the hills east of the city, and the Katsura Villa in its ten-acre pond-garden, which required forty years to build and is tended today by fifteen gardeners and a squad of ten swift woman weeders. Katsura was mostly used for imperial moon-viewing excursions that took place on just four evenings every year. Its series of four teahouses (the Moon-Viewing, Pine and Harp, Flower Appreciation, and Sense of Humor teahouses), each one with a quite different view, are designed so that not all of the garden-pond can be seen at once (the same is true of the stones at Ryoan-ji)—the "something hidden" creates a pleasing mystery and encourages the visitor to appreciate each detail. The frames of the teahouses are three centuries old, but everything else is changed every twenty years, including the cedar-shingled roofs with their bamboo nails.

About twenty of Daitoku-ji's eighty subtemples are still in

existence, and one of these, Ryoko-in, is distinguished by wonderful moss and rock gardens and exquisite paintings in the Chinese tradition. At Ryoko-in we were given tea by Sohaku Kobori-roshi in the exquisite Mittan tearoom, one of two tearooms in Japan that are national treasures.[4] The "perfect" dimensions of the small chamber are especially admired, as are its sumi paintings of mountain rocks in clouds, and of birds blown like petals from a large flock in a dead tree. The birds are placed upon the paper in a mind-arresting pattern, like the placement of the stones at Ryoan-ji.

Kobori-roshi, gold teeth and glasses flashing in a shrewd, clear face, tested our understanding in mild Dharma combat and chided us good-humoredly for our Zen-type answers. But when one student offered the opinion that Zen and psychotherapy had similar effects in helping suffering, the roshi observed tartly that the psychotherapist was just another patient. (Psychotherapy deals with the twigs, Eido-roshi says, whereas Zen aims straight into the root.) "Can he cure this bowl? This table? Zen can do." Kobori-roshi pointed sternly at a pair of American shoes dropped carelessly outside the tearoom door. "If you arrange a pair of shoes together neatly, that is curing the shoes." He pointed at the sumi painting. "Can psychotherapy cure birds? Or only, perhaps"—and the gold teeth gleamed in anticipation of a Japanese joke that might well have elicited nods and smiles in the Sense of Humor Teahouse at Katsura Villa—"some kind of . . . monkey?"

All the while, Kobori's deft hands served green tea, brought originally to Japan by Master Eisai.

Formal tea ceremony, Cha No Yu, was an expression of Zen culture developed in the sixteenth century by Sen no Rikyu (1521–1591), founder of the Urasenke Tea School here in Kyoto, who lived to see a statue of himself installed over Daitoku-ji's great roofed entrance gate. Unfortunately this honor gave offense to Toyotomi Hideyoshi, a feudal overlord who refused to walk beneath the likeness of a commoner, and his displeasure persuaded Sen no Rikyu to perform ritual suicide rather than bring down Hideyoshi's wrath upon his family.

Three of us were tea students at Urasenke in New York, and while in Kyoto, we visited the tea school, which has its own celebrated tearoom. Here long ago an early master, having invited a Zen priest for tea, became annoyed when the priest was late, and left a note which read, "Please come tomorow." Finding this note, the Zen priest wrote, "Lazy monk cannot come tomorrow." The tea master was so ashamed that he named this chamber "the Today Tea Room."

One sunny afternoon, with Urasenke friends, we attended a huge outdoor tea ceremony at the Omi Jingu shrine overlooking Lake Biwa. In a pageantry of white-and-black-robed Shinto priests, swept by a bright freshwater breeze, flags flying, a modern Mr. Sen[5] and his assistants offered a prolonged ritual tea to the Shinto gods, the graceful movements gracefully exaggerated in order to be seen by an enthralled audience of thousands. Later we dined at a lakeside hotel at the kind invitation of Mr. Sen, who left word that he would not obstruct our enjoyment with his own presence.

On the second day of the thirteenth century (January 2, 1200)[6] a child was born in Heian-kyo (later Kyoto, "the Capital") who would have a precocious experience of life's impermanence, since he seems to have been illegitimate and would soon be orphaned. "Buddhist Dogen, family name Minamoto, of Kyoto; and an heir to the gentry," as he was identified in the first known reference[7] to his genealogy, was apparently the son of Lord Kuga Michichika, a descendant of the tenth-century emperor Murakami and Keeper of the Privy Seal in the imperial court, who took leave of life when Dogen was just two. His mother, of the Fujiwara clan, died when he was eight. "At his mother's funeral, observing the smoke of incense, he intimately realized the impermanence of the world of sentient beings, and profoundly developed the great aspiration to seek the Dharma."[8] For the rest of his life, Dogen Kigen was concerned with the awakening of the enlightened state through penetration of the true nature of reality, and the consequent freedom from the bondage of life and death, as—in his own image—a fish escaping from the net. "At each moment," he would write, "do not rely upon tomorrow. Think of this day and this hour only, and of being faithful to the Way, for the next moment is uncertain and unknown."

After his mother's death, this young Minamoto was adopted by an aristocratic uncle, but eventually he ran away to her younger brother Ryokan, a hermit monk at the foot of Mount Hiei. No doubt to ensure his place in life, the boy's mother had urged that he join the priesthood, and in 1213 he trudged up Mount Hiei to Enryaku-ji, the huge Tendai monastery on the north face of the mountain, overlooking Lake Biwa, some 3,000 feet below. Here the Tendai abbot Koen gave him the precepts as the novice monk Buppo-bo Dogen in the Yokawa-chudo, a small temple on a wooded ledge under the north peak, on a steep hillside of giant cedars.

In Dogen's time, Enryaku-ji concerned itself with rituals and rich ceremonies that attracted the costumed aristocracy of Kyoto, paying small attention to the practice of the Buddha's teachings. It made much of Shakyamuni's realization that "all sentient beings have the Buddha-nature," since this seemed to eliminate the need for arduous training. Dogen (who would teach that Shakyamuni meant "All beings *are* the Buddha-nature") demanded of his mentors why, in that case, the Buddhist patriarchs had struggled so hard to attain this enlightened condition. Already he knew that priestly finery, ritual incense burning, sacrament and ceremony, sutra copying and even chanting— the mere veneration of the Buddha's words—all missed the point, that the structured hierarchies of Mount Hiei had lost the bold spirit of the quest for profound awakening.

"The masters I had seen all advised me to study until I was as learned as those who preceded me. I was told to make myself known to the state and gain fame in the world."[9] Such teachers were unqualified to answer the relentless probing of the young monk, and after one year he walked back down the mountain to Mii-dera, another extant Tendai temple on Lake Biwa. Here a teacher named Koin sent him on to Eisai, the Rinzai master in Kyoto. "I first developed the mind for enlightenment because of impermanence [mujo] and asked about it in all corners of the world. At last I left Mt. Hiei to study the Way and entrusted myself to Kennin-ji. In the meantime, I encountered no authentic teacher."[10]

Dogen's restlessness was symptomatic of a growing resistance to the decadent "aristocratic" Buddhism of the Heian period. At Nara, the older sects had enjoyed a mild revival by instituting strict monastic practice, and the Hall of the Great Buddha at Todai-ji, burned down in the civil wars of 1180, had been rebuilt ten years later by the shogun Yoritomo Minamoto. In the same period Honen Shonin (1133–1212) founded the Jodo or "Pure Land" school, which, as he said himself, was "nothing but the mere repetition of the name of the Buddha Amida without a doubt of his mercy, whereby one may be born into the Land of Perfect Bliss." To this simple-hearted teaching (which does not really contradict the Buddhist tenet of emancipation from within)[11] thousands of converts from the unlettered multitudes, denied access to the esoteric schools of Mount Hiei, gathered like "clouds in the sky," causing a fierce attack on Jodo by the threatened priesthood of both Nara and Kyoto. After his death in 1212, Honen's sect spread rapidly in influence, especially in the military government. The great Buddha of the Boundless Light at Kamakura, described earlier, is an Amida figure constructed by Honen's supporters in 1252.

Master Eisai apparently answered some of Dogen's questions. Yet it seems unlikely that he studied much with Eisai, who died in 1215, the year after Dogen's arrival, having spent most of his last years in Kamakura seeking the protection of the Kamakura regents for his new sect of Rinzai Zen. Still frustrated, Dogen embarked on two years of inconclusive wandering before returning to Kennin-ji to study with Eisai's first Dharma heir.

In 1221, this monk Myozen transmitted the precepts of the Oryu Rinzai school to Dogen, who accompanied him on a pilgrimage to the T'ien-t'ung Monastery in China two years later. Before departing, Myozen was asked by a former teacher to see him through the death that was soon to come. Myozen's other disciples felt that nothing would be lost by postponing the journey until after the old man's death, but Dogen was not of that opinion. "If you think your realization of the Buddha-Dharma is satisfactory as it is now," said Dogen—who clearly doubted it—"then you should stay." Apparently Myozen was impressed by his disciple's relentless attitude. At any rate, he told the others, "To spend time in vain just for one person is against the will of the Buddha. . . . I resolve to go to China now."[12]

In 1223, Myozen and his students sailed from the Port of Hakata on the "Western Sea Road" to the Land of Sung. Dogen, who had already begun the copious writing that provides so much insight into his character and life, took note of his own seasickness and diarrhea while "entrusting his ephemeral existence to the roaring waves."[13]

In the Land of Sung as in the Land of Wa, the Buddhist priesthood was enmeshed in politics, finance, and the imperial court. The Zen schools were still powerful, but the long spiritual decline from which Chinese Buddhism was never to recover had set in. Young Dogen, already contemptuous of the immature Buddhism in Japan,[14] was dismayed by its decrepitude in China. Especially was he critical of his own Rinzai school, which had now absorbed all other Zen schools except Soto; it seemed to him to have distorted the Buddha's teachings in its emphasis on koan study to the near exclusion not only of the sacred texts but of zazen. Although devoted to Myozen ("leading disciple of my late Master Eisai . . . unparalleled among his fellow disciples in learning and virtue"),[15] he soon despaired of finding a true teacher of the uncompromising kind he had read about in the ancient Chinese chronicles.

Indeed, the closest Dogen came to the pure spirit of Zen was an encounter with an old monastery cook in the first days after his arrival. This monk, who had visited his ship to buy Japanese mushrooms, declined Dogen's invitation to stay and converse, since he had to get back to his monastery to supervise the next day's meals. When Dogen protested, saying that other

164

cooks would surely take care of things, the old man said mildly that his job as tenzo, or head cook, was "my training during my old age. How can I leave this duty to others?" Incredulous, Dogen exclaimed, "Venerable sir! Why don't you do zazen, or study the koan of ancient masters? What is the use of working so hard as *tenzo* monk?" At this the cook laughed, remarking that the young Japanese appeared ignorant of the meaning of true training, much less Buddhism.

In the cook's reproof lay two important teachings which were later much emphasized by Dogen, that work for its own sake was fundamental in Zen practice, and that the state of enlightenment was manifest in even the most ordinary acts of everyday life. (In a later encounter, when Dogen asked, "What is the Way?" this old man said, "The entire universe has never concealed it.")[16]

After three months of living aboard ship, Dogen went to visit Myozen at T'ien-t'ung, south of the Yangtze River and not far inland from the East China Sea. T'ien-t'ung, where Master Eisai had studied, was an ancient shrine of the third century which had become one of the five great "mountains" or Zen monasteries of southern Sung. Here Dogen was given an inferior position in the monk's hall, despite his status as Myozen's Dharma successor. The outspoken Dogen fired off three letters to the emperor, protesting that the monks' positions should depend on seniority, not on nationality, and winning a certain notoriety when the emperor intervened on his behalf.

At T'ien-t'ung, Dogen received another lesson from a tenzo. This ancient monk, painfully supported by a staff, was drying mushrooms in the heat of summer noon. Asked why he did not use the help of others, the old man said, "Others are not I." Dogen said, "But the sun is scorching! Why must you work now?" And the old man said, "If not now, when?"[17]

Between 1223 and 1225, Dogen visited a number of the leading monasteries of southern China, after which, having failed to find a teacher, he decided to return home to Japan. But at T'ien-t'ung, where he went to say goodbye to Myozen, the Rinzai abbot had been replaced by a teacher of the Soto sect named Tendo Nyojo (Ju-ching), aged sixty-two, who until this time had led the life of a poor wandering monk, far from the influences of the government and court. More interesting still, so far as Dogen was concerned, was Tendo Nyojo's repudiation of priestly occupations and his insistence on strict training based on shikan-taza. "No more need," said Tendo Nyojo, "to burn incense, make prostrations, invoke buddhas, perform repentance ceremonies, or read scriptures—just sit and liberate mind and body."[18]

This "silent illumination" practice of the Soto sect was harshly criticized by Rinzai teachers as passive and ineffective, since no effort was made to attain enlightenment. In Tendo Nyojo's view, shikan-taza itself represented the enlightened state, because practice and realization of one's own Buddha-nature, when truly perceived, were no more separate from each other than the relative and the absolute, the fleeting and the eternal. That practice and realization were inseparable was to become the marrow of Dogen's teaching.

"I met Master Ju-ching face to face. This was an encounter between a man and a man!" Dogen wrote later, extremely moved by his first meeting (on May 1, 1225) with a severe master who shunned fame, fine robes, and monetary privilege, and who, in his enlightened old age, did zazen until late each night, beginning again early each morning, vowing "to wear out a diamond seat." According to Dogen's journals, Tendo Nyojo said, "What is the point of . . . entering a monastery if you are only going to waste time? Birth and death are vital matters. The impermanent world passes swiftly away. . . . With time so short, how foolish it is . . . to waste your time in sleep! This is what brings the decline of the Buddha Dharma!" Dogen, who had all but abandoned hope of finding an inspired teacher, immediately recognized this one "who regardless of old age or prestige, comprehends the right Dharma clearly and receives the certification of true master. . . . He is one in whom living and understanding correspond to each other." For the first time in his life, he perceived in a teacher the embodiment of the true Dharma, and was overjoyed. Nyojo, in turn, immediately recognized the Dharma in this very rare student,[19] instructing him to come to dokusan whenever he wished.

Dogen spent three years at T'ien-t'ung, entering whole-heartedly into rigorous zazen practice. One day during meditation, Tendo Nyojo shouted at a sleeping monk, "When you study under a master, you must drop body and mind! What's the use of single-minded intense sleeping?" For Dogen, seated right beside this monk, the shouted words "drop body and mind!" precipitated a profound kensho. He made his way to the abbot's quarters and burned incense in awe and gratitude, and after a brief exchange, Tendo Nyojo confirmed that his young Japanese disciple had indeed "dropped body and mind." The unrelenting Dogen said, "It might have been a temporary delusion; please do not give me the seal of approval indiscriminately!" Apparently this was his way of pleading that his teacher drive him deeper, which he did,[20] and eventually Dogen left after receiving face-to-face Dharma transmission: "The Great Matter of my life was thus resolved." He had now perceived that "Buddha-nature is not some kind of changeless entity, but is none other than the eternally rising and perishing reality of the world"—the wonderful precision of this present moment, moment after moment—*now!*—just as the old cooks had tried to teach him.

In 1227, encouraging Dogen to spread the true Dharma in his own land, his teacher presented him with further documents of succession, in a silk cover with a design of plum blossoms. At the same time he instructed him not to be "preoccupied with concern of limited time, limited life. . . . The succession of the buddhahood should not be studied that way. . . . It should be learned that Shakyamuni Buddha inherited the Dharma from Kasyapa and Kasyapa from Shakyamuni Buddha. When it is thus studied, we understand the succession of the Dharma by all the buddhas and all the patriarchs."

The ancient lineage of Dharma transmission traditionally began when Shakyamuni in dead silence held up a single flower before the assembly and Kasyapa smiled. The Buddha said, "I have the treasury of the true Dharma eye [*Shobogenzo*], the inconceivable mind of nirvana. This I entrust to Kasyapa." What Tendo Nyojo (and later Dogen) said was that Kasyapa was simultaneously transmitting the true Dharma to Shakyamuni—in short, that the lineage was not linear but circular; that buddhas or awakened ones, while not identical, were not to be separated either. ("Those who have passed the barrier [of Mu] are able not only to see Joshu face to face, but also to walk hand in hand with the whole descending line of Zen masters," says Mumon's commentary to "Joshu's Dog").[21]

Tendo Nyojo gave Dogen a document certifying his place in the circular lineage of the Soto school, from Shakyamuni to Bodhidharma and the Sixth Chinese Patriarch, and from Daikan Eno and his successors to Tendo Nyojo, Dogen, and Shakyamuni. He also gave Dogen certain Buddhist relics, including a portrait of himself and a copy of Master Tozan's *Five Ranks* (*Goi Kenketsu*) and *Jeweled Mirror Samadhi* (*Hokyo Zammai*), which, together with Master Sekito's *Identity of Relative and Absolute* (*Sandokai*), is the fundamental literature of Soto Zen: "With all sincerity, I give these to you, a foreign monk. I hope you will propagate true Buddhism throughout your country, thereby saving deluded people. You should not live in cities or other places of human habitation. Rather, staying clear of kings and ministers, make your home in deep mountains and remote valleys, transmitting the essence of Buddhism forever. . . ." Later Dogen would write a poem derived from *Hokyo Zammai*:

> A snowy heron in the snow.
> Winter grass hidden
> Hides itself in its own form.

Myozen had long since died at T'ien-t'ung—in good zazen posture, according to his former student—and Dogen attested to miraculous events surrounding Myozen's memorial service that caused people to venerate his old friend and erect a statue to his memory on T'ien-t'ung Mountain. Not until 1227 did Dogen

168

return his ashes to Kennin-ji. Otherwise, all Dogen brought with him out of China was the realization "that the eyes are horizontal and the nose is vertical; thus I am unable to be deceived by others. . . . I have returned to my native country with empty hands. There is not even a hair of Buddhism in me. Now I pass the time naturally. The sun rises in the east every morning, and every night the moon sets in the west. When the clouds clear, the outline of the mountains appears, and as the rain passes away, the surrounding mountains bend down. What is it, after all?"[22]

In effect, Dogen had freed himself of all ideas and preconceptions about Buddhism, about enlightenment, about the true nature of reality, all of which had "dropped away with body and mind." There was simply the fact of his vertical nose and horizontal eyes, of the sun and moon rising and falling, moment by moment, day by day. With the opening of his true Dharma eye, he perceived the extraordinary within the ordinary, and realized with all buddhas and patriarchs that everything, everywhere, in every moment, is "nothing special," as is said in Zen, being complete and perfect just-as-it-is.

The mountain was the mountain once again.

Having met with his own Buddha-nature, Dogen seems to have become less judgmental, less demanding. Asked what he had learned abroad, he said, "Not much except a tender spirit."[23]

The Buddhist trainee can be compared to a fine piece of timber, and a true master to a good carpenter. Even good quality will not show its fine grain unless it is worked on by a good carpenter. Even a warped piece of wood will, if handled by a good carpenter, soon show the results of good craftsmanship. The truth or falsity of enlightenment depends upon whether or not one has a true master. . . .

In our country, however, there have not been any true masters since ancient times. We can tell this by looking at their words, just as we can tell [the nature of] the source of a river by scooping up some of its water downstream. . . .

True Buddhism has not yet spread to this peripheral little country, and true masters have yet to be born. If you are unable to find a true master, it is best not to study Buddhism at all.

Points to Watch in Buddhist Training
—EIHEI DOGEN

CHAPTER FOURTEEN

ALTHOUGH Tetsugen had visited Kyoto on previous journeys, he had never seen the three great monasteries associated with Dogen Zenji which are still active to this day. Under the guidance of Yo Ishikawa-sensei (whose son Sho is a young monk studying with Tetsugen in New York), we drove up Mount Hiei to Enryaku-ji, which after twelve centuries remains the head temple of Tendai Buddhism in Japan. In the entrance temple on top of the mountain, large portraits commemorate Eisai, Dogen, Nichiren, and others who studied at Mount Hiei before moving away to establish their own schools. Here aged monks in stiff brocade, red, gold, and purple, were chanting the question-and-answer teaching in the *Lotus Sutra*. In a forest grove is the huge red building called the Kompon-chudo, built originally in 788 by Tendai's founder. Although the present Kompon-chudo, with its chancel of gold Buddha figures, was rebuilt in 1642, after a fire, the three dedicatory bronze lanterns that bring dim light to the ancient shadows of the hall are said to have been lit by Saicho and never extinguished to the present day.

The original Yokawa-chudo, down the mountain, lasted well over one thousand years—it burned to the ground in 1942—but because we were eager to experience the place where Monk Dogen received ordination, an obliging young priest led us downhill on the silent forest paths to the remains of the old temple, which is marked by an open-air altar scattered with needles from the tall and silent trees. Probably the oldest hoary conifers on this mountainside were already living when that thirteen-year-old boy, pate fresh and shining as an apple seed, received his monk's robe and monk's bowl from the Tendai abbot Koen, with the blue cloud mirror of the lake shining below. If he came in spring, the lavender bloom of these woodland azaleas would have freshened his eye, and doubtless a bold forebear of this blue Eurasian jay came squalling to the treetops to jeer at the priestly retinue in its brilliant robes.

From Enryaku-ji, by way of Mii-dera, on Lake Biwa, Dogen had traveled to Kennin-ji, which in those days was located in a wooded swamp along the Kamo River. Since then the Kamo has been rechanneled and the swampland drained, and the modern city has grown up around it, replacing the miasmal climate of the swamp with that of the Gion red-light district.

On the day of our visit to Kennin-ji, a special ceremony was in progress. Outside the entrance of the main service hall was a hallucinatory array of hundreds of small Japanese shoes, set out in intricate patterns to help the wearer locate the right pair upon emerging. Within, small, bright-robed, decorous figures moved ceremonially across a sun-filled hall. Opened screens and an outside platform overlooked a renowned stone garden of Kyoto—at least the equal of the stone garden at Ryoan-ji, or so we were assured by an American monk, who seemed glad of this rare opportunity to speak with countrymen. A number of comparable stone gardens, the monk said, are hidden away in cloistered courts of the thousands of temples in Kyoto.

The event in progress was an annual commemoration of the importation of green tea by Master Eisai, who had used it as a stimulant for his monks during zazen. Under the stern eye of elder roshis, four leading tea masters, each with eight disciples, were being served tea in high ceremonial fashion by the priests and monks, after which formal tea would be prepared for two hundred or more Japanese ladies in ornate combs and many-colored silks. Tiny feet in their white tabi peeped like mice from beneath the silks as the happy ladies, opening bright fans, sailed across the fresh-smelling greenish straw of new tatami.

In the stone garden, a turtledove's wings were the bronze color of wild cherry leaves after the spring fall of pink-white blossoms. Uninterested in the human pageant, it walked about beneath a red azalea bush, inspecting the raked earth for fat new grubs.

According to the American monk,[1] Kennin-ji under Sado-roshi is the most active Rinzai training center in Kyoto, and one of the few monasteries left in Japan that maintains a strict zazen schedule. Seven days a week, as in the old days, thirty-one monks arise at 4:00 A.M. for zazen, then go out into the city with their "begging bowls."[2] In the afternoon the monks perform their monastery duties, followed by zazen until near midnight. They are also expected to chant sutras every day, at two in the afternoon and at two in the morning.

The monk led us to the grave of Eisai, in a stone garden hidden behind old walls. Not far away was the grave of Myozen, where a very old man dressed in white sat on his heels among the mosses, paying the big gaijin no attention. "He was the head priest here," murmured our guide. "He's retired now, and spends his days pulling out the weeds in the stone gardens."

Returning here with Myozen's ashes in 1228, Dogen realized that Kennin-ji had deteriorated. "Every room of the temple was furnished with a lacquered case, and every monk had his own furniture, liked fine clothes, and stored away treasures. . . ."

Nevertheless, he remained here for three years while he composed *Fukan-zazen-gi (A Universal Recommendation for Zazen)*, which was in effect zazen instruction, a manifesto of Zen practice (as opposed to the "mixed practice" established by Eisai), and a challenge not only to Kennin-ji but to the entrenched Buddhist priesthood all over Japan.

> Need I mention the Buddha, who was possessed of inborn knowledge? The influence of his six years of upright sitting is noticeable still. Or Bodhidharma's transmission of the mind seal? The fame of his nine years of wall-sitting is celebrated to this day. . . . If you want to attain suchness, you should practice suchness without delay.

"In *Fukan-zazen-gi*, we see Dogen's desire to reach everyone," says Tetsugen, who sometimes seems to have the same desire. "Later he has to give this up." Not long before this document was written, the tomb of Honen, founder of the Jodo school, had been vandalized, and an extant letter of the period to the poet Teika Fujiwara suggests that the priests of Mount Hiei were debating the merits of destroying Dogen's house and also his expulsion from the capital. Dogen himself became aware that his ambition of spreading the Dharma must be put aside "until a time of rising tide." In 1230, unhappy (and no doubt unwelcome) at Kennin-ji, he moved south to the Fukakusa District, where he rebuilt Anyo-in, an abandoned hermitage of his mother's Fujiwara clan, known thereafter as Kannon-dori.

> *Births and deaths, coming and going—how pathetic!*
> *The path of ignorance, the road of awakening—I walk*
> *   dreaming!*
> *Yet one thing persists even at waking:*
> *The sound of rainfall in a hut at Fukakusa.*[3]

At Kannon-dori, Dogen accepted Koun Ejo as his first disciple. This monk, born a Fujiwara, had studied in the Nihon Daruma (Japan Dharma) school at Nara, whose temple had been burned down twice by the older sects. Two years older than Dogen, he had already received the seal of realization from a Rinzai teacher, but it is suggested[4] that his true realization came about through study of the koan "A single hair penetrates many holes," with which Dogen had tested him at their first meeting at Kennin-ji. One evening at Fukakusa, he passed through this koan with great enlightenment. He went to Dogen, made his bows, and said, "I do not ask about the single hair. What are the myriad holes?" Dogen smiled, saying, "It is penetrated." From that time forward, Koun Ejo was his attendant, serving to the end of Dogen's life, and requesting that his ashes be placed at the foot of his teacher's grave, so that he might attend him after death.

In the Fukakusa period, Dogen composed *Bendowa* (*The Practice of the Way*), which sets out the main principles he would deal with later. Here he states plainly the answer to the question that had plagued him as a boy at Mount Hiei: the Buddha-nature or enlightened state "is amply present in every person, but unless one practices, it is not manifested; unless there is realization, it is not attained."[5]

In 1235, with the completion of the monk's hall and the installation of Koun Ejo as first shuso, or head monk, Kannon-dori was renamed Kosho-Horin-ji. At the opening ceremony of the new monk's hall, designed specifically for zazen, Dogen discussed what he had "gained" from his studies in China, which was, in effect, the realization of his own true nature, his Buddha-nature, beyond all teachers and ideas, beyond enlightenment itself. Subsequently, he ordained a small number of new monks. In the next ten years, in the peaceful atmosphere of the beautiful Uji River and surrounding mountains, he composed a large part of *Shobogenzo* (*Treasury of the True Dharma Eye*), including the famous *Genjo-koan* (*Actualization of the Koan*), which contains the best-known passage in his work:

Seeing forms with the whole body and mind,
hearing sounds with the whole body and mind,

one understands them intimately;
Yet it is not like a mirror with reflections,
nor like water under the moon—
When one side is realized, the other side is dark.

To study the Buddha Way is to study the self.
To study the self is to forget the self.
To forget the self is to be enlightened by all things.
To be enlightened by all things is to be freed from one's
    own body and mind and those of others.
No trace of enlightenment remains, and this traceless
enlightenment is continued forever. . . .[6]

At Kosho-ji, Dogen also composed the *Tenzo Kyokun*, a discussion of the head cook's significance in the monastery (and by extension, the true meaning of the Dharma, Tetsugen says. The meal is our life, its ingredients the means we have available. Each of us is tenzo: what sort of meal do we prepare? Do we make the best of what we are given, or do we complain that the right ingredients are missing?). This fascicle recounts—and was doubtless inspired by—those thorny encounters with the two old tenzos in the Land of Sung. Meanwhile, Koun Ejo gathered Dogen's more informal sayings for the collection know today as *Shobogenzo Zuimonki*.[7]

Although he gave koans to Ejo and other disciples, Dogen felt that most Zen lineages using koan study—especially in the Rinzai school—had become "dead lines" that did not perpetuate the essence of the teaching. Yet *Shobogenzo* is a vast compendium of koans drawn from Dogen's voracious reading of the old texts. The *Mumon-kan*, or *Gateless Gate*, collection was put together during his lifetime, the *Shoyo Roku* (*Book of Equanimity*) commentaries by twelfth-century Soto master Tendo Shogaku had been recently completed, and apparently he was aware of the *Hekigan Roku* (*Blue Cliff Record*) put together in the eleventh century by Setcho Joken, of the Unmon-Rinzai school. The *Hekigan Roku* included eighteen original koans by Master Unmon, and beautiful commentary verses by Master Setcho:

> Overwhelming evening clouds
> Gathering in one great mass
> Endlessly arising distant mountains
> Blue upon blue.

Kosho-Horin-ji, a lovely white-walled monastery across the river from Byodo-in (a former Fujiwara villa at the edge of the old town of Uji), sits on a hillside just north of the bend where the Uji River flows down out of the mountains. The majestic location doubtless inspired the *Sansuikyo*, or *Mountains and Rivers Sutra*, which celebrates the manifestation of the Buddha-body in the mountains, rivers, and great earth, an ancient synonym for all things, fleeting and eternal, that are included in the emptiness, the void, the One. "I came to realize clearly that Mind is no other than mountains and rivers and the great wide earth, the sun and the moon and the stars." This phrase, from an early Chinese collection (*Zenrin*) used in koan study and often cited in *Shobogenzo*, precipitated the enlightenment experience of Yamada-roshi quoted earlier.[8]

In *Sansuikyo*, Dogen challenges head-on the Chinese teachers who (like so many today) claim that any talk which can be grasped by thought is not true Zen talk of the Buddhas and patriarchs. "At the present time in the Land of Sung there is a certain crude bunch who have by now formed such a crowd that they cannot be overcome. They maintain that talk such as this is incomprehensible. Consequently, they hold that Obaku's stick and Rinzai's roar, because they cannot be comprehended or grasped by thought . . . are impossible to comprehend. Those who talk in this way have never met a true teacher, and lack the eye of study. This is truly regrettable, for it represents the decline of the great way of the Buddhas and Patriarchs. . . . What these shavelings call 'incomprehensible talk' is incomprehensible only to them, not to the Buddhas and Patriarchs. . . ."[9]

"Dogen tried all of the known theories, from Shakyamuni onward," Tetsugen says. "He discarded them when his students got too caught up in theories and forgot about life itself. He spoke out against koan study, sutra-chanting—in fact, virtually everything except zazen—but only that aspect of them that was stereotyped and dead. Even as he condemns koans, he is using them in his own teaching."

Especially Dogen denounced koan practice that excluded sutra study. "In the country of Sung lately there are those who call themselves Zen masters. . . . Reciting a few words of Rinzai and Unmon, they take them for the whole truth of Buddhism. If Buddhism had been exhausted by a few words of Rinzai and Unmon, it could not have survived until today. . . . These people, stupid and foolish, cannot comprehend the spirit of the sutras, slander them arbitrarily, and neglect to study them. . . ."[10]

On the other hand, he is urgently aware that one must go beyond all words and teachings to the thing itself. "To read the words, unaware of the way of practice, is just like reading a medical prescription and overlooking the mixing of the compounds for it; it will be altogether worthless. Lifting your voice in endless recitation is like frogs in the spring fields, croaking from morning to nightfall."[11]

"In the great Way of the Buddha Dharma, all the sutra chapters in the Universe are contained within a dust mote. A blade of grass or a leaf are the Mind and Body."[12] And "Hundreds of grasses and myriad forms—each appearing 'as it is'—are nothing but Buddha's true Dharma body."[13]

"At Kennin-ji, Dogen studied koans under Myozen," Tetsugen says, "and received inka from Myozen, so he was familiar with koan study as it was then practiced in the Rinzai sect. In China he studied with Tendo Nyojo, a Soto master not much interested in koan study and giving precedence to shikan-taza. When Dogen came back to Japan, he started to criticize koan study, saying that, as practiced by Zen sects in China, it had become stereotyped, that there was no life in it anymore. In his opinion, koans had been reduced from expressions of enlightenment to tools or techniques to attain a desired end—that is, completion of koan study and formal approval from a teacher, without any real penetration along the way. Most scholars read these criticisms superficially, assuming that Dogen rejected koans as a valid method of Zen practice. But he continued to use koans. In fact, *Shobogenzo* contains so much commentary on koans that to read it properly, one must really be familiar with koan study; otherwise, it seems much less intelligent than it really is. *Shobogenzo* itself is one enormous koan: each word is an expression of the Way."

Directly opposite Kosho-ji's gate, a white egret alighted on a gravel bar in the bright torrent. ("Brighter than the fireflies on the Uji River are your words in the dark, Beloved," Amy Lowell wrote, in a haiku imitation that entirely lacks this Zen form's tension between the fleeting and the eternal.) From the riverside, the entrance road, carved through the wall of river rock, runs straight up the wooded hill, while twin rivulets run down stone ditches under the stone walls to either side. This place is called Koto (a stringed instrument), because of the water's purl. Sunlight descends through a canopy of delicate maple leaves, alighting here and there on yellow roses. Then the road ends at a white arch inset into the long white forewall of the temple court, which sits on a broad step of the mountainside above the river. On the portal arch, a sign identifies Kosho-ji as the earliest Soto training center in Japan. Inside this gate—so simple by comparison with the huge and dark-peaked entrance gates of the Rinzai temples—is a stone garden with an ancient temple bell.

Completed in 1233, Kosho-ji was the first Zen temple in Japan entirely free of influence from other Buddhist sects, having been specifically designed for the zazen training that Dogen had emphasized in *Fukan-zazen-gi*. Seven centuries later, it is still offering zazen practice. The simple zendo—maintained in the original style, says the present abbot—seats thirty people under the gaze of a striking Manjusri Bodhisattva, seated on his lion, whose blazing eyes seem to shine in the dim light. The Founder's Hall is dominated by a hard-faced Dogen, very unlike most Dogen representations. A second image, much more typical, portrays him as gentle and cerebral, with a broad, high forehead, pink face, and small mouth.

Tetsugen-sensei, who had never imagined that Kosho-ji was still so active, was moved by the feel and spirit of the place. Regretting aloud that we had not worn our formal robes this morning—we travel in the black work tunic of monks—he prostrated himself in three full bows to Dogen Kigen, touching his shaved head to the gray tile floor.

Because Tetsugen is so casual and so informal, I am taken by surprise, and touched, by his unselfconscious impulses toward devotion, just as I have been taken aback by his sudden sternness. At Kosho-ji he had undergone a change of mood, remaining silent much longer than usual as we walked a little in the temple grounds. However, his mind was as hard at work as ever, and when he spoke again, he entered directly and without preamble into the subject of Dharma transmission training and our own relationship.

"Maezumi-roshi often told me how Dogen developed shiho studies with *his* first Dharma successor, Koun Ejo, and how he had set such high standards for this face-to-face training, and the *broadness* of this training. In fact, my original admiration of Dogen came from these standards for shiho training, which is peculiar to the Soto sect and was mostly established by Dogen himself, at least in Japan. Koan study is very important in opening your Dharma eye and broadening your understanding, whereas shiho study is more concerned with teacher–student relationships, the closeness, the merging, as teacher and student become one. The first shiho document transmitted specifies that the point of training is for master and student to become one. And what *should* happen—it doesn't always—is a sort of father–son relationship, so that no matter what you do, it's all right, you're not dismissed for mistakes, there's no turning back."

Tetsugen looked at me seriously, then chuckled, as if to say, You're trapped! "It's not so simple for two people to become that close, even a parent and child. That's why there is this emphasis on face-to-face study of such matters as Dai-ji—'the

Great Matter'—enlightenment. But just living together, being together, as we are doing on this trip, is also very important. For that reason, I consider the trip itself much more important than how many dokusan we have together, how much koan study we accomplish. Even if nothing is going on, so to speak, there is a lot going on."

"Teacher and disciple studying simultaneously is twining vines of buddha ancestors," said Dogen.[14]

As Tetsugen's jisha, I nodded dutifully, letting him continue without interruption. While I found what he was saying fascinating, I also feared that I would be found wanting. Traditionally, a Zen teacher's first shuso should be a disciple younger than himself, not a student a decade older than the teacher. Also, I knew that he had "become one" with Maezumi-roshi in a way and to a degree that was probably not possible in our case, given not only my life apart from his Zen community (which meant that except in intense bursts, such as this journey, we spent too little time together), but also discrepancies in age, outlook, and temperament, including my stubborn resistance to authority and a notable lack of the proper devotional attitude. Not that Tetsugen's devotion to Maezumi made him blind to his teacher's human failings—on the contrary—but even when they disagreed, this didn't matter, their communication seemed like the internal dialogue of a single person. And inevitably Tetsugen was more steeped in Japanese Zen tradition than I would ever be, or felt like being (if I had found an American Indian teacher—not some media medicine man but a true teacher—willing to work with me, I might well have chosen a North American tradition over an Asian one). Ever conscious of Maezumi's standards, he was conservative and strict about his monks' observance of Soto customs despite his ongoing discussions with his teacher about forming their own school of American Zen.

Once, in Riverdale, a senior monk made a technical error while officiating at morning service. Embarrassed, this monk made an open joke of it right then and there. The joke was funny, and I, for one, had to struggle not to laugh out loud, but

Tetsugen went dark red in the face, saying nothing at all. When the service was concluded, he snapped at this monk very coldly, "To joke that way during this service is very disrespectful to our practice. You will do three full bows to the Buddha by way of apology to us all." I stood there guilty and unhappy while the humiliated monk performed his bows.

The episode was reassuring, since it put to rest certain lingering doubts about Tetsugen's mettle, so well hidden by his soft-voiced, teasing manner. Almost always, he controls his anger, but this "nice Jewish boy from Brooklyn" has a huge voice and power at his disposal, and when aroused—or pretending to be aroused—is a fearsome Dharma guardian indeed.

"In Rinzai, there is intimacy and face-to-face contact through dokusan," he is explaining, "and by the time of inka, student and teacher are one. The cell splits, and after that, both can give dokusan. The master is the center of the circle, the student is the circle, becoming smaller and smaller until they become a single point. In Soto, this process takes place in shiho training. There's a lot of correspondence with koan study, so that if you understand koans, shiho study will be quite straightforward. There are three basic documents to be transmitted, which Dogen was permitted to see in China. In fact, several teachers showed him their Dharma, which is rare; he must have been an exceptionally powerful student. Dogen was very impressed, and set up his own study system, based on these documents, which he used with Ejo, his successor.

"This system has since been strengthened by other teachers. But the need for priests as Soto spread caused a lowering of standards, since priests had to have finished shiho training to qualify. The system deteriorated, and these days only a few Soto teachers try to maintain Dogen's standard, and only then with a few students. Most Soto priests receive shiho without serious study. It is scarcely more than a form they have to know to go through the motions of Dharma transmission."

It is impossible to give the seal of realization without being a buddha, and it is impossible to become a buddha without receiving the seal of realization from a buddha. . . . When chrysanthemums inherit from chrysanthemums and a pine gives the seal of realization to a pine, the preceding chrysanthemum is one with the following chrysanthemum, and the preceding pine is one with the following pine. Those who do not understand this, even when they hear the words "correct transmission from buddha to buddha," have no idea what it means. . . . My late master, abbot of Mt. Tiantong, strictly prohibited students from unjustifiably claiming to have received dharma heritage.[15]

Being-Time, which had first attracted Tetsugen to Dogen, was set down here at Kosho-ji in 1240. The seventeen fascicles of *Shobogenzo* composed in 1242 included *Unbroken Activity*, which was read at the Kyoto residence of Lord Yoshishige Hatano, of Echizen Province, in the remote "Snow Country" to the north and east. Hatano, a samurai attached to the Kyoto headquarters of the Kamakura shogunate, is the man who is thought to have persuaded Dogen to remove himself entirely from the Kyoto region.

Dogen's growing reputation as a teacher had attracted more students than Kosho-ji could maintain, and had also increased the resentment of the other sects. Although he had shown some of his writings to the emperor Gozaga, Dogen—unlike Eisai—apparently made no political overtures to win those in power over to his side. Toward the end of his stay here at Kosho-ji, he intensified his attack on Rinzai Zen, attributing the ideas that he expressed to his late teacher, "the old buddha," Tendo Nyojo, whom he described as the greatest master to appear in China "in two or three centuries"—that is, since Zen's Golden Age in the T'ang dynasty. But far from criticizing Rinzai, Nyojo had followed the lead of Sekito Kisen in belittling sectarian disputes, ignoring the five separate schools of the Zen sect, and the Zen sect itself, for that matter. What he had endorsed was "the Great Way of All Buddhas" and the transmission of the true teaching from Buddha to Buddha. Denying that Zen was (or was not) what Bodhidharma had called "a separate transmission outside the scriptures," Nyojo observed that the Great Way was not concerned with "inside" or "outside."

Very likely, Dogen's fresh resentment of Rinzai was caused by government sponsorship of Tofuku, the new Rinzai monastery in Kyoto, since it was only a few weeks before Tofuku-ji was opened that he would leave the area for good. (Dogen's criticism of the Rinzai school did not lessen his great admiration for Rinzai himself, whom he praises repeatedly, even favorably compares to the great Soto master Tokusan. "It has been said that the best of the partiarchs were Rinzai and Tokusan, but how can Tokusan be put in the same category as Rinzai? Truly the Zen man Rinzai was without an equal in the whole crowd.")[16]

Perhaps his political difficulties interfered with his work on *Shobogenzo*, or perhaps he realized it was time to heed the instruction of his teacher: "Do not stay in the center of cities or towns. Do not be friendly with kings and state ministers. Dwell in the deep mountains and valleys to realize the true nature of man." In any case, he accepted Lord Hatano's invitation to relocate himself in the far north, where Hatano proposed to build him a new temple. Leaving Kosho-ji in the care of his student Gijun, he departed in 1243 for the remote Snow Country on the Sea of Japan. Not long thereafter, Kosho-Horin-ji was destroyed by fire, whether by accident or by ill-wishers is not known.[17]

Emptiness is bound to bloom, like hundreds of grasses blossoming. Although originally having no flower, it now has flowers. It is, as it were, a plum tree that some days ago did not have flowers but blooms when spring arrives. It is the time of flowers, and flowers have arrived. . . . The flowering of plums and willows happens to plums and willows; that of peaches and damsons to peaches and damsons. The way the flowers of emptiness [kuge, literally "sky-flowers," the illusory forms of the relative world] open is also like this.

Sky Flowers
—EIHEI DOGEN

CHAPTER FIFTEEN

FROM the train northward from Kyoto, the gray tiles of the shore villages and the gray waters of Lake Biwa turn a weary shine to the misty light. We wonder if Monk Dogen, on his way to the Snow Country in Echizen province, came this same way along the western shore, under the steep sides of Mount Hiei, which in those days must have been mirrored in a clear blue lake. And Biwa was surely the inspiration of Dogen's poem, called "On a Portrait of Myself," in which the poet presents the "original face" of our Buddha-nature:

Cold lake, for thousands of yards, soaks up sky color.
Evening quiet: a fish of brocade scales drifts to the bottom,
then goes this way—that way.
The arrow notch splits:
  endless water surface, moonlight, brilliance. [1]

Behind the old villages, small gardens rise in terraces to the edge of coniferous forest that climbs into the mists on Mount

Hiei. Bursts of spring color in the dark corridors between the evergreens are lavender sprays of wild azalea. Toward the north end of the lake, which is forty miles long, the train enters a region of harsh, sudden peaks and inhospitable ravines. Then the land opens out again, descending to the coastal city of Tsuruga. The blue distance is the great Sea of Japan.

Eventually the train comes to Fukui, not far from Dogen's first habitation in the Snow Country. At a temple called Yoshimine, near the coast, he completed nearly thirty chapters of *Shobogenzo* in scarcely more than a year. It was at Yoshimine "in three feet of snow" that the remarkable *Baika*, or "Plum Blossoms," was first presented as a teisho. The preliminary verse, attributed to Tendo Nyojo, sounds very much like Dogen himself:

> *Old plum tree bent and gnarled*
> *all at once opens one blossom, two blossoms,*
> *three, four, five blossoms, uncountable blossoms,*
> *not proud of purity,*
> *not proud of fragrance;*
> *falling, becoming spring,*
> *blowing over grass and trees,*
> *balding the head of a patch-robed monk,*
> *whirling, changing into wind, wild rain,*
> *falling, snow, all over the earth.*
> *The old plum tree is boundless.*
> *A hard cold rubs the nostrils.*

Because of what Dogen calls *zenki* ("unbroken or concerted activity" or "total exertion"—the free, spontaneous *being* of anything at all, which in that moment is the whole expression of the universe), the absolute and relative, the fleeting and the eternal, appear instantaneously, in the blossoms and ancient trunk of the old tree: "When the old plum tree suddenly opens, the world of blossoming flowers arises. At the moment when the world of blossoming flowers arises, spring arrives. There is a single blossom that opens five blossoms. At this moment of a single blossom, there are three, four, and five blossoms—countless blossoms. . . . Blossoming is the old plum tree's offering. . . ."[2]

On June 15, 1246, Dogen moved inland to Daibutsu-ji, the new temple built under Mount Kichijo by Lord Hatano. Upon its completion, this temple was renamed Eihei-ji, or Temple of Eternal Peace, which Dogen envisioned as an earthly Buddha paradise. "The mountain landscape was the sound of streams: all is the form and word of Shakyamuni," he wrote, in one of the poems composed in a wild land of deer and bears. The new monastery was based on monastic specifications laid down in the first years of the ninth century by the Chinese master Hyakujo, who, like Dogen, put great emphasis on physical labor as inseparable from Zen practice: "A day of no work is a day of no eating," said the venerable Hyakujo, who refused to eat after his monks hid his tools. His ideal monastery was located like this one "in the bosom of mountains and waters."

Near the end of Basho's classic *Narrow Road to the Deep North*, the poet-monk arrives at Eihei-ji: "I thought it . . . a miracle that the Priest Dogen had chosen such a secluded place for the site of the temple." Today one travels by small electric train, sixteen kilometers inland from Fukui, ascending the valley of the Nine-Headed Dragon River to the steep village that has accumulated over the centuries at Eihei-ji's gates. Here a wood plaque inscribed with Chinese characters reads, "Only those concerned with the matter of life and death need enter here." Rebuilt after a fire in the fifteenth century, Eihei-ji today is composed of some seventy buildings, yet this huge place seems overwhelmed by the looming hoary cedars on the mountainside, the rush of water. Dogen wrote,

> I won't even stop at the valley's brook
> For fear that my shadow may flow into the world.

At the guest hall we are given formal tea by Hirano-sensei, guest master of Eihei-ji, a cool, urbane, and handsome priest who had paid a visit to the Zen Center of Los Angeles a few years before, when he was head of a Zen group in Seattle. Subsequently two apprentice monks, or *unsui*,[3] lead us to the baths, then bring a simple supper to our room. Tetsugen is much bemused by the hospitality we have received in this strict place. "Maezumi-roshi must have called ahead from Tokyo," he has decided. "Roshi is very well regarded here in Japan; you can see that from the treatment we receive wherever we go."

However, I feel out of place, a gaijin or barbarian of unseemly height, and the only monk in this great monastery whose hair, though short, is not shaved to the skull. When he had joined us at Los Angeles Airport, Maezumi-roshi (who makes an annual trip to Japan on a fund-raising mission for the Zen Center of Los Angeles and on Soto business) had made a sour comment on my hairiness, but he had the tact to leave the final decision to Tetsugen, and Tetsugen—though keenly sensitive, as ever, to his teacher's disapproval—was confident enough to pass the decision on to me. Having no wish to embarrass my teachers, I told Tetsugen I would shave my head more or less cheerfully if he felt strongly about it, but otherwise would prefer not to. I do not live in a Zen community but am very much out in the world, where my work these days is among American Indian people and commercial fishermen. A shaved head would draw unwelcome attention, making people uneasy and flaunting my "Zen" in a way that I very much dislike. It is also true that self-consciousness and vanity are too much with me.

For American Zen students who choose to become monks, this "being in the world" presents serious, unmonkish problems, which include in my case not only the demands of a large family and the role of money but also my chronic involvement in social causes—the environment and peace movements, the migrant farm workers, the Indians. Activism is not antithetical to Zen practice in Japan since in Zen it is critical to be "who you are" (Suzuki-roshi, among many past and present masters, was a strong pacifist); on the other hand, Eido-roshi used to say that, until one's Dharma eye is opened, such activities are "the blind leading the blind."

In America, despite the counterculture reputation that Zen acquired in the "Beat Zen" days, no Zen group formally espouses any cause which sets one group against another, or involves itself in politics or world affairs. Tetsugen has never been an activist, though he hopes to involve ZCNY in social welfare programs in the poor neighborhood of the Zen bakery which, with the help of Richard Baker-roshi and the San Francisco Zen Center, will become the livelihood of our Zen community. For individual students (and some teachers, too), the situation is more troublesome. Robert Aitken-roshi, for example, has been an antiwar activist since the 1960s; Baker-roshi, in recent years, has been active in the antinuclear campaigns. I feel as (I imagine) they do. Since from a Zen point of view, the absolute and the relative are not different, I cannot dwell in the absolute calm of my black cushion and ignore the chaos of the relative world pounding past the zendo doors.

Finally, there is the consequential matter of my "literary endeavors" of nearly forty years, which place me at once in the most hopeless category of Zen student, according to the Rinzai master Muso Soseki (1275–1351): Muso names three grades of disciples, then concludes, "Those who befuddle their minds in non-Buddhist works and devote their efforts to literary endeavors are nothing but shaven-headed laymen and are not fit to be classed even with those of the lowest grade."

Presumably Master Muso railed at dilettantes, not true poets—though the work of both is an expression of their Buddha nature. Since the ground of Zen is life itself, neither murderers nor poets are excluded.

Eihei Dogen Zenji is so named because of his identification with this monastery, which even today maintains the strictest discipline in the Soto sect. "Undefiled practice," Maezumi-roshi says, "is the very spirit of *Shobogenzo*," and this practice is manifest at Eihei-ji. At 3:00 A.M. a monk is tapping on our screens, and we are scarcely in our robes when Hirano-sensei's jisha comes to lead us up the mountain, through old, dank passages to the old halls. No outsiders are permitted into the zendo. Here the novice monks sleep, eat, and do zazen on the single tatami mat, six feet by three, which serves as their home during years of arduous training. We are shown to a raised platform along the corridor outside the zendo hall.

In the darkness, deep in the April mountains, it is very cold. A bell awakens the unsui, and there comes a hushed stir as the monks clamber about, folding their bed rolls into the lockers on the tatami platforms. Within ten minutes they are dressed and seated in zazen, and soon the monitor is making his rounds with the narrow-bladed stick that represents Manjusri's delusion-cutting sword. The old timbers echo the monotonous *whack-whack* on each pair of shoulders. The somber priest does not spare the gaijin—*whack!*—the pain rings in my ears. Then he is gone, and each black-robed figure sits alone in the cold gloom of the old brown hall with what Maezumi-roshi calls "the Real One inside ourselves."

At the end of zazen, while still seated, we put on the toga-like Buddha's robe, or *kesa*, and also white *bessu* on our bare feet, after which we climb the steps to the main service hall. Waiting for service to begin, we stand outside on a platform overlooking the monastery below. Dawn is coming, and still it is very cold. The gray-tiled roofs are dim in the night's shadow, but the climbing sky high overhead, behind evergreen turrets on the ravine walls, is turning pale, and already a solitary bird sings in the forest.

"It's not just a deep respect I have for Dogen," whispers Tetsugen, who has scarcely stopped talking about Dogen during our stay here. "More than that, I feel an *affinity* with him. His universality affects me strongly, the feeling and thinking behind his conviction of the single Dharma, the everything-as-it-is-now, not in a superficial sense but as the true expression of the Dharma or Law in every instant, every object, every phenomenon of mind and matter.

"For Dogen, the Zen of our everyday life, moment after moment, is truly the way of enlightenment. His teachings hammer that idea over and over, and at the same time, his *practice* manifests it so sincerely that it serves others as a model. Dogen's great contribution—and his own life was an example—was the perception that daily practice and enlightenment are one. That's why his system here at Eihei-ji became so ritualized—so that his whole life and being could become a model for what our life should be. Part of Dogen's plan in ritualizing Eihei-ji—and Japanese Soto derives from his ideas—was the emphasis he put on everyday life, on work and personal conduct, as opposed to koan study, teisho, and dokusan. So many teachers say 'All is the Dharma,' but I don't feel that they truly mean it, or live their lives that way.

"The one way to be *truly* universal is to be very particular, moment by moment, detail by detail. If you are merely 'universal,' you lose the feel of life, you become abstract, facile. All is the Dharma, everything is enlightenment! Or everything is okay!—according to Beat Zen, which lacked that vital particularity. But if the emphasis on everyday detail is too rigid, our existence loses the religious power of the universal. To walk with one foot in each world—that was Dogen's way, and Dogen's life. In a single sentence, he talked from both points of view, the absolute and the relative, the universal and the particular. He was not only living in both, he was switching so fast between the two that he was in *neither*! He was entirely free! And this is wonderful, just as it should be! Form *is* emptiness, emptiness *is* form. Relative *is* absolute, absolute *is* relative. But *all of reality* is in the *is*—the *now* of this very moment! Generally we favor one realm over the other, but our *real* existence is that '*is*.'"

In the great hall we take our place in rows of gold-robed priests and black-robed monks. The chanting and invocations of the morning service last almost two hours, most of it kneeling, sitting on our heels. For one unbroken stretch of nearly an hour we maintain this position, which the Japanese use all their lives but which for most Westerners is painful quickly. (American students never last long at Eihei-ji, which has small tolerance for lack of fortitude. For years, this place refused to accept Americans, who were not worth the bother of having to deal with their complaints.) The long service is choreographed against the golden altar, the cascades of small golden bells, the scarlet carpeting on the tatami mats. The pageantry, the bells, the pound of voices to the ancient drums is stirring, and we, too, chant those parts of the service that, in our training, we have memorized in Japanese: the *Heart Sutra* (the essence or "heart" of the great Prajna Paramita literature of Mahayana Buddhism); the *Sandokai* (*Identity of Relative and Absolute*, attributed to the Chinese ancestor of Soto, Sekito Kisen); the *Names of the Patriarchs*; the *Daihishin Dharani*, paying homage to Avalokiteshvara Bodhisattva. Toward the end, an old priest beckons us, and I follow Tetsugen to the main altar, where we make our bows and offer incense.

After morning service, we go to a rock outcrop above the lower buildings where Dogen Kigen is said to have performed outdoor zazen. Even in bright morning sun, the power of the place is not dispelled. Most monasteries are located at the base of mountains, but here the old buildings sit in a compact mass in the deep V made by the mountainsides, high up in the valley of the Nine-Headed Dragon River. Because its buildings are necessarily close together, the old monastery has great force, for as Dogen teaches us, Eihei-ji itself is doing zazen, hurling its power down the canyon and out into the world on every toll of the old mountain bell. This is the bell that each new monk must sound upon arrival, requesting to be let in ("What do you want here!" they bellow at him, in the first test of his resolve). From that day forward, the unsui run barefoot from duty to duty and from job to job. ("A monk is like the clouds and has no fixed abode; like flowing water he has nothing to depend on.")[4] In black work denims, white cloths wrapped around their naked heads, squads of grim youths attack the ceaseless cleaning of the stairs and corridors, stopping short to bow almost to the waist to the lowliest priest, then resuming their arduous and redundant work, performed barefoot even in the winter.

Tetsugen resists the "military" practice at Eihei-ji, which

191

he feels is ill-suited to American Zen. The stern atmosphere is reinforced by the monastery's oppressive location in a dark mountain ravine in the northern Snow Country. In winter the snow here is so deep that even from the downhill side, says Hirano's jisha, one can walk from the ground up to the roofs, and the enclosed corridors between the buildings are dark all day because of the drifts piled high above the windows.

It seems appropriate that in the Buddha Hall, above the altar, a wood frieze illustrates the legend in which Monk Jinko, standing all night in the snow, cuts off his arm to prove his zeal to Bodhidharma, who appears as a cowled figure in zazen, facing the wall. The famous koan based on this episode—the forty-first in the *Gateless Gate* collection—is the one I happen to be working with this very day. Tradition relates that the only text permitted his students by Bodhidharma was the mighty *Lanka-vatara Sutra* ("Things are not what they seem, nor are they otherwise. . . . Deeds exist, but no doer can be found"), which later became the main document of the Kegon (Hua Yen) sect of Buddhism, and was given to Jinko when he received Dharma transmission. Dogen wrote:

Snowdrifts like those at Shorin, in the old days.
Whole sky, whole earth, whole spring—new.
Inheriting the robe, attaining the marrow—
To join the ancestors
Who would spare himself standing in snow through the night?

Tetsugen feels that because Bodhidharma was so old when he came to China, he had no time to found a monastery or school. He was fierce and severe in order to maintain high standards and attract strong students like this Jinko, who felt obliged to cut off his arm to attract the old man's notice. Traditionally, Bodhidharma found just four successors, among whom Jinko was the best. (You have my skin, my flesh, my bones, he tells the other three who grasp his teaching, in a famous story; to Jinko he says, You have my marrow—though in saying this, he does not mean that marrow is "superior" to skin.) And all this time, so it is said, two rival teachers were trying to murder the Blue-Eyed Monk with poison so powerful that it burned his teeth out—hence the broken-toothed look in certain portraits. By the time of the sixth attempt upon his life, he had already chosen Jinko as his successor and, being tired, decided to go along with his own assassination, dying in good zazen posture about A.D. 536. Jinko (known later as Taiso Eka, the Second Patriarch) was also persecuted, but he, too, transmitted the Dharma before being killed for his unorthodox Zen teachings.

As the sun peers down over the east wall of the ravine, lighting silver fires in the stream above the monastery, two wagtails teeter on river stones of shining black, stuck with pink blossoms, and a dipper flutters on the water sparkle, rounding a bend. This is the stream referred to in a story[5] used for teaching at Eihei-ji in which a young monk who tossed unused water onto the stream bank was chastised by Dogen. The stream water had *inochi*, or "life integrity," as stream water and should therefore have been returned into the stream with gratitude and as little waste as possible (in the same way that an American Indian who is still in touch with Indian way will return even a pebble to its own place).

"As more and more of Dogen's work becomes available in English," my teacher is saying, "we can really appreciate his thinking, such as his notion of what one critic[6] refers to as 'cosmic resonance.' In effect, this is the Kegon concept of Indra's net—the One Body, which is very important to grasp. 'Cosmic resonance' is what Dogen called the oneness of the universal; when I am enlightened, at that moment the mountains and rivers are enlightened, and vice versa. Shakyamuni said it first: 'Alone above and below heaven, I am the honored one.' Dogen brought this idea into practical use: as I practice, everything is practicing. To realize this invests each moment of our life with great significance. This moment is not just for 'us,' just for right now, but for all space and time. When we *really* perceive that, we can *feel* the trees and rocks doing their enlightened practice."

And the wagtails, too, think I, watching the birds. But it is difficult to interest Tetsugen in wagtails, short of pointing them out as expressions of the One.

At the graveyard, in dappled April light, we pay our respects to Dogen Zenji's memorial stone, a rough, plain rock sheltered by a small hut from the weather. Soon two unsui come with an offering of fresh yellow flowers.[7] For more than seven hundred years here at Eihei-ji, Priest Dogen's recommendations for zazen (*Fukan-zazen-gi*) have been chanted every evening as an inspiration to the monks, and only those priests who have had shiho, or Dharma transmission, are permitted to rise at 2:00 A.M. each morning to wash the calm features of Dogen's face on the statue in the Founder's Hall. In their gold kesas, they offer this buddha green tea and dried plums, as well as kaya nuts from the surrounding forest.

> All my life false and real, right and wrong tangled.
> Playing with the moon, ridiculing the wind, listening to the
>   birds . . .
> Many years wasted seeing the mountain covered with snow.
> This winter I suddenly realize snow makes a mountain.

In another poem of this period, Dogen would speak of the "shining forth, true Buddhism all over the world." But the great labor of establishing Eihei-ji interfered with his progress on *Shobogenzo*, and scarcely eight chapters were completed after his arrival on the Nine-Headed Dragon River.

In 1247, in what seems to have been a belated attempt to justify his new school to the authorities, Dogen accepted the invitation of Tokiyori Hojo, the new regent at Kamakura, to teach in the military capital. The invitation testifies to his prestige as a teacher, since there was no "Soto school" as yet and since Rinzai was very strong in Kamakura. Before leaving that city seven months later, Dogen conferred the Buddhist precepts on Tokiyori, who was a sincere practitioner.[8] Dogen also presented ten small poems to a lady of the court, including "Original

Face" (from the classic koan "What was your face before your parents were born?").

> Spring flowers.
> Summer cuckoos.
> Autumn moon.
> Winter snow.
> Cool. Serene.

Dogen returned to the Snow Country in March of the year 1248; he was not to leave Eihei-ji again until the last month of his life. In 1249 he composed a poem to accompany his best-known likeness, "Portrait of Dogen Viewing the Moon":

Fresh, clear spirit covers the old mountain man this autumn.
A donkey stares at the sky ceiling; glowing white moon floats. . . .
Buoyant, I let myself go, filled with gruel, filled with rice.
Lively flapping from head to tail.
Sky above, sky beneath, cloud self, water origin.

In 1250, Dogen Zenji was finally prevailed upon to accept an honorary purple kesa from the emperor Gosaga in Kyoto, but like Tendo Nyojo (who had inherited a brocade robe from his own teacher), he refused to wear a garment which signified pursuit of fame and profit: "If an old monk here wore a purple kesa, he would be laughed at by monkeys and cranes."

Dogen fell ill in 1252, apparently of some ailment of the heart, and the following January he wrote *The Eight Aspects of the Enlightened One*, in which he explicates the Buddha's last words to his disciples. This was the ninety-fifth and final fascicle of *Shobogenzo* ("Unfortunately," as Koun Ejo comments, "we cannot see a one-hundred-chapter version [which Dogen had intended]. This is a matter of deep regret.")

To the end, Dogen Kigen returned to the theme of mujo, the transience of existence, evoked by the eternal wind, the eternal moon:

> *On a grass leaf, awaiting the morning sun*
> *The dew is melting.*
> *Do not stir the field so soon, wind of autumn!*

> *To what may this world be likened?*
> *Moonlight in a dewdrop*
> *Falling from a duck's beak.* [9]

By midsummer, seriously ailing, Dogen was persuaded by Lord Hatano to travel to Kyoto to seek medical advice. Before leaving, he appointed Koun Ejo as the next abbot of Eihei-ji and presented him with a robe of his own making. Ejo escorted him to Kyoto. On the 15th of August, [10] under the full moon he had used so often as the symbol of the awakened state ("the moon abiding in the midst of serene mind"), [11] he wrote his final verse:

> *Even when I hope to see it again in autumn,*
> *How, this evening,*
> *Can I sleep with such a moon?*

Tradition has it that Dogen died on August 28, 1253, at Seido-in or Sonen-in, a temple now vanished from the Takatsuji District, but Hirano-sensei tells us that he died at the house of his student Kakunen, located somewhere near the edge of what is now Maruyama Park.

The forming of mountains, rivers, and the earth is all dependent on the Buddha-nature. It being thus, seeing mountains and rivers is seeing the Buddha-nature. Seeing the Buddha-nature is seeing a donkey's jowls or a horse's mouth. . . .

The very impermanence of grass and tree, thicket and forest, is the Buddha-nature. The very impermanence of men and things, body and mind, is the Buddha-nature. Nations and lands, mountains and rivers are impermanent because they are the Buddha-nature. Supreme and complete enlightenment, because it is the Buddha-nature, is impermanent. . . .

Our present moment-to-moment activity is the opening of a gate. . . . Completely utilizing life, we cannot be held back by life. Completely utilizing death, we cannot be bothered by death. Do not cherish life. Do not blindly dread death. They are where the Buddha-nature is.

For infinite kalpas in the past, foolish people in great number have regarded man's spiritual consciousness as Buddha-nature, or as man's original state of suchness—how laughably absurd! . . . Buddha-nature is a fence, a wall, a tile, a pebble.

Buddha-Nature
—EIHEI DOGEN

CHAPTER SIXTEEN

EIHEI DOGEN, as he became known, had developed a religion that drew its energies from his own insights and devotion, rather than from thin-blooded imitations of Chinese tradition that had characterized Japanese Buddhism before this time. Nonetheless, it remained too "Chinese" in character to win wide acceptance from the common people. Koun Ejo, Dogen's loyal successor as abbot of Eihei-ji, did his best to record and maintain his teacher's words in his *Shobogenzo Zuimonki*, and the third abbot, Tetsu Gikai, encouraged the dissemination of the teachings, which in the early years after Dogen's death were little known beyond Eihei-ji.

Like Ejo, Gikai had come with their teacher from Fukakusa and Kosho-ji, where he had awakened upon hearing Dogen say, "This [absolute] truth abides in the world of objective reality. . . . In the spring, the hundred flowers are red; doves are crying in the willows."[1] Gikai founded a Zen monastery at Daijo-ji, a spare, beautiful temple on a wooded rise overlooking Kanazawa on the northern coast, which is the birthplace of D. T. Suzuki. On the afternoon of our visit, a hard sea light on the pines in Daijo-ji's inner garden was softened by the mist of cherry blossoms, the sad warmth of weathered wood. A solitary monk weeding the mosses, who did not look up or greet the only visitors, reminded me of that old head monk tending Myozen's grave at Kennin-ji, and also the old monk raking leaves (described at sesshin years ago by Eido-roshi), who embodied profound realization without ever having experienced a kensho.

In feudal times, Kanazawa was already a wealthy city, and remnants of the great castle of the Maeda clan still stand. Kenroko-en, a miniature landscape of streams and ponds, bridges and paths, stone lanterns, and flowering trees, required two centuries to put together, and is now regarded as one of the finest gardens in the nation. On our travels in Japan, songbirds have been few in species as well as numbers, and so I was pleased, in late afternoon, to encounter in Kenroko-en a small party of Eurasian tits or "chickadees," three different species, gleaning new bugs from the old handcrafted trees.

Soto priests say that if Dogen is the father of Japanese Soto Zen, Keizan Jokin (1268–1325) is its mother. Like Gikai (who once struck him in the mouth as he struggled to answer the koan question "Can you show me ordinary mind?"), Keizan founded a temple (Yoko-ji) which has survived in Kanazawa. Then, in

1321, he became abbot of another temple far out on the remote Noto Peninsula to the north and east. This temple, which he renamed Soji-ji, is the one associated with the spread of Soto Zen. Like Dogen himself, Keizan had studied with an accomplished Rinzai master, and this master's successor, in his turn, came to study with Keizan in Kanazawa. A decade later, the same monk turned up at Soji-ji with ten Dharma questions from the emperor Godaigo, who was apparently so delighted by Keizan's answers that he made Soji-ji an imperially approved temple and presented its abbot with a purple robe. At the end of his life, according to one ancient account, Keizan "wandered around with a broken rainhat and a skinny cane, meeting people wherever he went, and crowds of people submitted to him."[2]

In his efforts to adapt Dogen's "Chinese" teachings to the Japanese people, Keizan and his successors felt obliged to give these teachings a name. Like Tendo Nyojo, Dogen had put much more emphasis on the way of everyday enlightenment then on the Zen sect and its various schools, but his successors, attempting to claim him by setting his teachings apart, established a Japanese Soto school, naming Dogen and Keizan its cofounders. Dogen would surely have abominated the proselytizing of his teachings, not to speak of the defiling of the Dharma in the esoteric prayers and tantric incantations adapted from Shingon by his followers to broaden Soto's appeal. Yet but for Keizan and other missionaries, Japanese Soto and Dogen's teachings might never have endured to the present day.

"Dogen's ritualizing of Zen practice at Eihei-ji ran the same risk as systematizing koan study," Tetsugen says. "The life can go out of the ritual, and merely the structure is left. Yet the structure is very important. In Judaism there were brilliant mystics but no structure to their teachings, and Judaic mysticism died away. A similar thing happened to the Gnostics, who also refused structure. On the other hand, the Christian churches have retained their structure while losing most of their vitality. It is necessary to maintain a balance between structure and creativity; both are needed. In Soto, Dogen was the germinal seed, but without the structure established by Keizan, Soto might not exist today.

"I see it as an endless, intertwining dualism, in which one element seeks to maintain its structure and the other tries to keep it from petrifying; if either fails, the whole will die. This is why it is so crucial to maintain the lineage, perpetuate the teaching, knowing that a Dogen will appear once in a while to bring new life."

At the time of Dogen's death, the Buddhist hierarchy at Nara and Kyoto was still trying to suppress Zen teachings, all the more so because of Zen's refusal to extend any special privilege to its own priesthood, far less the aristocracy. The abbots worked in the gardens and kitchens with the monks, and the head cook, or *tenzo*, was usually the second-ranking figure in the monastery. In addition, Soto dared to state that the Buddha's true teachings could be transmitted to illiterate peasants without benefit of incense, ceremonies, or sutras, far less the priestly hocus-pocus by which the older sects had ensured their power.

The popular rejection of the Buddhism of the aristocrats coincided with the rise of the military government in Kamakura. The new warrior class, intent on an alternative to the Heian court, was attracted by Zen's spare, self-reliant style, its lack of interest in fame and worldly affairs, its avoidance of esoteric doctrine and abstruse study, and its ethical precepts, which were an implicit rejection of the corruption of the older Buddhist schools. It was also drawn to Zen's philosophic attitude toward life and death, which had a strong influence on the development of the samurai warrior class and the stoic code of bushido, "way of the warrior."

The struggle between popular and esoteric Buddhism was intensified by the emergence of the Hokke or Lotus sect under a reformer with violent political views. Like Eisai and Dogen before him, Nichiren (1222–1282) had studied with the Tendai priests at Enryaku-ji and later denounced the court-corrupted doctrine; while he was at it, he attacked the Nara schools, the meditational approach of Zen, and the simplistic *nembutsu* ("Take shelter in Amida Buddha") chanting of Jodo, for which he sub-stituted the equally simplistic *Namu-myoho-renge-kyo*, "Take shelter in the *Lotus Sutra.*" Nichiren's dire predictions about the future of a nation contaminated by false teachings were borne out in 1257–58, when Japan was racked by floods and earthquakes, famine, plague, and crime. From Kamakura, to which he would retreat in 1260 like Eisai before him (Dogen had retreated to the Snow Country), he denounced Zen as "a doctrine of fiends and devils" and all the other schools as even worse.

In this troubled period, China's Kublai Khan wished to subjugate the Land of Wa. When the Great Khan's envoys were executed by the Kamakura government in 1275, Nichiren com-mented, "It is a great pity that they should have to cut off the heads of the innocent Mongols and left unharmed the priests of Jodo, Shingon, Zen, and Ritsu who are the enemies of Japan." (This view was not so wrong-headed as it appears. The previous year, while the Kamakura government was trying to organize resistance to a Mongol invasion, armed monks were busy rioting in Kyoto to advance the fortunes of Tofuku-ji; in Nara, just prior to a second Mongol invasion a few years later, similar riots were encouraged by Enryaku-ji.) But when the Mongol fleet was destroyed by storm, credit was given, not to Nichiren, but to the ancient Shinto gods and goddesses, and Nichiren, thwarted in his aim to make his Lotus sect the national religion, retired to a mountain hermitage, where he soon died. An inspired and courageous reformer, he is commemorated in the name of his sect (Nichiren Buddhism) and remains a great figure in the history of Japan.

The Tendai sect, still very strong, had been the main enemy of Nichiren, and in 1537, in a great battle in Kyoto, all of the Lotus sect temples were burned down. Nichiren never recovered its former energy, and Tendai itself began to waver. Today this sect has little influence beyond the confines of its own great temples. Jodo and Zen Buddhism became dominant, together with Shinto, which was faithfully credited with foiling the nat-ural calamities, anarchy, and widespread wars that continued to threaten the old order of the nation. But already the Zen schools had begun a long decline that would continue for three hundred years.

With the death of the regent Tokimune, the Kamakura government began to weaken, having drawn too close to the aesthetic attractions of the Heian court, and in 1333 it was overthrown by Emperor Daijo II, abetted by some disgruntled Minamotos. One Minamoto clan, the Ashikaga, promptly deposed their imperial ally in favor of a Minamoto lineage, which was consolidated after a half century of struggle known as the Age of the North and South Dynasties (1336–1392). The government was returned to Kyoto, "the Capital," where a new court was established by the Ashikaga shoguns in the city district which gave the name "Muromachi period" to the next two centuries of Japanese history. The Ashikaga shoguns and the imperial court were strong sponsors of Rinzai Zen, which had established five "mountains" or main temples in Kyoto. The cultured priests spent less time in zazen then in composing stilted Chinese verse, but they were useful as arbiters of taste and in diplomatic relations with the mainland nations.

Although none became true Zen practitioners, the Ashikagas interested themselves in poetry and painting, upon which Zen—unlike the other Buddhist schools—would have an influence "so subtle and pervading that it has become the essence of Japan's finest culture."[3] While Dogen's teachings strengthened the development of the strong identity with nature that lies at the heart of Japanese sensibilities, the superb brush painting and calligraphy, tea ceremony and flower arrangement, stone gardens, Noh theater, haiku poetry—all of them made more exquisite by artistic ideas and artifacts from China—were brought to their present eminence by Rinzai Zen. If Master Eisai introduced green tea, Daio Kokushi introduced tea ceremony, which was later taught by Master Ikkyu, developed by his disciple Shuko, and perfected by Sen no Rikyu, who became the most celebrated tea master in Japan. As D. T. Suzuki has made clear, Zen is "so adaptable to the character of the Japanese people,

especially in its moral and aesthetic aspects, that it has penetrated far more widely and deeply into Japanese life than into
Chinese."[4]

Without question, the infusion of Zen principles into the
arts produced an extraordinary flowering of Japanese culture, but
the effect of the Zen arts on Zen itself was less beneficial. Many
if not most of the monks and priests were primarily painters and
calligraphers, tea masters and poets, and very often all of these
at once. Daito Kokushi (perhaps inspired by the appearance of
the *Mumon-kan*, or *Gateless Gate*, in 1228) had assembled his
own koan collection, but in the next century koan study became
mere literary analysis of heretofore secret confrontations in the
dokusan room. As for zazen, it was scarcely mentioned, and the
Rinzai teachers who are best remembered from the next three
centuries were all "heretics" in their unconventional attempts
to return to zazen and the true spirit of the Dharma.

The first of these was the poet-calligrapher Jakushitsu
(d. 1367), who wrote wistfully of the "intimate" Buddha-nature
all around us, if only our eye would open and we could see:

Didn't I tell you it was there?
You could have found it without any trouble.
The south wind is warm, the sun shines peacefully. . . .

Another was Ikkyu (d. 1481), bastard son of the emperor,
pauper, poet, twice-failed suicide, and Zen master, enlightened
at last by the harsh call of a crow. At eighty-one Ikkyu became
the iconoclastic abbot of Daitoku-ji. ("For fifty years I was a
man wearing straw raincoat and umbrella-hat; I feel grief and
shame now at this purple robe.") His "mad" behavior was perhaps his way of disrupting the corrupt and feeble Zen he saw
around him: "An insane man of mad temper raises a mad air,"
he wrote.[5] He also said,, "Having no destination, I am never
lost." One infatuated scholar[6] has called him "the most remarkable monk in the history of Japanese Buddhism, the only
Japanese comparable to the great Chinese Zen masters, for ex-

ample, Joshu, Rinzai, and Unmon." Ikkyu found no one he could approve as his Dharma successor. Before his death, civil disorders caused the near obliteration of Kyoto, forcing Rinzai Zen to follow Soto from the decadent capital city into the countryside.

For three centuries after Dogen's death, the Rinzai school would continue to construct large temples in Kyoto and Kamakura, but eventually its power was rivaled by Soto, which had achieved a broad expansion in the north and west. Keizan's successors had carried on Dogen's tradition of avoiding institutionalized Zen in favor of seeking seclusion in the mountains and offering the Way to the common man. Dogen's symbolic identification of "mountains, rivers, and the great earth" with Buddha-nature suited the animistic ideas of the local people and the traditional mountain religion called Shugendo. More important, it exposed his countrymen to the idea that awareness of the inochi, or life spirit, in everything-just-as-it-is was crucial to a religious sense of our existence through which the beauty of "mountain, rivers, and great earth" might be revealed. Not that Dogen's respect for all things in nature was animistic, far less pantheistic reverence or nature mysticism; it was clear-eyed homage to the absolute identity of each phenomenon, from dust mote to mountain, from sky-flower to dream.

In the middle of the sixteenth century, the first traders from Europe had reached Kyoto, already a city of 96,000 houses or a half-million people. As usual, the Christian missionaries were hard behind. Spanish Jesuits, arriving in 1549, exploited the unsophisticated nation's desire for European manufactures and manipulated the opinion of the shogunate not only against other Europeans but against Buddhism, all sects of which were attacked and suppressed in 1571. By the end of the century, Buddhism had lost almost all its political power and prestige in the capital city. But in 1612, Ieyasu, the first Tokugawa shogun, prohibited the practice of Christianity, which in a few short decades had converted some 300,000 impressionable Japanese. Ieyasu had already removed his government to Edo, a small settlement at the head of Edo Bay that was protected by the swampy terrain behind it, and with the consolidation of his power, based on sworn fealty from local overlords and their samurai, the political status of Buddhism was restored. (This tumultuous period is a popular subject of Japanese theatre and films, especially the story of the ritual suicide of young Lord Asano and the forty-seven *ronin* in 1702, which was the basis for the great Kurosawa film, *Chushingura*.)

Nevertheless, Zen had become a decrepit teaching. In 1620, while still vigorous, Zen master Takuan, poet, painter and calligrapher, master of swordsmanship, tea, and ikebana (and the inventor of the sour "takuan pickle"), retired from his position as fifty-fourth abbot of Daitoku-ji rather than "flatter people for the love of wealth, sell Buddhism for a living, and drag the teachings of the patriarchs down into the mud."[7]

During the feudal Tokugawa period, the Zen schools were able to reconsolidate and spread their influence. Dogen's original monastery at Kosho-Horin-ji was rebuilt and the Obaku Zen School founded by Ingen Ryuku (1592–1673) was established a short distance to the north down the Uji River. An anti-Christian persecution culminated in a general massacre in 1638; two years later some Portuguese trade envoys were beheaded. For the next two centuries the Tokugawa shoguns would carry out a national policy which excluded foreign influences almost entirely.

From Kanazawa northeastward to the Noto Peninsula, the local train crosses a plain of rice fields among humble mountains. The paddies in wet browns and greens are set off by lone white egrets, like sentinels. Spring comes late to this northern land, and the rice is in several stages of seasonal cycle: a cracked winter earth of withered stalks is side by side with dark rectangles of froggy water and patches of intense fresh green. In this old landscape of Japan, the rice fields are harrowed by small motor plows, then worked by hand and heavy mattock before flooding.

The elder peasants in the fields wear old-fashioned wide conical straw hats—the oldest women wear white bonnets—while the younger men, who operate the small red plows, prefer white overalls and Western tractor caps. What is noticeable in Japanese farm country on this main island of Honshu is the near absence of livestock—cows, horses, sheep, pigs, goats, and even chickens—as well as a seeming scarcity of dogs and cats.

From the town of Nanao, on Noto Bay, the train follows around the shore through a series of small fishing towns stuck to the coast between the hills and sea. Small rice fields abut the sea walls, even the beaches, and one paddy, scarcely twenty feet across, is pinched between the railroad tracks and a row of pines along the cliff, above blue water. To the northeast is the open sea, but a circle of faraway islands protects the calm waters of Noto Bay, where fields of stakes are sign of extensive aquaculture in kelp (nori) and oysters. The kelp and oyster beds are tended by small boats, while solitary old women of another epoch, bent by big baskets, up to their hips in water, forage for shellfish in the tidal rocks. Far out on the bay, a small, still boat on the silver sea, against the islands, evokes that immemorial solitude that has always drawn the painters and poets of the East.

Waves recede.
Not even the wind ties up a small abandoned boat.
The moon is a clear mark of midnight.

Once again, the ephemeral and the universal: Dogen called this poem "On the Treasury of the True Dharma Eye" as if to point out that these simple lines conveyed the whole import of his mighty work.

Small flocks of sandpipers on their way to Kamchatka and the Siberian tundra cross back and forth over the gleaming fields, and a Japanese pheasant flutters across a ditch, cocks its head in the spring sun, then sneaks into a thin margin of weeds. A man planting his new field casts grain from side to side as he wades the shallows in bright yellow boots, and the quick seeds, wrinkling the bland surface like puffs of wind, startle a band of Siberian buntings; the birds flit away along the grassy strips between rectangles of water. But there is no wind, and as soon as man has gone, the rice paddy mirrors a fair-weather white cloud reflected on the earth between sea and mountain.

The local train stops at Anamizu on the bay, from where a small bus huffs uphill over the dry wooded ridge of the Noto Peninsula and wheezes down again on noisy air brakes to the valley of the Haka River. Here at the base of a small mountain stands the monastery that Keizan founded in 1321, the last year of his life. Since then the village of Monzen has grown up around it, while the Haka delta was transformed into broad rice fields. The old monastery, an airy and open place around a long court at the base of the hill, was rebuilt after the most recent fire in the late 1800s. It has been called So-in Soji-ji or "Old Soji-ji"[8] since 1907, when Soji-ji was officially moved to its present location in Yokohama, south of Tokyo, as one of the two head temples of the Soto sect.

At So-in Soji-ji the abbot was away, but his assistant and the ten-odd monks who take care of the old monastery were friendly and hospitable, offering green tea and nori crackers in a guest chamber that overlooked an enclosed garden of ilex and small pines. At Eihei-ji there had been no contact with any unsui except those who served us, but here we slurped thin Japanese noodles in exuberant Japanese style at the monks' table and took the morning meal with them after zazen and sutra-chanting service the next day.

That afternoon we walked down the valley of the Haka to the sea. Gulls, terns, herons, and an osprey had convened around the calm waters of an estuary pool behind the beach, and a pretty fishing village sat perched at the river's mouth, but the beach was disfigured by the wrack of plastic and industrial flotsam which even on this remote coast, so far from cities, is left stranded on the sand after each tide. The eager materialism of a small and crowded country has deprived the Haka delta of its "life integrity" as an ocean shore, and yet—from a Zen point of view—the ocean coast has always been here, no more altered by such fleeting phenomena as man and plastic than this ocean sky by the atomic clouds from Hiroshima.

Behind the monastery a steep path climbs the hill to numerous bodhisattva shrines, like Stations of the Cross. In quest of solitude, I followed a narrowing path high up the mountain, pursuing the lovely song of an unknown bird. A sea wind thrashed the points of the great cedars, but the forest floor was quiet, and in high fields along the path were not quite familiar spring flowers—buttercups, mints, violets, cinquefoil, and mustard, Eurasian species not the same yet scarcely different from closely related forms in the New World genera. The trees looked vaguely familiar, too, and of course they were, as Palearctic kin of the trees of home. I saw buntings and a thrush and yellow grosbeaks, but was unable to locate the mysterious bird.

Being unstained is like meeting a person and not considering what he looks like. Also it is like not wishing for more color or brightness when viewing the flowers or moon. Spring has the tone of spring, and autumn has the scene of autumn; there is no escaping it. So when you want spring or autumn to be different from what it is, notice that it can only be as it is. Or when you want to keep spring or autumn as it is, reflect that it has no unchanging nature. . . .

Only Buddhas to Buddhas
—EIHEI DOGEN

CHAPTER SEVENTEEN

IN a well-loved story of Japan, a beautiful young girl who would not tell her angry parents who had made her pregnant finally pointed at an old and revered Zen master, who until now had been praised for his pure life. Accused by the parents, all the old man said was, "Is that so?" When the child was born, he accepted it into his house and took good care of it, unconcerned about his loss of reputation. Not until a year had passed did the remorseful girl admit to her parents that the good old man was entirely innocent, that the real father was a young man in the fish market. The embarrassed parents rushed to fetch the child, apologizing to the old master and begging his forgiveness for the great wrong that they had done. "Is that so?" was all the old man said.[1]

This story is one of many about Hakuin Ekaku, born in 1686 at Hara village under Mount Fuji, on the old Tokaido high road between Kyoto and the Tokugawa stronghold known as Edo. Like Dogen, nearly five centuries before, Hakuin had hurled his life into the practice of Zen in the fierce tradition of the great masters and restored respect to the Zen schools, which had been weakened by long centuries of decline. Concentrating on Mu, this monk once went into deep samadhi on a boat in hurricane, while others vomited and cried out to high heaven. Afterward he was chastised by the boatman: "In all my long life, I have never come across such a rascal as you!" Hakuin experienced a number of profound awakenings, the first of which was brought about by the chirping of a cricket. ("The cricket is just a cricket and the bird is just a bird—nothing else!" Soen-roshi says. "All the cricket does is chirping. Our great master Hakuin was very grateful to the cricket.")

Inspired by the Soto example, Hakuin emphasized work in the fields and kitchens, and did much to revitalize Rinzai Zen by making it more accessible to the common people. He also recommended to his students the study of the *Jewelled-Mirror Samadhi*, "that supreme treasure of the Mahayana," even though the teachers who had developed it, from Sekito Kisen to Tozan Ryokai, had been patriarchs of the rival school: "For the past eight or nine years or more, I have been trying to incite all of you who boil your daily gruel over the same fire with me to study this great matter thoroughly, but more often than not you have taken it to be the doctrine of another house and remained indifferent to it." Hakuin went on to explicate Dogen Zenji, which Dogen's own Soto priests were unable to do: "Eihei [Dogen] has said, 'The experiencing of the manifold dharmas through using one's self is delusion; the experiencing of one's self through the coming of the manifold dharmas is satori.' This is just what I have been saying. This is the state of 'mind and body discarded, discarded mind and body.' It is like two mirrors mutually reflecting one another without even the shadow of an image between. Mind and the objects of mind are the same thing; things and oneself are not two. A white horse enters the reed flowers . . . snow is piled up in a silver bowl. This is what is known as the Jewelled-Mirror Samadhi."[2]

In his *Song of Zazen*, Hakuin wrote:

Not knowing how near the Truth is
We seek it far away—what a pity! . . .
We are like him who, in the midst of
  water,
Cries out in thirst so imploringly.
We are like the son of a rich man
Who wanders away among the poor. . . .

At this moment what more need we seek?
As the Truth eternally reveals itself,
This very place is the Lotus Land of purity,
This very body is the Body of the Buddha. [3]

In 1760, Hakuin founded Ryutaku-ji, the Dragon-Swamp Temple, a few miles east of his own temple of Sho-in, at Hara. He was already one of the great painters and calligraphers of his time (his are the best-known portraits of Bodhidharma), but his foremost accomplishment was the renewal of koan study, which in both Rinzai and Soto had declined to dead "formula" teaching that certified indifferent monks for the Zen priesthood. ("The ancestor's garden has become desolate, and the teaching is trampled down.")[4] In Hakuin's view, kensho or satori was of primary importance, and his students were given the koan Mu and also One Hand, a now-classic koan of his own invention ("I have asked everyone to listen to the sound of one hand").[5] These mighty koans, leaving no room for intellectual maneuver, brought the sincere student straight up against the iron wall. Hundreds of others that expressed the teachings followed these preliminary koan, and all were accompanied by vigorous teisho and dokusan. Hakuin's methods were organized into a system by his disciples and remain the basis for Rinzai koan study to this day.

"By Hakuin's time," says Tetsugen, "both Zen and koan study were in a bad way. D. T. Suzuki said that Hakuin's system revitalized koan study, which is true, but inevitably it led to stereotyping, decadence, and collapse. Hakuin made a beautiful system, but in the end, the problems that Dogen had spoken of five centuries before emerged again."

In Hakuin's time, *Shobogenzo* was still neglected by the Soto priesthood, and not until late in the seventeenth century (about 1690) did Kozen, the thirty-fifth abbot of Eihei-ji, arrange the several extant versions according to date of composition and assemble the ninety-five-fascicle form. But this arrangement received no more circulation than the others, to judge from the fact that an earlier, incomplete version was the basis for the first commentary on the text since the fourteenth century. The Zen master who challenged the priestly notion that Dogen's masterpiece was too esoteric and profound to explicate was Tenkei Denson (1648–1735), a contemporary of Hakuin Zenji, who had already written a piercing analysis of the *Heart Sutra*. Tenkei Denson was "one of the most brilliant masters of our lineage," says Maezumi-roshi. "Not having access to all the original texts, he made some mistakes in his interpretations[6] of *Shobogenzo*, which only Dogen's immediate successors really understood, but at least he attempted to set it free, bring it out into the fresh air. It took him three years to prepare, and when he did it, he was already eighty years old! A very rigorous and profound person!"

In response, the Soto priesthood, mindful of official Tokugawa resistance to a work so seemingly critical of Rinzai Zen, continued to stifle the circulation of *Shobogenzo* for six decades after Tenkei's death, and a printed edition commenced in 1796 remained unfinished until 1811, by which time Zen was once again decrepit. The dull and repressive atmosphere of Japan's feudal administrations, encouraging orthodoxy, reaction, and plain laziness in the Soto priesthood, permitted sectarian study of Dogen's thought to lapse once more into mere veneration of a temple relic.

In a poem called "Reading the Record of Eihei Dogen," the poet and Zen priest Ryokan commented in vain on this neglect:

On a somber spring evening around midnight,
Rain mixed with snow sprinkled on the bamboos in the
   garden.

212

I wanted to ease my loneliness, but it was quite
impossible. . . .

I remember the old days when I lived at Entsu Monastery
And my late teacher lectured on the True Dharma Eye
[Shobogenzo]. . . .
Inside this teaching, there's never any shortcoming. . . .

Nobody was asked whether it is a jewel or a pebble.
For five hundred years it's been covered in dust. . . .
For whom was all his eloquence expounded?
Longing for ancient times and grieving for the present
My head is exhausted.[7]

The temple associated with Tenkei Denson is Jogo-ji, built five hundred years ago in the tea country near Shimbara, southwest of Mount Fuji, in a landscape of small and abrupt hills terraced neatly with green hedges of clipped tea. Between the stiff tea groves, tall green waves of yellow-green Asian bamboo[8] flow with spring sea winds off the Pacific coast.

At Jogo-ji, Dogen's painted statue is on the altar in the founder's hall, and as in all the best-known representations, this one is pink-faced, with prominent brow and small, sensitive mouth. Tenkei Denson, on the other hand, seems dark with anger, as befits a man who at the age of eighty defied the Soto establishment in a courageous but forlorn attempt to resurrect a hidden treasure. Up the hill from the temple, an unusual "sutra treasure house" contains a huge cylinder holding drawer upon drawer of rolled-up sutra scrolls. As in the prayer wheels of Tibet, these Vajrayana teachings may be cast upon the world by turning the cylinder, in one of the many Tantric innovations brought into Japan by the Shingon ("True Word") sect in the ninth century and later adopted by the Soto school in its efforts to attract a wider following.

In the gardens all around, tiger-striped wasps have set up a low humming, and frogs clack like wood blocks in an abandoned rice paddy behind the temple. High overhead in the blue sky, a pale brown falcon sets its wings and stoops in a steep glide beyond the ridges. Otherwise there are no birds in view, although that one I can never seem to locate sings its beautiful and solitary song. "That is *uguisu*," says our guide, Hoichi Suzuki-sensei. "The nightingale!" But since the nightingale does not occur in the Land of Wa, I am no wiser than before. Suzuki-sensei whistles this elusive bird's melodious song. "*Ho-ho-ke-kyo*, it says—the *Lotus Sutra*!"

Suzuki-sensei is the son of Shunryu Suzuki-roshi, former abbot of Rinso-in at Yaizu, on the southern coast, who later founded the Zen Center in San Francisco. In 1971, at Tassajara, the Center's retreat deep in the Coast Range, I worked briefly as an assistant to the carpenter monk who was putting a new roof on the cottage of Suzuki-roshi. Although he was dying, the roshi evinced the keenest interest in our progress, and this interest provided a wonderful opportunity to observe the comings and goings of this gentle teacher, who still offered teisho in the evening. Suzuki-roshi was already frail, and one day his jisha, cleaning his room, set down his teacup a little too hard in her rush to assist him at the doorway. "Take care of my cup!" he warned her mildly. And when she protested that her only wish was to take care of her teacher, the roshi said, "When you take care of my cup, you are taking care of me."

The carpenter monk was engaged to marry this young woman, who was rich. Since he himself had always been penniless, the prospect of money worried him; he told me he had expressed this worry to Suzuki-roshi. "Rich or poor, it does not matter," the roshi told him. "It only matters if you *cling* to being rich." He smiled in warning. "Or poor." The monk nodded uncertainly, saying he understood. "Since you understand," the roshi said, "then you may as well be rich."

"My father wished to bring zazen way to other countries," says Suzuki-sensei, an appealing man with a sad face and a quick laugh who had welcomed us the previous evening to Rinso-in, near the fishing village of Yaizu. The night wind of April off the north Pacific was dank and cold, and we were grateful for Hoichi-san's green tea, sweet cakes, and Napoleon brandy. Expressing regret that he could not speak English as well as his father, he defeated Tetsugen-sensei in a game of *go*. "First my father went to China, but under that government, the people are only coming back very slowly to Buddhism, and it does not work there. So the Soto headquarters in Tokyo suggest San Francisco, and my father is willing. He studied some English in middle school, and maybe he wanted to use it. So in San Francisco he put up just a little card outside. It said, 'Everybody welcome, come and sit zazen.' That was, I think, in 1962. And it built up slowly, slowly, in a natural way."

Seven young Japanese students were visiting at Rinso-in, and early next morning Suzuki-sensei gave them zazen instruction in one of the few active zendos left in the Soto and Rinzai temples of Japan. After morning service—attended only by Tetsugen and me—we enjoyed a merry breakfast with his friendly family. Afterward, in the temple yard, I had a game of catch with Shungo, aged perhaps six, who wore a blue T-shirt with the inscription "Boston Sports." The boy lugged his rubber baseball and a fielder's mitt into the founder's hall, where Tetsugen and I inspected a peculiar statue of Bodhidharma—the first benevolent-looking replica of the fierce wall-gazer we had ever seen. While we made our bows, our baseball buddha rolled his ball against the altar, then clambered up to seat himself in front of the statue of the temple founder,[9] making a loud sound of one hand and smacking the ball into his mitt.

Together with Maezumi-roshi, who preceded him by a few years in America, Suzuki-roshi is revered as the founder of Soto Zen practice in the United States, and his gentle teisho, assembled in *Zen Mind, Beginner's Mind*, are widely read by Zen students in the West. In December 1971, a few months after my visit to Tassajara, this wonderful teacher died of cancer. Eido-roshi, who had gone to California to attend him not long before his death, was extremely impressed. He told his students upon his return to New York City, "Shunryu Suzuki was a true-ue-e ro-shi!"

Shunryu Suzuki's grave lies under evergreens up the small

stream that comes down the forested ravine behind Rinso-in, a pretty temple built in the fifteenth century. In April the shady margins of the stream are lighted by large blue-and-yellow orchids. We offer incense in spring morning light as swallowtailed butterflies come and go in red-striped arabesques, mindlessly offering the bold red dots on the undersides of their black wings.

Since 1907, when it moved from the remote Noto Peninsula to Yokohama, Soji-ji has replaced Eihei-ji as the largest temple of the Soto sect. The new monastery's location in a pleasant, open, parklike area of a big city denies it the power of that ancient place on the Nine-Headed Dragon River, in the mountains; the atmosphere is less severe, and all but novice monks may greet and smile. But the 200-yard corridor that links the monastery to the entrance building is cleaned and shined three times a day by the squads of unsui, who, as at Eihei-ji, must lock into deep bows each time a superior sweeps past.

With one thousand tatami mats (three by six feet each), Soji-ji's main hall is the largest in Japan. The services are precisely orchestrated by drums and bells and a huge *mokugyo*, or wooden fish gong; a monk must stand up on a platform and swing a mallet like a sledge in order to deal this instrument a worthy blow. The main drum, on a raised platform in one corner of the hall, is struck by three men simultaneously. The red carpets and gold canopies of bells, the yellow, white, red, green, and dark blue Buddhist colors on the curtains and banners, are set off by the glowing wheat of the new mats, which mingle the scent of incense with a new-mown hay smell from the countryside.

On an ivory seat in a reliquary behind the altar in the old service hall is the dried corpse of Sekito Kisen, presumed author of the *Identity of Relative and Absolute* and the great eighth-century Chinese ancestor of the Soto lineage. Seven feet tall during his lifetime, so a priest informed us, Sekito once intervened to save an ox that was being sacrificed in an aboriginal ceremony, and later he would try in vain to heal the schism between Zen schools brought about by the Sixth Patriarch's fierce disciples. Today he sits, sunken-eyed and hunched, in a kind of terminal zazen, brown-shined wrists protruding from pale bamboo-leaf-colored robes. Sekito said, "A sage has no self, but there is nothing that is not himself."[10] His earthly face, black with dehydration, is twisted tight into a smile or grimace, as if he knew that eleven centuries later the exaggerated differences between Rinzai and Soto were still being perpetuated by an unwise priesthood.

Once when Yakusan was sitting, Sekito saw him and asked, "What are you doing here?"

Yakusan said, "I'm not doing anything."

Sekito said, "Then you are just sitting idly."

Yakusan said, "If I were .idly sitting, that would be doing something."

Sekito said, "You said you are not doing; what aren't you doing?"

Yakusan said, "Even the saints don't know."[11]

On the first evening of our visit, about forty new monks, one nun, and one-hundred-odd laymen and laywomen received the Buddhist precepts in a huge and stirring *jukai* ceremony in the main hall. Six visiting roshis in red robes sat on each side of the great altar, and on the altar itself loomed the hooded figure of the acting *zenji*, or temple head (the real zenji, we were told, is too old and frail to conduct this great mass service). In their four groups, the preceptors were led by priests up narrow steps onto the altar, joining Shakyamuni, Bodhidharma, Dogen, Keizan, and the other patriarchs in the circle of buddhas. Then the six roshis, led by the zenji, circumambulated the raised altar. "Buddha becomes Buddha!" the red figures chanted, to the bang of the zenji's stave. "Buddha bows to Buddha!" Hands clasped on their chests, the new buddhas bowed in return, then returned down the steep steps—the novice monks, then the solitary nun,[12] the men, the women, one by one by one.

All but a few of the laypeople were old, with bright-eyed, weathered faces and bent backs, shuffling and bowing shyly as the priests herded them along. In the flickering candlelight, to a beautiful, sad chant, they descended from the great altar of no birth, no death, into the darkness. There was nothing sad here, only a hushed joy, for in this moment everyday life and nirvana were not different. When their turn was finished, the small, thickset figures reformed their lines, kneeling on the ta-tami as simple and close as swallows gathered for the journey south.

Before daylight, roused by an old and crippled monk, we were led by lantern to the guest zendo across the corridor from the monks' hall. Dawn zazen was followed by morning service in the *hondo*, where Tetsugen and I, on our knees in the gold-and-black-robed rows, could study the intricate precision of the ritual. Swift monks ran backward from the altar, snatching up sutra books in stacks for presentation to the priests, who deftly flared the saffron pages in symbolic readings of the sacred texts. At this altar, just five years ago, Tetsugen-sensei had officiated at the morning service, having been installed as temporary abbot of Soji-ji the night before. When repeated at Eihei-ji, this *zuise* ceremony completed his priestly training in the Soto school.

With the new nun (a young person of great presence) we were given tea in the abbot's magnificent stone garden. The garden includes a sculpted rock pool inhabited by multicolored carp, those huge "goldfish," black, white, and red and gold, that are prized like tea bowls and wild river rocks by Japanese collectors. A single one of these illustrious creatures may cost more than the small family car.

Outside the main hall in midmorning, in a fresh sun that followed April rains, Japanese robins, heads cocked, ran a little, sounding the softened earth for worms, as covies of school-children in tulip-red and daffodil-yellow caps chased and laughed among the buildings. Inside, the monks and preceptors had

218

gathered for Dharma combat. Whoever wished to benefit from the zenji's Dharma might now rush forward between ranks of priests to face the zenji in his staff and hood, high on the altar. Each cried out his question, and the zenji answered in a calm and measured voice, then banged his stave as the aspirant ran backward from the altar, crying out shrilly once again in gratitude.

Traditionally, the final question in this Dharma combat is asked by the shuso, or head training monk, and I "watched with my ears, listened with my eyes," hoping to pick up a few pointers. In the autumn I shall be shuso myself, and my three-month training period will conclude with my first Dharma talk, based on a koan. The talk will be followed by Dharma combat, in which other students will have at me with tough questions in an effort to test my understanding.

Here at Soji-ji, the shuso's koan is invariably Bodhidharma's exchange with Emperor Wu, and both questions and answers are provided in advance to all participants, to make certain that the Dharma wheel turns smoothly. In this baseball-loving country, the questions are lobbed up like softballs, and the happy shuso knocks each one out of the park. Perhaps this is appropriate, since the great majority of Japanese monks have no ambition to become Zen teachers, being content to take over as Buddhist priests in the family temple back home. The ritual combat, which has nothing to do with Zen, reflects great credit on all concerned, and is no doubt very gratifying to the doting relatives, who may have traveled a long way for the great occasion. I, too, will explicate a koan,[14] but the questions and answers of the Dharma combat will be unrehearsed.

At Soji-ji, where all four were trained, and where their father was a high official, Maezumi-roshi and his brothers are very well known.[15] One of them, Takeshi-sensei, an energetic, cultured man, very interested in art and music, seems destined for a high place in the Soto hierarchy and will certainly follow his father as a Soji-ji official. At present he is abbot of Zenko-ji, a large new temple under a hill in Yokohama, the seaport adjoining Tokyo to the south. After our visit to Soji-ji, Takeshi-sensei and his kind family offered his brother's students the generous hospitality of his house, including an astonishing array of sushi and sashimi from a Yokohama restaurant, "the best sashimi restaurant in the whole world."

By 1907—the year that the Soto sect established this main temple—Dogen's *Shobogenzo* had been reduced to an anthology of digestible "principles" put together a few years earlier by the priesthood. Its obscurity was the more profound because Soto teachings were still little known in intellectual circles of Tokyo and Kyoto, which depended on Rinzai for their Zen. Although more widespread than Rinzai, Soto was thought of as a rural Zen of the smaller towns off to the north. Even when Soji-ji was transferred here to the Tokyo region, the complacent priesthood made no effort to exhume their extraordinary Dharma ancestor, and his resurrection eventually occurred because Tetsuro Watsuji, one of Japan's most eminent philosophers, happened upon, not *Shobogenzo*, but Koun Ejo's *Shobogenzo Zuimonki*, a much less vibrant and exciting work. Even so, Watsuji was astonished. In a series of outspoken articles called "Monk Dogen," which appeared between 1920 and 1923, he stated flatly that "Dogen has been killed thus far in the Soto sect." A few years later, Watsuji's peer, the philosopher Hajime Tanabe, described this "great metaphysical thinker" as the precursor of Japanese philosophy. Since then the scholars of Japan have competed in their praise of Dogen, and four translations of *Shobogenzo* into modern Japanese have been produced in the last twenty years.

But "once we turn our eyes from Japan to the Western scene, we find that virtually nothing has been introduced about Dogen," says the Korean scholar Hee-jin Kim, (who describes Dogen's "exquisite mythopoeic imaginings and profound philosophic visions"). "Obviously ignorance of Soto Zen is tantamount to ignorance of Dogen, its founder. The scholarship of Zen Buddhism in the West has chiefly relied upon D. T. Suzuki's brilliant introduction of many invaluable texts and his own interpretation of them, based primarily on Rinzai Zen in which

Suzuki was nurtured. Overshadowed by Suzuki's brilliance and reputation, the Soto tradition has been treated like a stepchild of Zen in the West. Perhaps this situation has been aggravated by the extreme difficulty of presenting Dogen's thought in a form intelligible to the Western mind. His language and thought are forbiddingly difficult and subtle, yet irresistibly intriguing, and more often than not, exasperate the students of Dogen, who alternate between hope and despair."[16]

As Tetsugen says, "Almost all of *Shobogenzo* are teisho that Dogen gave his monks, which is why non-practicing scholars have such problems with them. To listen to a teisho is not to figure out what is being said, but simply to allow the mind and body to remain receptive and open, to listen with our entire being. If the words strike sparks and cause something to happen, that's fine; if they don't, that's all right too. The mistake is to try to analyze what's coming in. Teisho is like zazen—whatever comes from whatever direction, from the five senses or the mind, just let it come, just let it go—the mirror mind. Listening to teisho should be that way. The words flow through us. We do not cling to them, afraid we'll miss something, or try to 'understand.' We allow the words to come in through all our senses, hearing them with our eyes as well as ears, with our whole body, everything but our brain. That is the way Dogen intended them to be received, not read and analyzed in an intellectual fashion.

"Everything in *Shobogenzo* is dealing with the unity of the absolute and the relative, the universal holistic sphere and the sphere of moment-to-moment phenomena. His sentences shift back and forth between the two, and if you try to follow him intellectually, you're lost. The only way you can accompany him is to flow freely with his words, to just *become* each of these sentences, in the same way that you must 'become' your koan in order to penetrate it thoroughly. Dogen lived simultaneously in the relative and absolute, and we have to join him in both worlds if we are to know what life really is—not moving back and forth from one to the other but traveling in both at the same time."

The first translations of Dogen into English appeared in

The Soto Approach to Zen, a rendition of *Shobogenzo Zuimonki* by Reiho Masunaga, who referred to Dogen's "incomparable depth of thought." A few years later, Heinrich Dumoulin, in his *History of Zen Buddhism*, claimed that Dogen belonged "among the great creative figures of mankind." In 1968 the novelist Yasunari Kawabata (author of *Snow Country*, *One Thousand Cranes*, and other works), in his acceptance of the Nobel Prize, commented on Dogen's influence on the poetry of Ryokan, whose deathbed poem ("What shall be my legacy? The blossoms of spring / The cuckoo in the hills / The leaves of autumn") was a near echo of Dogen's "Original Face," pointing directly at the common miracles of everyday life.

In the last decade, many fascicles of *Shobogenzo* have appeared in English in texts related to Zen Buddhism, and in recent years, Maezumi-roshi and the Zen Center of Los Angeles's Kuroda Institute have sponsored two Dogen conferences in the United States. American scholars have begun to reconnoiter Dogen, attempting comparisons with Heidegger and Whitehead. But as Tetsugen says, the first definitive analysis in the West will probably be done by a Zen practitioner with profound experience of koan study and the silence of zazen, from where Dogen's own primordial intuitions seem to come.

Know that within the innumerable things which are in yourself there is birth, and there is death. . . . Birth is just like riding in a boat. You raise the sails and row with the oar. Although you row, the boat gives you a ride and without the boat no one could ride. But you ride in the boat and your riding makes the boat what it is. At such a moment, there is nothing but the world of the boat. The sky, the water, and the shore are all the boat's world, which is not the same as a world that is not the boat's.

When you ride in a boat, your body and mind and the environs together are the concerted activity of the boat. The entire earth and the entire sky together are the concerted activity of the boat. Thus birth is nothing but you, you are nothing but birth. Both the entire earth and the entire sky appear in birth as well as in death.

Entire Activity
— EIHEI DOGEN

CHAPTER EIGHTEEN

EARLY in the twentieth century, a great scandal was caused in Zen circles in Japan by the publication of hundreds of the best-known koans in a collection which differed from all others by supplying the so-called koan "answers." Its unknown author was accused of seeking to destroy the koan study system and thereby bring ridicule on Zen. His defenders perceived it as an attack, not on true Zen, but on "dead" koan study, in which stereotyped answers were offered by uninspired students and accepted by inferior teachers as a kind of perfunctory examination for candidates for the Zen priesthood. Whatever their view of his intentions, almost everyone agreed that the author of this book was an accomplished master, and the teacher whose name came up most often was Sogaku Harada-roshi (1871–1961), Soto abbot of Hosshin-ji, a remote monastery near the town of Obama on the northwest coast.

At twenty, after thirteen years as a novice in the Soto school, Sogaku Harada had yet to meet an enlightened teacher. Dissatisfied, he entered a Rinzai monastery for seven years, then attended Komazawa Soto University in Tokyo, pursuing his Buddhist studies for some six years after graduation. Still unfulfilled, he continued to visit various Zen masters, asking about the great matter of life and death. ("Clarifying birth, clarifying death, is the matter of greatest importance," Dogen wrote.) At Engaku-ji, in Kamakura, he was told by Soyen Shaku, "If you experience kensho, your question will be answered all by itself." Resolved to pursue koan study, Harada went to Toyota Dokutan-roshi at Nanzen-ji, in Kyoto, one of the strongest Rinzai teachers of the day. Under Dokutan, his eye was opened, and eventually he received inka.

Thoroughly trained in Hakuin's koan system, Harada-roshi taught at Komazawa for twelve years. Eventually he became a full professor, conducting sesshins in the summertime and writing an excellent commentary on the brief 1890 anthology of Dogen's phrases which did much to help bring Dogen to light.[2] In 1921, when he was fifty, he accepted the post of abbot at Hosshin-ji, where he would teach for the next forty years.

Before long, this small monastery on a dark and inhospitable coast won a reputation as the strictest in the country. Here the best of the Soto and Rinzai traditions had been merged in a fresh new manifestation of true Dharma. "Nobody has done real shikantaza since Dogen Zenji," Harada would declare, exhorting his students to ignore sectarian disputes and intensify rigorous zazen through koan study, which had all but disappeared from Soto Zen.

Because Harada-roshi is revered in Maezumi's lineage (which has based its teaching methods on those adapted from Harada by Yasutani-roshi),[2] Tetsugen and I had visited Hosshin-ji, taking the local train west from Tsuruga under the small, solitary mountains that break away from the inland range and scatter down to the blue coves of Watsuga Bay. At Obama, on the Sea of Japan, we were given tea by Harada-roshi's last Dharma successor, Harada Tangen-roshi, abbot of Bukko-ji, a small temple under the steep hill behind the town. Here Harada Sogaku had lived as a small boy and received tokudo in the home-leaving ceremony at the age of seven. Tangen, a warm, spontaneous man with whom we wished we could have spent more time, had been a student, friend, and young Dharma brother of Yasutani. He summoned his jisha to escort us on foot to Hosshin-ji, a mile away.

Built in the early sixteenth century, Hosshin-ji surrounds a pretty court of stone lanterns and pines. Inside the walls, a stone bridge crosses a small stone-lined canal. These days the monastery has twenty students, five of them foreigners; the Canadian monk who showed us about seemed at once eager and ill at ease, as if voices from home in this far place might dispel the effect he had come so far to find.

In the old days Hosshin-ji, like other Zen monasteries, gave novice monks no instruction of any kind. The unsui was supposed to keep his eyes lowered, looking at nothing, yet be so totally aware of everything taking place around him that he was prepared at any moment to fulfill any duty or take any service position, even in complicated rituals. Without guidance in zazen or any sort of preparation for koan study, the monk was supposed to make what he could out of the teisho, and often spent years going to dokusan only to be peremptorily dismissed and sent away.

In Harada's opinion, what was left of the true Buddhist spirit in Japan could not sustain the ruthless severity of the ancient methods. Zen practice, he felt, should be illuminated by introductory talks and explanation: it should be less dogged, less perfunctory, more inspired and alive. At the same time, he was very strict. Using the kyosaku as Manjusri's delusion-cutting sword, he applied it unsparingly to the shoulders of his students, a habit emulated with enthusiasm by his disciples. (Tetsugen believes that the use of the kyosaku—and probably sesshin itself—began since Dogen's time, with the decrease of fierce urgency among Zen students.)

"Harada talked a lot about listening," Tetsugen told me as we walked in the court garden at Hosshin-ji. "How when you go to teisho, you should be the only listener in the room. If there is just you and the teacher, you will listen: otherwise, you tend to give responsibility to others. And as you listen, doing zazen, there will no longer be two people in the room, no subject and object, just the One. And that is the way to read Dogen Zenji, too."

In an important sense, Harada-roshi was the first modern Zen master, and because he offered preparation for koan study —unheard of before this time—the more ferocious Zen students from all over Japan made winter pilgrimages to Hosshin-ji for the annual Rohatsu sesshin. The meditation hall, which seats perhaps thirty-five people, would overflow into the courtyard, all the way down to the small stream that crosses the lower court; at times there were several hundred monks doing zazen in the snow. Such conditions seemed ideal to the master, who approved of the wind and cold on this northern coast, the relentless rains, extinguishing snows, the dark, wild typhoons that came roaring in off the Sea of Japan. Rude weather, he felt, lent itself nicely to introspection and the deep study of "the universe in the pit of one's own belly" that would eventually lead to letting the self go. Not surprisingly, a high percentage of his students attained a kensho.

On the mountain slope just opposite Hosshin-ji is the small hermitage where the roshi lived after the age of eighty. His grave above the hermitage, on a moss-green knoll strewn with fallen cherry blossoms, is set about with yellow daffodils. Sogaku Harada died on December 12, 1961, and the moment of death at ninety-one coincided precisely with the moment of mean low tide, as if, as was said, he had ebbed away with the ocean waters. On the altar at his funeral service hung a calligraphy prepared several years before, expressing the realization of not-knowing, of nothing to "understand" or "learn":

> *For forty years I've been selling water*
> *by the bank of a river. Ho, ho!*
> *My labors have been wholly without merit.*

Harada once said that zazen clarified the bones, and his own bones turned out to be pure white, according to Etsudo ("Delight in the Path") Nishiwaki-roshi, one of Harada's four living successors, who saw to the cremation. When Nishiwaki arrived at Hosshin-ji for Rohatsu sesshin at the age of twenty, the head of training told him his face was too soft, that he should try to look more severe, but at the end of sesshin, Harada had said, "Your face is too severe! Put that stress into your efforts in zazen!" The master himself was very strict until he was over seventy, but in his last years he was gentle, and tried to transmit to his monks all his not-knowing.

Harada sent Nishiwaki to study at Kennin-ji, and Nishiwaki recalls with approval the rigorous Rinzai schedule, which included five dokusan each day. (Later, when Nishiwaki became head training monk at Soji-ji, he reinstituted dokusan, which had been neglected in the Soto school for many years.) In Nishiwaki's opinion, the Soto school was revitalized by koan study, for which most of the credit goes to Harada and two of his disciples, Watanabe, who established koan study at Soji-ji, and Ida Toin, who was Harada's favorite, despite an implacable alcoholic nature. Ida Toin had already received inka from two teachers, one of them an outstanding Rinzai master, yet he came to Harada because he still felt "incomplete." Harada considered that, among his disciples, this layman alone had really "broken through," that only Ida Toin saw more clearly than Harada himself. Ida Toin inhabited a horrible little room, subsisting on sake and old salt fish hung from the rafters, his poems and papers all over the floor. Once (says Nishiwaki-roshi) when Harada turned up at his door, Ida Toin was so ashamed that he hid himself beneath a pile of papers. Ida Toin received inka from Harada at the age of sixty-one.

His students agree that Harada-roshi—who was never close to the seats of power at Soji-ji or Eihei-ji—was the greatest Zen master yet to appear in the twentieth century, not only because of the brilliance of his teaching but because he lacked those flaws of character that would keep great teaching from taking healthy root. For Harada, as for Dogen and Hakuin, realization of the Buddha Way was not different from its actualization amid the tumult and temptations of everyday life. "Because of his virtue, so much is able to happen," Nishiwaki says.

"Such masters are very rare," says Tetsugen with a sigh, comparing Harada with other teachers whose clarity of insight may be unsurpassed, yet whose private weakness—usually drink or women—will disillusion the more idealistic students, and sometimes turn away from Zen those who confuse the teacher with their own notion of a "true" spiritual leader. "They want to dehumanize the teacher so that he reflects some personal deity of their own." Tetsugen smiles. "We try to improve a little, but we are who we are."

If Harada-roshi never quit the priesthood, as he threatened, neither did he give up his battle with the Soto bureaucracy, which continued to obscure the purity of Dogen's teachings with petty sectarian disputes and rigid structuralism, setting up needless impediments to true Zen practice. Harada offended the Soto priesthood by placing so much emphasis on "Rinzai" koan study. At the same time, his views on formula responses that had made a mockery of koan study were very well known. As one of his students, Soen Nakagawa, liked to say, "If the answers to koans are all that interest you, just bring a pad and pencil to the dokusan room and I will give them to you." Even after he became abbot of Ryutaku, Soen-roshi did not hesitate to put on his old monk's robe and travel across the main island of Japan to study with Harada-roshi at Hosshin-ji, causing a great clicking of fans in the Rinzai hierarchy.

Nishiwaki-roshi says that Soen first asked to study with Harada while still a hermit on Dai Bosatsu Mountain, near Mount Fuji, in the early thirties, but because Soto lacks Rinzai Zen's long, honorable tradition of "eccentrics,"[2] Harada had refused this bearded poet. Soen studied instead with Yamamoto Gempo-roshi at Ryutaku-ji, but even when he had completed his studies and received inka, he felt (like Ida Toin) "incomplete." Eventually he returned to Harada-roshi, who admired the power in the young Rinzai abbot's voice, and said he would go far. Nishiwaki, who was head monk at Hosshin-ji in this period, also "liked him very much." After Harada's death, Soen resumed study of the koan Mu with one of Harada's Dharma heirs, Hakuun Yasutani. Not until this study was complete did he feel qualified to be a teacher, nor would he give a student any koan that he himself had not passed through.

Although a Soto novice monk at age thirteen, Yasutani had spent years as a family man and schoolteacher, longing all this while for a true Zen master. Not until the age of forty did he find Harada-roshi, and at his first sesshin with Harada in 1925, he attained kensho with the koan Mu. Before meeting Harada, he recalled, "I was altogether a blind fellow, and my mind was not yet at rest. I was at a peak of mental anguish. When I felt I could not endure deceiving myself and others by untrue teaching and irresponsible sermons, my karma opened up and I was able to meet . . . Sogaku Harada-roshi. The light of a lantern was brought to a dark night, to my profound joy."

At Hosshin-ji, some years later, Yasutani encountered Soen Nakagawa, who was already in touch with a teacher in Los Angeles, Nyogen Senzaki, and was familiar with the pioneering work of D. T. Suzuki. Soen convinced Yasutani that Zen must travel to the West, and meanwhile it was Yasutani who transmitted Harada's teachings to Soen and Eido, Yamada and Maezumi, Aitken and Tetsugen. In this way Sogaku Harada-roshi, whose nonsectarian teachings were carried to the New World by these Dharma heirs, became a great spiritual ancestor of American Zen.

In the opinion of Nishiwaki-roshi, who became head of training at both Eihei-ji and Soji-ji after his teacher's death, the Soto sect had been dead for two centuries before the advent of Harada, and even today he has his doubts about Zen masters who are not in Harada's line. He agrees with Yasutani and Yamada that most Japanese teachers and students are not serious, and refuse to undergo vigorous training. Instead of true seeking, the monks ask such questions as "How do I run my temple?" and "How do I get married?," which Nishiwaki would answer with thirty swift blows of his stick.

Heading east along the coast from the Noto Peninsula, the train crosses a rice plain between the Sea of Japan and the snow peaks of the island's central mountains. There is a flower culture here, and west of Uozu, mats of vivid red and yellow tulips are set off by the livid green of the new rice plants in the paddies, in misty light under soft blue snows of Mount Shironina. On the rock shore at Itoigawa, we walk along the beach in the chill twilight, observing the Pacific gulls ("The sea darkens," wrote Basho of this place, "the cries of the gulls are faintly white") and collecting wild sea rocks colored by the earthen fires and smoothed by ocean storms. After steambath and fish supper, we watch one of the samurai dramas that are almost always running on TV, for Japan is even more addicted to these national epics than America once was to "cowboys and Indians."

At Naoetsu railway station early next morning, tulips and pansies bloom in boxes on the station platform, and the railway food vendors form a line to bow to the coddled travelers as the train departs. Because trains are frequent, clean, and so efficient that watches may be set by their departure times, the railways are the chosen mode of travel for most Japanese, who seem dedicated to visiting during their lives as many as possible of their country's points of scenic interest.

From Naoetsu, our way turns inland, for we are leaving the Sea of Japan and returning across Honshu to the Pacific. The railroad climbs a long broad valley to wooded hills under Mount

Myoko. At higher altitudes, the spring trees are still bare and the soil is dark, but the day is hot in the mountain valley of Nagano, where we descend from the train to pay a visit to Zenko-ji, a huge Tendai-Jodo temple, at the summit of the town's main street, against the mountains. "Four gates, four different sects sleep as one under the bright moon," said Basho, an early visitor to the unfinished temple, which was completed in 1707, in the Edo period (1603–1886).

Tendai-Jodo emphasis on an afterlife makes Zenko-ji a place of pilgrimage for eight million Japanese each year, despite the decline of both these schools of Buddhism. The high priest of Tendai and the high priestess of Jodo are resident at Zenko-ji, and on this April day, both are officiating at a huge service for the thousands who come in formations up the central street, flowing in endless and orderly lines past the smoke-breathing dragon-dog guardian. A young woman assists her mother or grandmother up the steep steps; although of ordinary size, she is at least twice the height of the child-sized figure beside her. In the decade since I first visited Japan, the average height of the younger generations has increased so markedly that I no longer loom over the passengers in a crowded bus or subway.

At the temple entrance the pilgrims pause to touch the wood statue of Honen, which is smooth after centuries of adoration. One woman touches his heart and pate, and then her son's breast and her own head. A group of young men laugh too loudly when they rub the statue's loins and then their own.

Further eastward, late that afternoon, as the train crosses the central range and begins its descent toward the Pacific, Mount Asama is sending forth a high white plume of smoke, and later that day Asama erupts for the first time in years. (Basho wrote, "A sudden storm on Mount Asama blowing stones all over me.") West of Yokokawa, Mount Myogi juts misshapen towers into the sunny mist as a man stands up on his seat to change his trousers for the city. The train emerges on the broad Kanto Plain that extends southeast to the Tokugawa capital at

Edo, called Tokyo since the last shogun resigned and the imperial house was resurrected, in the Meiji Restoration of 1868 that introduced the era of modern Japan.

At that time, the nation's reverence of Western "progress" undermined its culture and old values, and it was questioned in public debate whether a tradition so archaic as Zen Buddhism should continue to exist in the new Japan. But Eido-roshi says that a Zen monk, chanting the *Diamond Sutra* in its entirety, awed the officials, even those of "big head and small hara," who wore their ceremonial swords over Western clothes.

An imposing wood statue of Harada-roshi may be seen at Tosho-ji, in Tokyo. We paid a visit with Maezumi-roshi, who had joined us briefly in Kyoto and met us again here. Founded by Harada before World War II, Tosho-ji is administered by Tetsugyu Ban-roshi, seventy-two, who is one of Harada's four living disciples. According to Ban, a small, merry man with big false teeth who never had any other teacher, the sculptor[4] of this statue practiced zazen under Harada and once sat sleepless through the entire eight days of Rohatsu, falling unconscious at the end. Ban-roshi, who keeps as souvenirs on a long rack the many kyosaku he has broken on the shoulders of his students, offered this story as evidence that the man was qualified for the job. The statue is thin-lipped and severe, although later in life, Maezumi says, Harada-roshi gained a reputation for compassion, kindness, and a playful way with dogs and children.

Harada's purpose in coming to Tokyo was to start a children's school where the true nonsectarian spirit of Zen practice might be taught, but because he refused to ask for any financial assistance from his supporters, the first school closed within the year, and the establishment was moved three times before it put down secure roots at this location. Yasutani and two other disciples devoted most of every day to trying to salvage their teacher's dream, but it was no use. Apparently Harada had assumed that conditions in the middle of Tokyo—at that time the largest city in the world—were similar to circumstances at Obama,

232

where the monks could grow vegetables and go out with their collecting bowls on *takuhatsu*, and where the monastery was largely self-supporting. "He had a wonderful Dharma spirit!" laughed Ban-roshi, who radiates the same spirit himself, "but a very poor sense of administration!"

When this temple was built in 1940, Harada still refused to solicit money (which inspired certain suspicious people to call him a fake), but during World War II, when even Hosshin-ji was going into debt, he finally asked Ban to take care of the matter. The young disciple, who became Tosho-ji's second abbot, immediately instituted a fund-raising program. Eventually he made the place self-sustaining, after many hard years in which he rose at 3:00 A.M., conducted morning service, went out all day on takuhatsu, then returned in the late afternoon for evening service and zazen. After 9:00 P.M. he devoted a few hours to editing Harada's writings and other duties. Throughout most of these hard years, he said, he subsisted on pickles.

Maezumi-roshi, translating Ban's discourse for our benefit, was elated to realize the extent to which Harada had been innovative in both practice and teaching. Harada's attitude affirmed Maezumi's feeling that almost all of the most qualified Zen teachers since the time of Dogen were those trained in both koan study and shikan-taza. Such people paid little or no attention to the petty differences between Rinzai and Soto, being determined to locate a true teacher who revitalized and maintained the true Dharma. Both of Maezumi's principal teachers, Koryu and Yasutani, had refused to submit to the stultifying influence of sectarian thought, and for some time now, Maezumi himself had considered founding his own White Plum lineage as a pillar of American Soto Zen.

Ban-roshi recalled with broad-toothed glee Yasutani's opinion that scarcely ten among the hundreds of so-called Zen teachers in Japan, Rinzai or Soto, deserved to be called roshi. He had greatly admired Yasutani, who was teaching in the monk's hall at Hosshin-ji when Ban turned up as a novice monk in 1931, and who gave Ban a final teaching forty-two years later, in the year he died. In his poem commemorating Yasutani's death, Ban said, "How momentous it is, leaving such great footsteps! You changed your place to teach in the New World. . . ." To Tetsugen he said, "Make your own *honzan*—'original mountain'—in America."

("Harada's mind is now with Maezumi-roshi and Tetsugen-roshi in the United States," says Ban's Dharma brother Nishiwaki-roshi, who would be the senior priest at Tetsugen's abbot installation[5] in June 1982, on the first of what were to become annual visits. "We hope this mind will go all over the United States and around the world." Harada had given Nishiwaki "a last koan," which he intends to pass on to Maezumi. "We owe ourselves to our roshis, but we must know ourselves, too. We must understand how to make Zen in our own style.")

In Japan, one waves until one's friends are out of sight, and Ban-roshi stood in the narrow Tokyo street until we reached the corner, perhaps one hundred yards away. There we turned to make our parting bows, as he bowed, too.

You should know that the entire heaven and earth are the roots, stem, and branches, and leaves of the long bamboo. Thus heaven and earth are timeless . . . a wooden walking staff is both old and not old.

A plantain has earth, water, fire, wind, emptiness, also mind, consciousness, and wisdom as its roots, stems, branches, and leaves, or as its flowers, fruits, colors, and forms. Accordingly, the plantain wears the autumn wind, and is torn in the autumn wind. We know that it is pure and clear and that not a single particle is excluded.

Painted Cake
—EIHEI DOGEN

CHAPTER NINETEEN

THE train from the Ueno station, north of Tokyo, crosses the great flat Kanto Plain, a heavily populated region of small houses and well-tended gardens, diminutive haystacks and low plastic greenhouses. In every free space between road and railroad track, amid factories, stacks, towers, and power lines, the barefoot householders, pants rolled to the knee, hack at the dark spring earth with the heavy mattocks of long centuries past. In the factory yards as the train rolls past, the workers play baseball in the noon hour, for this eerily adaptive land quickly adopted the national game of the big gaijin who reduced thousands of its citizens to atomized "shadows" on the fallen walls of Hiroshima and Nagasaki. From food advertisements to the design of children's clothes, the baseball motif is everywhere in Japan, in celebration of the deft fielders and spry hitters of such teams as the Hiroshima Carp and Tokyo Giants.

The rivers of this region are much diminished by industry

and agriculture, even in this season of spring torrents, but at a river edge stands a white egret, the elegant bird so beloved of Oriental artists. Even from the train, the yellow feet on its black legs are visible in the gravel shallows. Here and there a lone fisherman stands well back from the bank, as transfixed as the solitary bird. The stillness of the human figure, the length of the wispy pole, are signs that the last fish in these shrunken streams are scarce and shy. Small Japanese salmon once ascended Honshu's streams, but today these lovely silver fish, like the Japanese crane and the last native bears, are confined to the northern island of Hokkaido, together with the remnant aborigines, or "Hairy Ainu," tall, blue-eyed, bearded hunter-gatherers, at one time considered a relict population of the early *Homo sapiens* known as Cro-Magnon.

In the seventeenth century, this endless plain north of the Tokugawa capital at Edo must have been desolate, since in the first pages of his last, best work, *The Narrow Road to the Deep North*, the poet Basho observed no place of note on his journey across it. "The faint shadow of Mount Fuji and the cherry blossoms of Ueno . . . were bidding me a last farewell," says he as he sets off on foot. A few lines later, he is already ninety miles northward at Mount Nikko (Mount Sun Rays), site of "the holiest of shrines"—a temple established early in the ninth century by Kobo Daishi, founder of the Shingon sect, and rededicated in 1636 to Ieyasu, the first Tokugawa shogun. Some of these huge cryptomeria or "cedars," planted three centuries ago, were on this mountainside when Basho came here. Mount Kurokami, so admired by the poet, was engulfed today in clouds and sweeping rains, but the Toshogu shrine is still in good repair, and so is the poet's great waterfall, which "came pouring out of a hollow in the ridge and tumbled down into the dark green pool below in a huge leap of several hundred feet." On the rocks below the fall, a dipper teetered. Even in April, snow patches cling to deep, dark places in the gorge.

From Nikko, the poet proceeded east to Kurobane, on the Naka River, in a soft valley not far south of the flat-topped hills called the Yamizo Mountains. Apparently Basho liked this region, where he lingered for some time. His wanderings are locally commemorated by his haiku, which are carved into flat erected rocks, like wild, rough gravestones. At Daiyo temple, an old thatch-roofed building withdrawing year by year into its shaggy grove of evergreens, the caretaker told us that Basho had lingered here for fourteen days.

> Yama mo hiwa mo   Mountain garden
> Usani hidoya   A rabbit came
> Natsu zaski   (Its) summer living room.

Just as we read this commemorative stone, an accipitrine hawk, pearl-mantled with rufous breast, dove through the mountain orchard in cherry blossom light and vanished in the blackness of the pines. Perhaps this sudden hawk pursued that unseen bird of melodious bent whose song I had heard a few moments before, the elusive thing which, in our hurry, we have never tarried long enough to find.

Basho also visited Ungan-ji, a Rinzai temple of the late thirteenth century, which like Engaku-ji is built into a grove of evergreens against a mountain, and remains today very much as he described it: "The temple was situated on the side of a mountain completely covered with dark cedars and pines. A narrow road trailed up the valley between banks of dripping moss, leading us to the gate of a temple across a bridge. The air was still cold, though it was April." The gate of Ungan-ji is bright red, gathering up light out of the forest, and the mountain torrent between gate and temple is clear and strong, entirely unlike the weary rivers draining the flatland below.

Ten miles to the south, across the Jabi River from the town of Otawara, is Maezumi-roshi's family temple, called Koshin-ji. Originally a sixteenth-century edifice, Koshin-ji was entirely reconstructed by Baian Hakujun Kuroda-roshi in 1933. A large complex of temple buildings surrounds three sides of an extensive court, perhaps 300 by 150 feet, entirely bare except for a few stone figures and stone lanterns and big evergreens. After four centuries the steep hillside behind the temple is mostly taken up by graves.

Tetsugen-sensei, who first met Baian Hakujun in 1970, was very impressed by "his emphasis on *aigo*, loving words. It was very rare for him to be harsh with anyone. He always had guests at this temple, and his staff and family were always serving. Privacy was never an issue, since they had none; theirs was a life of giving and serving. He never accumulated money, but spent it on the members, guests, and temple. Money was an energy source that flowed. This kind of lived patience and lived caring is very rare. I feel a special affinity for Baian Hakujun. His teaching was his life, lived in everyday situations, the kind of undramatic teaching that seeps into the blood and marrow of a student and transforms him. Of course such transformation takes many years, but it is the transmission of the true Dharma."

Although a high Soto official, Baian Hakujun (who was Maezumi's *honshi*, or "root teacher," and a strong influence on his son's style) had not hesitated to invite Rinzai teachers to lead sesshins at his own temple here in Otawara. One of these teachers, Joko-roshi, fed up with the bureaucratic attitudes of the Rinzai priesthood, was not only willing to teach in a Soto temple but had forsworn Rinzai temple training in favor of simple dojos, or meditation training centers, one of which we visited while near Mount Nikko. Today these dojos are directed by Joko's disciple Osaka Koryu-roshi, whom the American monk at Kennin-ji had referred to as "the best lay Rinzai master in Japan." Maezumi's older brother Kojun became Koryu's leading student, and Maezumi himself, at age fifteen, left Otawara for Tokyo in order to live and study with this powerful teacher.

After four years under Koryu-roshi, Maezumi studied at Komazawa Soto University, in Tokyo. Subsequently he enrolled at Soji-ji, where Harada's contemporary Watanabe was then zenji, after which he was asked by the Soto administration to go to Los Angeles to assist in the Soto temple founded there in the 1920s. Since his brother Kojun would inherit the family temple here at Otawara, their father approved of this idea, and Maezumi did, too. "I just wanted to go!" he says, and off he went in 1956, at the age of twenty-five. Because the Los Angeles temple had no serious Zen practice, he was happy to learn of "the floating zendo" led by Nyogen Senzaki, with whom he studied until Nyogen's death in 1958.

When Yasutani-roshi came to Los Angeles in 1962, the young monk Maezumi, after asking a few questions, "knew immediately that I should study with him." Yasutani told Maezumi what Harada-roshi had told him—that Harada had *not* been the author of that koan "answer book," and had strongly disapproved of it. While convinced that feeble koan study had done great harm, Harada felt that such a book did more harm still, burdening foolish students with preconceptions instead of urging them to let go of their ideas.

Since Baian Hakujun's death in 1979, Koshin-ji has been directed by Kojun Kuroda-roshi, a broad, strong-shouldered man with thick neck creases who looks more like a *sumo* wrestler or farmer than a Zen master. Though he does not speak English, his kindness and good nature come shining through a bluff and shy demeanor. Like his father, he is much beloved in Otawara, and at one time was asked to be its mayor; he fills the role of the feudal overlord, or *daimyo*, who lived in a castle on the next hill in the days when Koshin-ji was first constructed. His wife, Miyoko, a pretty woman of strong, quiet presence with a sudden, quick, appealing laugh, directs a school for young children of Otawara that adjoins the temple.

As the second son, Maezumi-roshi took his mother's family name—a traditional custom that keeps an old family from dying out—but he still regards this temple as his home. With Kuroda-roshi's family, and Baian Hakujun's sprightly widow, known as Obachan (Grandmother), we relaxed at a fine homecoming supper, toasting the coming together at Koshin-ji with copious amounts of sake. Then we drank more in celebration of the coming of Buddhism to America, Europe, and Israel, which would one day be recognized as a great historical event.

After supper, Maezumi-roshi led me on a tour of Koshin-ji, which is constructed around two main service halls connected by long enclosed corridors. Besides the usual temple appointments, Koshin-ji has an esoteric atmosphere due to his brother's interest in tantric practice, and Maezumi pointed out each detail with the greatest delight. I had never seen this sad-faced, detached man so relaxed and animated. "My father rebuilt it entirely when he was only thirty—isn't it amazing? Nobody thought that his sangha would raise the funds, but they did. And it was he who established this tantric hall, which is more . . . bold? . . . than the other one." He wandered on, gazing about him. "As a kid, I ran up and down these halls, climbed on the roof—I was a rascal!" His diminutive mother, who now joined us, confirmed that her second son had been a rascal, and Maezumi laughed in glee at her expression. To prove that he was a rascal still, he imitated her frown and even her stoop as they walked together down the long corridor: "Look!" Taizan Maezumi cried. "Look! Obachan!"

In a family regimen which the Kuroda brothers have made famous in Soto Zen circles, Maezumi celebrated with sake and whiskey until after midnight, then rose next morning before dawn. Peevish, he expressed annoyance that his American students had not risen in time to do zazen before morning service. When I murmured that our sluggishness might be accounted for by all that drink, Maezumi snapped, "Sake is one thing, and zazen is another! They have nothing to do with each other!"

Kuroda-roshi led an elaborate service in which we moved from altar to altar, hall to hall. A young disciple performed the rapid tantric chants as Kuroda kept time with hard, quick pounding on the drum. Afterward we went outside and climbed the hillside to the grave of Baian Hakujun, on a rise overlooking the old town. Obachan, out early to cut daffodils, hobbled stolidly up the steep hill behind us, and Maezumi-roshi, already recovered, called out happily, "Ho, Obachan!" in affirmation of his mother's doughty existence.

At the grave, we offered water, incense, flowers. The north wind of recent days had died, and the clear skies were thickening with a change of weather. All the way up to the evergreen forest on the ridge, soft, shifting light filled the cherry blossom clouds that covered the hillside. The earth was sprinkled with the blue of violets, and the mist of pale pink cherry blossoms was quickened here and there by blood-red and bone-white camellias. Noisy flocks of bulbuls, with a few bold jays, crossed the high trees, and the wild pigeons mourned their ancestors back in the wood.

Within the forest, at an ancient Shinto shrine watched by stone foxes, the three teachers in their golden robes rang the bell that banishes malevolent spirits. From this height, the blossoming trees flowed down in waves to the Jabi River and the town, and Maezumi spread his arms, exclaiming, "The trees are at their very *best!*"

Dogen said:

> As *usual*
> Cherry blossoms bloom in my *native place*
> Their color unchanged. [1]

From the thicket in the early light came the melodious sweet voice of that unknown bird, and Maezumi-roshi, who had been talking to his brother as they walked along, turned around on the path ahead, as if anticipating my question. "That is the nightingale," he informed me, and I nodded wisely, no wiser than before, in my useless knowledge that nightingales are not encountered in Japan.

On the train south to Tokyo, Tetsugen analyzed the system of koan study in which we were engaged. Before Hakuin Zenji, koan study had been arbitrary, with koans assigned at random. In Hakuin's system, sets of koans were given that dealt with specific questions, and they were progressive in difficulty. Although this is the system in general use today, Hakuin had two "Dharma grandsons" who had different temperaments and developed different traditions, and Maezumi had studied in both. Osaka Koryu-roshi was in one of these traditions, and Yasutani, as a student of Harada (who did koan study with two Rinzai masters but introduced some Soto ideas), was in the other. Their teaching emphasis was different, and so were the koans themselves. Yasutani insisted on meticulous examination of the koan, with a lot of probing; Koryu emphasized the *spirit* of the koan, without bothering to break it down, to analyze it. Inevitably, people complained that Yasutani took too long in the dokusan room. Others asserted that Rinzai teachers such as Koryu neglected true penetration of the koan. With a good teacher, in Tetsugen's opinion, either approach worked well. A lot depended on the nature of the student and the teacher's judgment.

Although Maezumi and Tetsugen used Koryu's ideas, their teaching reflects the Harada–Yasutani system, which begins with about fifty preliminary koan, followed by the fifty-odd koan in the *Mumon-kan* (*Gateless Gate*). Next came the *Hekigan Roku* (*Blue Cliff Record*), the *Shoyo Roku* (*Book of Equanimity*), the *Denko Roku* (*The Transmission of Light*),[2] the *Go-i* koan,[3] and the precept koan, about five hundred koan altogether. Many of these koan are also found in the system used in Koryu-roshi's lineage.

Yasutani-roshi was forty-eight when he began koan study with Harada, and was in his late fifties when he finished. Even after he became a roshi, in 1943, he remained for some years at Hosshin-ji, transcribing Harada's introductory talks.[4] "Of Maezumi's three teachers," Tetsugen says, "Yasutani had the most influence on our teaching style in the dokusan room, and this style derives from Harada-roshi. Harada and Yasutani would not settle for half-understood koans, and neither will Maezumi nor his disciples."

Like Maezumi, Tetsugen is a firm believer in keeping his students off-balance, unaffixed, and he offered me an enigmatic buddha smile. However, I am glad of his strict attitude. If American teachers failed to maintain the highest standards, American Zen would always be weak-rooted, and would certainly die in a few generations.

Kirigaya-ji, where we stayed during our several stays in Tokyo, is an old temple restored to prominence by Maezumi's father in the 1950s and now administered by Junpu-sensei, the youngest of four Kuroda brothers who are prominent in the Soto priesthood. Junpu-sensei, a slight, boyish man with a mischievous smile, his wife, Tamiko, and the kind aunts and delightful children of his household were unfailingly hospitable, offering us the unusual honor of permitting us to share in their family life. Our airy chamber of shoji screens, tatami mats, and comfortable futon bedding (tucked away in cabinets each morning) looked out on the temple crematory and graveyard, with its loud mynah birds, bare wintry trees, and old stone buddhas. In the fresh spring wind, wood memorial plaques were nagged by the soft, sad clacking of the hungry ghosts.

In Tokyo we paid calls on Zen teachers, bought temple supplies for ZCNY, attended the kabuki theater, and frequented hot baths and good restaurants as happy recipients of our hosts' abundant hospitality. One afternoon we visited Sengaku-ji, built in 1612, a redoubt of rock and pine erupting like an old root of Edo through the bright chemical-colored crust of Tokyo. In passing beneath the old dark eaves of its mighty entrance gate, one leaves behind the surrounding city to enter another century. Under high pines on the granite outcrop of the hill behind, the graves of the forty-seven ronin are grouped around the larger memorial to their leader, the young Lord Asano. In this small fern-ringed well set in the rock, says Maezumi-roshi, the head of Asano's persecutor had been cleansed of blood before being presented to Asano's gravestone altar as an offering.

At the time of the ritual suicide of the forty-seven ronin, in 1702, Sengaku-ji was part of the Tokugawa Imperial Palace, and its temple treasures, which were on display on the day of our visit, include wonderful scrolls, drawings, and paintings. One painting was done by the celebrated Sesshu, creator of the extraordinary *Long Scroll*, and two of the drawings are by Hakuin Zenji. On this spring afternoon of sun and showers and falling wet blossoms, the visitors bring incense and daisies to the graves, and children offer little candy packets, the unnatural colors running in the rain.

Maezumi-roshi wished to visit his last living teacher, Osaka Koryu-roshi, who lives at Hannya [Prajna] Dojo, a Zen training center constructed a half century ago in what is now Inogashira Park, in northern Tokyo. The modest building, like a hermitage, lies half hidden in dark woods that overlook a narrow, leafy pond. At the age of eighty Koryu-roshi is still noted for his powerful teisho and dramatic dokusan, and continues to maintain stern discipline with his students. In November 1981, Koryu-roshi suffered a bad fall, and now he must offer teisho and dokusan from a chair. Also, he is nearly blind from a deteriorating eye condition apparently caused by exposure to the first atomic blast at Hiroshima, which burned out his hair before he could jump into a shelter. "My eyes maybe got some kind of effect, since I saw that bright explosion and felt that heat," he murmurs with a shy, sweet smile that recalled accounts of Hiroshima victims, courteous even in death agony, asking passersby to please lift the wreckage that crushed and suffocated them.

Koryu-roshi attributes his survival at Hiroshima to his daily homage to a Kannon Bodhisattva that had been entrusted to him for protection; the temple that formerly contained the figure was destroyed in the atomic holocaust. From an altar behind him, on which yellow chrysanthemums have been placed, the enigmatic deity looks down in mercy as we join Koryu at a low table. To the Roshi's left, on the wall of the small room, is a scroll painting of a hunched night heron on a dead limb, awaiting evening. Bird shadows flit across pale shoji screens, and a turtle-dove sings *cuh-coo-coo* from the spring trees of the park.

Happily the old teacher relates how his excellent student,

244

Taizan Maezumi, cataloged the dojo library of 60,000 volumes. The soft voice falls and rises like the spring wind that murmurs all around the old wood house as the Roshi's wife offers a light repast of sashimi—raw sea bass, tuna, mackerel, crayfish, fish roe, and squid, served with soy sauce, green mustard, radish, and raw ginger—set about with pickled cauliflower and carrot, mustard tofu, nori, and early strawberries.

Koryu's jisha brings in an ancient manuscript of the Rinzai koan collection, *Hekigan Roku*. The manuscript contains annotations, comments, and capping phrases written in by Hakuin Zenji and other eminent Rinzai teachers. This precious volume was once saved from fire, the roshi whispers, by a Zen master who willingly risked and received severe burns. In recent years a second copy has been made that he has given to Maezumi for safekeeping.

"When koan were made, there was the attempt to put all of Buddhism into a single phrase," Koryu-roshi has said. "What is the Buddha, What is Bodhidharma's fundamental spirit, Why did the Patriarch come from the West. . . . Zen seeks to speak the entirety of the Buddha's teaching in a single phrase. . . . But the odor of 'Buddhism' remains: 'What is the Buddha?' 'Why did the Patriarch come from the West?' and so on. Hakuin simply put out one hand and said, 'Hear *this*!' This is truly put directly to us, completely apart from all the trappings of 'Buddhism.' To hear the sound of one hand, our fundamental nature must clearly come forth. Without using the word 'Buddha,' without using the word 'Zen,' we throw ourselves directly into the recesses of the mind."[5]

Obeying the injunction of his teacher, Joko-roshi, Koryu has never joined the Rinzai priesthood. He agrees with other nonsectarian teachers that the Japanese priesthood, regardless of sect, has done its best to kill the true Zen spirit. Yet when nearly seventy, Koryu-roshi considered becoming a Soto monk and sincerely discussed the possibility of having his head shaved by his student Maezumi, in tokudo, the ceremony of "leaving home."

Hearing of this now, I am very moved. My own tokudo from Maezumi (in 1981), though momentous, seemed frivolous by comparison to such a step. I remember a crazy exhilaration, an airy feeling about my new blue head, but, as it is said, the hairs or delusions on the *inside* of the skull are the ones most difficult to remove. After years of Zen practice, I am still beset by the "greed, anger, and folly" referred to in the Gatha of Purification, still woefully deficient in that simplicity of spirit, that transparency of heart, that is evident in many people who have never heard of Zen at all.

Tetsugen-sensei makes it clear that one day he expects me to be a teacher. I do not feel ready. ("Generally speaking," Dogen said, "if you have still not sufficiently clarified the Buddha Dharma, you ought not to preach the Dharma rashly and heedlessly to others.")[6] "Be more simple," Soen-roshi always said, and how I long to simplify myself. The secret of well-being is simplicity, which is here for the taking in this very breath, and also as elusive as the air.

Over the room falls a soft sepia light, as if suffused from the master's old brown robes. He sits there quietly, all but motionless, his dim eyes seemingly filled with tears due to thick lenses in his glasses, the big ears set low on the close-cropped but not shaven head, the big hands working his wood beads.

"The seed of Zen was sown in India, its flower blossomed in China, and in Japan it bore fruit," Koryu-roshi has said. "In Japan we savor Zen through an extraordinarily wide range of things. In this room flowers have been arranged, bringing nature in, and if we open the screens here a garden will lie before us. Nature is constantly being brought in. . . . I think that in putting a vast world into something small there is the 'wondrous flavor' of Zen."[7]

(Koryu-roshi died on July 27, 1985.)

Buddha ancestors' heart and words are buddha ancestors' everyday tea and rice. Ordinary coarse tea and plain rice are buddhas' heart and ancestors' words. . . . You should leap over the summit of the question, "Besides tea and rice, are there any words or phrases for teaching?" You should try to see whether leaping is possible or not. . . .

Each and every extraordinary activity is simply having rice. Thus sitting alone on Daiyu Peak is just having rice. . . . To fill yourself is to know rice. . . . Now what is the monk's bowl? I would say, it is not wood and it is not black lacquer. . . . It is bottomless. . . . One gulp swallows the vast sky. It accepts the vast sky with its palms together. . . .

Inheriting the buddhas' essential wisdom is realizing the activity of having rice. . . .You cannot tell how many layers of misty clouds this sitting penetrates. Even with the sound of roaring thunder, in spring apricot blossoms are just red.

Being Ordinary
—EIHEI DOGEN

CHAPTER TWENTY

ON his last visit to the United States, in 1975, Nakagawa Soenroshi had scribbled on a scrap of paper his address at Ryutakuji. Whether I asked for it or whether he just gave it to me, I cannot recall. On another scrap he had scratched one of his haiku in quick Japanese characters:

> *In the light of flowers*
> *I travel*
> *Just for the sake of traveling.*

In 1981, Soen-roshi had refused to see Eido-roshi and a group of American students when they arrived at Ryutaku-ji. Early in 1982, when I wrote to my old teacher that I would like to visit him in April, I received no answer. One of his disciples, Kyudo-roshi (who as Monk Dokyu had visited my house in 1972, later led a Zen group in Israel, and was now accepting students in New York City), assured me that his teacher would see no one. Sochu-roshi, Soen's successor as abbot of Ryutaku-ji, had informed Maezumi-roshi (who telephoned from Tokyo) that his old teacher was still in seclusion in his chamber high above the monastery, that he had let his hair grow long and had a beard, as in his hermit days on Dai Bosatsu Mountain, and that sometimes he was not seen for weeks at a time. This cloud-hidden state was confirmed by Soen's friend, Koun Yamada-roshi, at Kamakura. Yet my instinct was to pay my old teacher a visit "just for the sake of paying my old teacher a visit." If he would not see us, that was all right, too.

I sense in Tetsugen mixed feelings about the visit, and yet he has no wish to interfere. Soen-roshi's erratic appearances, his long periods of withdrawal, have denied to his students the continuity of study that Soto masters feel is critical, and therefore Tetsugen has doubts about his ultimate effectiveness as a Zen teacher. "He *ignites* his students, but he does not keep that fire burning. He has not gone to America since 1975, and people who come to Ryutaku-ji to study with him may not set eyes on him for years." Nevertheless, he admires Soen as a great eccentric master, "in the traditional sense, probably the greatest Zen master of modern times."

Throughout our travels in Japan, we have mostly stayed at monasteries and temples, but because I am traveling as jisha to a Soto teacher, it seems inappropriate to ask if we might stay at Ryutaku-ji. Instead we will stay at Fuji Hannya Dojo, one of the lay meditation centers established by Joko-roshi, where Koryu-roshi still comes occasionally to give sesshin.

Chido-sensei, who administers this dojo, was a friend of the late R. H. Blyth, the eminent British translator and interpreter of Japanese literature[1] who was interned as a Japanese prisoner during World War II (with Robert Aitken, whom he started on the path of Zen) and who lived at this dojo for a while thereafter. Erudite, brilliant, cranky, and opinionated, Blyth decreed that the four greatest Japanese Zen monks were Ikkyu, Takuan, Hakuin, and Ryokan, all of them poets; Ikkyu was rated highest of all. "I omit Dogen," Blyth informs us, "because I think him infatuated, incoherent, and unlovable." Simplistic judgments such as these enliven without illuminating a volume[2] dedicated to D. T. Suzuki, "the only man who can write about Zen without making me loathe it." (This opinion is not so wrongheaded as it might seem, since anything written *about* Zen—including Blyth's own numerous volumes, and this one—inevitably separates itself from Zen's "instantaneous" spirit. In using dead words to *say* that Zen is this or that, a separation is created, and the freshness of the Zen moment is lost.)

A small, sturdy man with beetling brows in a kind country face toughened by weather, Chido-sensei dresses simply in a black beret and dark blue sweat suit that seem to emphasize his isolation from the priesthood. With his daughter and pretty grandchildren, he lives among overgrown gardens of abounding roses, washed by restless winds in the tall evergreens, soothed by the rushing of the Kise River. The Kise flows down from the eastern slopes of Fuji-san,[3] as this shining volcano, symbol of Eternal Mind, is known to the Japanese. "Oh! This beautiful Fuji-san! I am so happy living near!" cried Chido-sensei's friend, Mr. Sakuma, at one time a student of Soen-roshi at Ryutaku-ji. Chido-sensei, too, has known Soen for many years. Like all of Soen's friends and students, he and Mr. Sakuma have many memories of that quixotic and beloved teacher, and laugh affectionately over old stories. "He hides himself now," Mr. Sakuma said, collecting himself with a polite sigh. "I have not seen him for some years."

That night I steamed with my knees up like a fetus in a round wooden vat heated from beneath the shed by a smoky log fire stoked by Chido-sensei. At dawn our host led us in meditation in the small zendo, and afterward we carried flowers to Joko-roshi's grave on a wooded rise above the Kise River. His daughter served us a big country breakfast, and after breakfast Chido-sensei offered *chanoyu*. He served the ceremonial green tea precisely and correctly, yet simply, without mannerisms, the worn napkin small in his rough brown hand. His tea was "ordinary" in the sense so much admired by Zen masters, with nothing showy, "nothing special," nothing that drew attention to itself. ("Be more *ordinary*," Soen-roshi used to say to some of my more literary koan answers.)

A fresh wind down off Fuji-san, high to the west, made a rushing sound in the great cryptomeria and strong bamboo, and the one sound strong enough to carry over wind and river was the light, sweet song of that unseen bird, lost in the leaves of a maple overhead. A moment later I laid eyes on it at last. The bird had none of the magical colors with which I had painted it in my imagination, "nothing special." It was small and plain and brown, the *uguisu* or bush warbler (known to English-speaking Japanese as "nightingale"). Ryokan wrote:

> Illusion and enlightenment? Two sides of a coin.
> Universals and particulars? No difference.
> All day I read the wordless sutra;
> All night not a thought of Zen practice.
> An *uguisu* sings in the willows along the river bank,
> Dogs in the village bay at the moon. . . .[4]

Chido-sensei's household accompanied us to the main road to wave goodbye. *Sayonara!* they cried—a lovely word in the voices of young children. We followed the old man across the river. Below the bridge, big white geese of the village sailed on windy pools between shining gray stones, rubbed smooth by centuries of Fuji-san's spring torrents.

From the village, a small local bus climbed the terraces of the high farm country to smaller villages inset in the foothills. The villages sat at the edge of the montane forest that climbs to the snow line on Mount Fuji. Throughout our journey up the mountain, through fields and crossroads, orchards and pine-wood, the great white cone of Fuji kept reappearing, rising ever higher in the blue sky; snow blew from the peak in pursuit of swift white clouds. "Because mountains are by nature high and broad," Dogen Zenji said, "the right way of riding the clouds is reached from the mountains, and the inconceivable virtue of following the wind is not hindered by mountains."[5]

At these altitudes, the spring was new. Wild cherry and andromeda were just coming into blossom, and the low scrub hardwoods were still bare. The grass was straw-colored, parted here and there by yellow-edged leaves of small native bamboo. On the cold earth there were no flowers, but on tall poles above each mountain hamlet, tubular pennants in the form of heaven-colored carp swayed, tossed, and danced in the mountain wind. The huge fish, cloud-pink and sky-blue, swam like dragons against the snows, against the sky.

The road passed a closed amusement park with soiled pastel walls banged by the breeze. A chemical-colored polar bear was king of a plastic ice floe in the middle of a large plastic lagoon. Higher still, in the "Fuji Safari Park," a few chilled golfers swatted balls across last winter's novice ski slope. The road came to an end well below the snows at a "Wildlife Protection Area," a small forest without the smallest sign of life. In vain did I scan the silent woods for ashy minivets and red-flanked bluetails, green woodpeckers and copper pheasants, while Tetsugen, who discourses as freely as the uguisu sings, kept up an animated conversation. Chido-sensei walked ahead of us, hands tucked up behind his back, muttering a little, and seeing the snow cone through the trees beyond him, I was reminded of a story told by Soen-roshi, to show how words get in the way of the natural expression of the thing itself.

One day a young monk at Ryutaku-ji had a kensho, and his teacher, seeking to deepen this experience, led him on a long walk up Mount Fuji. Although the monk had seen the great snow mountain many times before, he truly perceived it now for the first time (like the monk who *truly* perceived that the sun was round), and all the way up, he kept exclaiming over the harmony and colors of the wildflowers, the flight of birds, the morning light in the fresh evergreens, the sacred white mountain rising in mighty silence to the sky. "Look, Roshi, this pine cone! See how it is made? This stone, it's so . . . so *stone*! Isn't it wonderful? Do you hear the nightingale? It is a miracle! Oh! Fuji-san!"

Muttering a little, the old master hobbled onward, until finally his student noticed his long silence and cried out, "Isn't it so? Aren't these mountains, rivers, and great earth miraculous? Isn't it beautiful?" The old man turned on him. "Yes-s-s," he said forcefully. "But what a pity to *say* so!"[6]

On the way down the mountain, we descended from the bus at the small Fuji museum. The kind curator endeavored to explain the geological mysteries of the volcano but, failing to penetrate the language barrier, presented me instead with a small transparent arrowhead, minutely fashioned by the aboriginal Jomon people of three to five thousand years before. Out of reverence for Chido-sensei, or so it appeared, the curator then drove us the rest of the way down the mountain into Mishima, on Suruga Bay.

In the early afternoon, as we walked off a fine lunch of baked eels and cold beer, Chido-sensei displayed the botanical gardens, children's park, and zoo of his fair city. One cage containing Siberian cranes (which wander to Japan in winter) was being hosed down by a hasty keeper, and the huge birds pressed frantically against the bars, lifting their wings and feet in consternation. Here in Mishima, in 1973, my bad knee had been treated by two aged acupuncturists, a man and wife, both blind. Before inserting the long, wispy needles, the old couple had run unabashed hands over every inch of me, without exception, chirping innocently as uguisu over their findings. When I returned to Ryutaku-ji, Soen-roshi said, "Have you been punctuated?"

Ryutaku-ji, the Dragon-Swamp Temple, is set on a steep slope of mosses and evergreens on the south side of the foothills of Mount Fuji. (The dragon symbolizes one's own true nature, or Buddha-nature, as in Dogen Zenji's exhortation, "Do not be afraid of the true dragon!") At the entrance a monk said, "Soen-roshi is not so healthy now; he rises, falls. But he is feeling better today, and he will see you." Chido-sensei translated these words, but because his English is haphazard, we wondered if the opposite message had been intended.

After making our bows in the main service hall where I sat sesshin in 1973, we went to the Founder's Hall to pay respects to Hakuin Ekaku, whose intensity animates an old wood statue that leans forward to peer into the eyes of those who look upon it. "His figure is extraordinary, he glares at people like a tiger, he walks like a bull; his power is fierce and difficult to approach," wrote Hakuin's disciple Torei Enji, who relocated the temple on this mountainside in 1761, the year that Hakuin came here to lecture. In this same place, two centuries later, at his *shin-san-shiki*, or abbot installation, Soen-roshi had worn Hakuin's robes.

Soen's successor, Sochu-roshi, had offered dokusan during the sesshin that preceded the formal opening of Dai Bosatsu, six years before, but our confrontations had been inconclusive. I remembered him best as one of the ringleaders on that lawless rowboat voyage to the Buddha on the farther side of Beecher Lake, and he had no reason to remember me at all. Though large, rounded, and thickset to the degree that Soen is small, erect, and trim, he resembles his teacher in his no-nonsense manner, his quick, cryptic humor, and his all but disreputable brown robes. Without bothering about greetings or introductions, he led us at once on an inspection of the new zendo, now under construction. The wood was still unstained and aromatic, and new copper tiles shone on the roof. At tea in the old monastery office, Sochu-roshi had little or nothing to say, and after a short time he rose rather abruptly and departed.

Quite suddenly, as if he had waited in the corridor for this moment, an old monk in a plain black robe stood in the doorway. He wore no sign of ordination, yet the robe was clean and his head was freshly shaven, and he stood erect in that authoritative way that had always made him seem larger than he was. Having expected an unkempt old man with long hair and beard, we were taken aback, and bowed in silence. Bowing briefly in return, Soen-roshi snapped, "All stand up, follow me." He turned on his heel and walked away toward the narrow stairs that led up the hillside to the abbot's rooms and eventually to his own small private chamber.

By these ancient stairs, as the foot of the mossy hillside behind the monastery, lies the small goldfish pond that—perhaps because of my old teacher's love of Basho—I associate with that most famous of all haiku:

> Old pond
> A frog jumps in
> The sound of water

Basho was a Zen student, and his old pond is the vast emptiness, the eternal. The frog is the quick glint of fleeting life. The splash is the instantaneous NOW! that makes them one.[7]

In 1973, returning from Kyoto, we had gone for a walk into the foothills, but Fuji-san was hidden in the clouds that wandered down among the daisies and wild rose on the hill terraces. At tea Soen-roshi had presented us with red demon paintings, and on one of these shikishi I found inscribed "Nowhere is now here: Soen." (The message startled me, having already appeared in a hallucinatory dream in one of my own novels, published eight years earlier; where Soen-roshi came by it I never asked.) The evening service commemorated his teacher, Gempo-roshi. Next morning we rose at 3:30 A.M. to begin sesshin.[8]

That first morning, Soen-roshi led his American students out of the service hall during dawn zazen, just as the first wand of light touched the old pond behind the monastery. At the foot of the stairs he pointed in silence at a dragonfly nymph that had crawled out of the lily pads and mud and fastened itself to the stair post. The nymph is a mud-colored water dweller of forbidding aspect and rapacious habit that preys on small fish and other creatures until the day comes when it hauls its heavy body from the water, affixes itself to wood or stone, and struggles to cast off its thick carapace, permitting its translucent, sun-filled dragonfly nature to take wing.

At sunrise, the new dragonfly was almost free, a beautiful golden thing, silvered by dew, resting a little, twitching its transparent wings, yet not quite liberated from the crude armor of its former life. When I gasped like the young monk on the mountain, unable to repress a delighted comment, Soen-roshi pointed sternly at the meditation hall: "Now do your *best!*"

In the first day, there was great pain and weakness in my injured knee, causing teeth chattering and even nausea, but within one day—it seemed miraculous at the time—the acupuncture treatment had taken hold. Though I still had pain, I no longer feared that I had come this great distance to Ryutaku-ji sesshin for nothing. At dokusan the roshi said, "In any event, in any moment, and in any place, none can be other than the marvelous revelation of . . . Mu! If your knee hurts, where is Mu?" Mu is just MU!, I declared, and he said sharply, "Never mind all this Mu! If your knee hurts there is only OUCH! If your car cracks, there is only BANG! Do you understand?"

If the frog jumps, there is only SPLASH: do you understand?

At next dokusan, I asked for a koan, but the roshi was relentless. "Mu practice is enough koan. You will die someday. What is Mu on the day of your death? You must work on Mu more diligently, more sincerely, more *completely.*"

I was still a new student, and therefore ashamed of my weak and stupid answers. At work period, avoiding the harsh stare of those bald eyes, I cleaned Hakuin's altar; another day I peeled onions in the sun. And later in sesshin, as my mind cleared, there rose from the great stillness of zazen the irrefutable not-knowing that Hakuin's eye, the onion smell, knee pain, tea taste, pine whisper, bells, the flutter of temple doves dusting in sunlight, were in no way different from myself, all one, all Mu.

Knee taste, tea pain, bell whisper, bald dust fluttering, nowhere, now here, all one, all eternal Mu.

During teisho for the Japanese, we listened upstairs to recorded teisho in English—scarcely teisho at all, since true teisho depends on a live buddha presence. But there was live teisho from the ratcheting frogs in the temple pool, the sudden silence at the nearing of the heron, hard-eyed, wet glint on its taut bill—the frog, the heron stab, the silver water splash all one, the rolling red color and the taste, the pain, are not separate from this excitable student who carried his frog tales into dokusan. Soen-roshi nodded vigorously. "Ripening, ripening! March on diligently! Expect nothing!"

> Moon glint on a heron's bill.
> . . . eep!
> Silverness.

During zazen, making his rounds with his delusion-cutting sword, the roshi smacks me smartly twice (though I do not ask for it), then says to us, "There is only one thing to win, and all of you may win it in this sesshin!"

At dokusan he demands again, "What is Mu on the day you die?" I fall back in a descending moan of death, and he nods, saying quietly, "*This* Mu is the true enlightenment."

Now it is 1982, and once again, in the same reception room, Soen-roshi led us in the *Kannon Sutra*. Still very stern, the old teacher rose and we trailed him up the stair to the little chamber in the evergreens, overlooking the mossy hillside, the old fish pond, the old monastery. Once again I made my bows to the magnificent thousand-armed, thousand-eyed Kannon figure, a national treasure, which at the time of that 1973 visit was destined to go to Dai Bosatsu, in America. Once again we chanted the Four Vows and the Gatha of Purification.

Only then did the roshi's stern expression soften in welcome. Greeting us one by one around the circle, he smiled, then laughed aloud in childlike pleasure. When my turn came, he took both of my hands and squeezed them three times, very hard, tears in his eyes, then rose to his knees and gave me a great hug. He laughed with Tetsugen, gazed at his old friend Chido-sensei with a happy smile. Then he went back around the circle, touching our heads in blessing, after which—just as he used to do—he commanded us to slap his shaved head *hard*, to knock some sense into it. By now, remembering his tricks, we were all laughing in delight.

Then, as if his eyes had died, he withdrew behind the remote expression I remembered so well from dokusan, in which his mouth sets as in a mask and his eyes disappear behind two slits. Without a word, he got up, bowed, and led us back down the crooked stair. At the entrance he took up his long wood staff and marched along the woodland paths of Ryutaku-ji, leading the way down the mountainside to the public road where the cab would be waiting.

Nine years before, departing this place, his American students were accompanied by Soen-roshi on an excursion to Atami, on the coast, where the hotelkeeper would not suffer any students of this renowned Zen master, poet, and calligrapher to pay for anything. We devoured fresh fish, glowed in fountain baths, danced on the hotel roof at dawn, bowed to the sun. In a rock-ledge house set among treetops on the mountainside, a beautiful woman, Soen's old student, offered our feet shiatsu massage, a hot face cloth, and a delicious cold sesame drink, preparing us for koicha tea in a delicate straw room that hung like a sun lantern in the old dark branches. From the leaf canopy, in the long June twilight, came a fluting birdsong. To my inquiry, the roshi said, "That is the nightingale."

A silver sake bottle, silver cups. In ancient dress, the mandarin lady offered in black lacquer bowls the delicate courses of *kaiseki* supper—hot and cold soups, egg tofu, kelps, tempura of lotus bulb and lilac root. Afterward we improvised a dance on the tatami, until the roshi raised his hand, summoning silence, and pointed through the trees at the ocean sunset. "Please appreciate," he murmured. "Dragon clouds."

One afternoon we visited a temple on the hills above Atami

and the sea. On one of the roofs in the temple court sat a motley of street pigeons, one hundred strong. In the midst of this discolored mob shone a lone white bird. While the roshi gave instructions to the cab driver, his guests walked across the square, then turned around on the far side to await him. When the small, brown figure set out alone, all but one bird in the pigeon flock, which had risen in a burst as we left the car to wheel in a tight circle overhead, returned in a sudden swirl onto its roof. The white bird circled round and round over Soen's head.

Not bothering to follow our gaze upward, Soen-roshi smiled at our awe-struck faces. Murmuring "Won-derful! Won-derful!," he continued on into the temple.

Nine years later, on the forest path, he was still offering appreciation of his life, cheering a late-blooming cherry, pointing his long stave at the sun. "The sun, the moon are buddhas, all the human beings of this earth are buddhas, *all* is Buddha! Everything and everybody is a teacher. Sometimes you are my teachers, *you* are so-called roshi! Everybody is so-called roshi, okay? *All* is enlightened, as-it-is-now!"

All are nothing but flowers
In a flowering universe. [9]

A little boy running uphill on the path, head down, was startled when he bumped into us, and more startled still when Soen-roshi, pointing his long stick, cried, "Monju! Here is Monju!" Monju is Manjusri, the Bodhisattva of Great Wisdom. The roshi was entreating us to perceive the Bodhisattva in the clear, undefended gaze of the little boy. Then the instant passed. Seeing the gaijin, the child's eye clouded in bewilderment, and the old man rubbed his head in blessing, saying sadly, "No, it is not Monju after all." The child ran off, and the roshi fell silent, walking on.

At the bottom of the hill where the cab was waiting, Soen-roshi was courtly and quiet. He inclined his head in recognition of our goodbyes, no longer with us, impatient to retreat into his solitude. Feeling incomplete, I told him how happy his students in America would be if he came to see them. I did not mention Eido-roshi and neither did he. "Perhaps," he said, "I shall appear soon in New York, but it is not a promise." He raised his staff and kept it raised as long as we could see him through the car window, a small, black-robed figure at the end of the path that led uphill into the forest.

Even before arriving in Japan, I had faith that Soen-roshi would see us, and this morning, as we drove up toward Mount Fuji, I felt sure of it. Tetsugen was mildly surprised that the visit had worked out so well in the face of so many obstacles and warnings. Tetsugen, too, perceives that Soen, with his ancient, innocent, and other-worldly ways, has the power of some old shaman from the Gobi Desert, and comes and goes, accountable to no one. Eido-roshi perceived him as "my greatest koan, truly ungraspable": Soen-roshi would say, "If I am caught, it is the end of me."

At seventy-five, Soen-roshi still seemed animated, but Tetsugen felt—and I had to agree—that he had been going on memory and nerve; his wild, spontaneous inspiration had dimmed. "He was almost like a ghost," Tetsugen commented as elation died in the journey down the mountain, "the perfect ghost of Soen-roshi, like a ghost in a Noh drama, which for some reason was allowed to reappear."[10]

In the sadness attending our visit there was also freedom. The wonderful teachers who had brought the Dharma from Asia to the West would appear no more, but in another sense, they would be with us forever. In Western as in Eastern lands, the Buddha Way might need centuries to become established, so the sooner we got on about it, the better. It was time to step forward from the hundred-foot pole as the fortunate student of this America-born buddha who sits here beside me in this present, first, last, past, and future moment of my life.

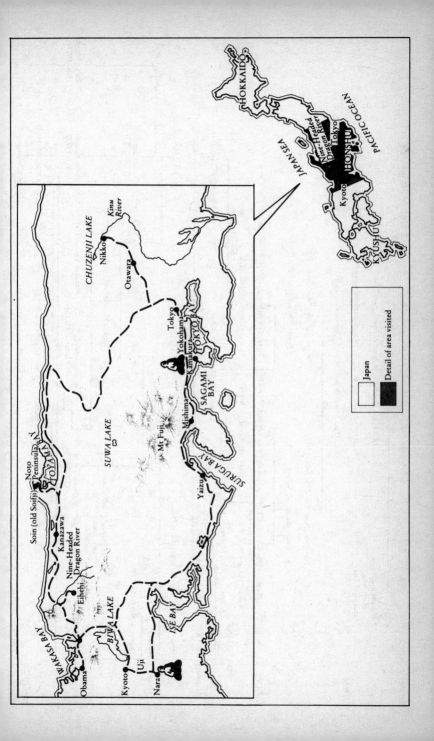

HOKKAIDO

JAPAN SEA

Nine-Headed
Dragon River

HONSHU

Tokyo

Kyoto

PACIFIC OCEAN

KYUSHU

Japan

Detail of area visited

Kinu
River

CHUZENJI LAKE

Nikko

Otawara

Tokyo

Yokohama

TOKYO BAY

Kamakura

SAGAMI
BAY

Mishima

SUWA LAKE

Mt. Fuji

SURUGA BAY

Yaizu

Noto
Peninsula

Soin (old Soiiji)

TOYAMA

Kanazawa

Nine-Headed
Dragon River

Eiheiji

WAKASA BAY

BIWA LAKE

Obama

Uji

Kyoto

ISE BAY

Nara

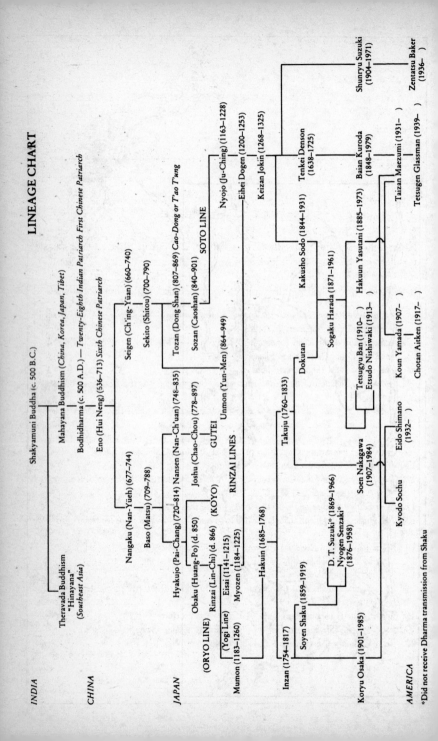

LINEAGE CHART

INDIA

Shakyamuni Buddha (c. 500 B.C.)

Theravada Buddhism "Hinayana" (*Southeast Asia*)

Mahayana Buddhism (*China, Korea, Japan, Tibet*)

CHINA

Bodhidharma (c. 500 A.D.) — *Twenty-Eighth Indian Patriarch First Chinese Patriarch*

Eno (Hui Neng) (536–713) *Sixth Chinese Patriarch*

Nangaku (Nan-Yüeh) (677–744)

Baso (Matsu) (709–788)

Seigen (Ch'ing-Yüan) (660–740)

Sekito (Shitou) (700–790)

Hyakujo (Pai-Chang) (720–814)

Nansen (Nan-Ch'uan) (748–835)

Joshu (Chao-Chou) (778–897)

Tozan (Dong Shan) (807–869) *Cao-Dong or T'ao T'ung*

Sozan (Caoshan) (840–901)

SOTO LINE

Unmon (Yun-Men) (864–949)

Nyojo (Ju-Ching) (1163–1228)

Eihei Dogen (1200–1253)

Keizan Jokin (1268–1325)

GUTEI

KOYO

RINZAI LINES

JAPAN

(ORYO LINE)

Obaku (Huang-Po) (d. 850)

Rinzai (Lin-Chi) (d. 866)

(Yogi Line)

Eisai (1141–1215)

Myozen (1184–1225)

Mumon (1183–1260)

Hakuin (1685–1768)

Inzan (1754–1817)

Takuju (1760–1833)

Dokutan

Sogaku Harada (1871–1961)

Kakusho Sodo (1844–1931)

Tenkei Denson (1638–1725)

Soyen Shaku (1859–1919)

D. T. Suzuki* (1869–1966)

Nyogen Senzaki* (1876–1958)

Koryu Osaka (1901–1985)

Soen Nakagawa (1907–1984)

Tetsugyu Ban (1910–)

Etsudo Nishiwaki (1913–)

Hakun Yasutani (1885–1973)

Baian Kuroda (1848–1979)

Shunryu Suzuki (1904–1971)

AMERICA

Kyodo Sochu

Eido Shimano (1932–)

Koun Yamada (1907–)

Chotan Aitken (1917–)

Taizan Maezumi (1931–)

Tetsugen Glassman (1939–)

Zentatsu Baker (1936–)

*Did not receive Dharma transmission from Shaku

Chapter Epigraph Sources

Note: Scholars differ markedly on translations of Dogen's titles, and in this text certain titles have been changed after consultation with Taizan Maezumi-roshi and Tetsugen Glassman-sensei. In such cases, the translator's title (in brackets) precedes his initials. Complete source information follows below.

1. *A Universal Recommendation for Zazen* (*Fukan-zazen-gi*) ["A Universal Promotion of the Principles of Zazen"] (A-W).
2. *Actualization of the Koan* (*Shobogenzo Genjokoan*) (TM).
3. *Birth and Death* (*Shobogenzo Shoji*) (A-W).
4. *One Bright Pearl* (*Shobogenzo Ikka Myoju*) (A-W).
5. *On the Clarification of the Way* (*Shobogenzo Bendowa*) ["On the Endeavor of the Way"] (KT).
6. *Unbroken Practice* (*Shobogenzo Gyoji*) ["Continuous Practice"] (FC).
7. *Mountains and Rivers Sutra* (*Shobogenzo Sansuikyo*) (CB).
8. *Arousing the Supreme Mind* (*Shobogenzo Hotsu Mujo Shin*) (FC).
9. *Body and Mind Study of the Way* (*Shobogenzo Shinjin Gakudo*) (KT).
10. *Pilgrimage* (*Shobogenzo Henzan*) ["All-Inclusive Study"] (KT).
11. *Bowing, Penetrating the Marrow* (*Shobogenzo Raihai Tokuzui*) ["Paying Homage and Acquiring the Essence"] (FC).
12. *Deep Faith in Cause and Effect* (*Shobogenzo Jinshin Inga*) (FC).
13. *Precautions for the Tenzo* (*Shobogenzo Tenzo Kyokun*) ["Instructions for the Tenzo"] (KT).
14. *Points to Watch in Buddhist Training* (*Gakudo Yojin-shu*) (YY).
15. *Sky-Flowers* (*Shobogenzo Kuge*) (HK).
16. *Buddha-Nature* (*Shobogenzo Bussho*) (A-W).
17. *Only Buddhas to Buddhas* (*Shobogenzo Yuibutsu Yobutsu*) ["Only Between Buddhas and Buddhas"] (KT).
18. *Entire Activity* (*Shobogenzo Zenki*) ["Concerted Activity"] (KT).
19. *Painted Cake* (*Shobogenzo Gabyo*) ["Painting of a Rice Cake"] (KT).
20. *Being Ordinary* (*Shobogenzo Kajo*) ["Everyday Activity"] (KT).

A-W: Masao Abe and Norman Waddell, various Dogen translations, in *Eastern Buddhist*, 1971–1975.

TM: Taizan Maezumi, *The Way of Everyday Life*. Los Angeles: Center Publications, 1978.

KT: Kazuaki Tanahashi, *Moon in a Dewdrop*. Berkeley: North Point Press, 1985.

FC: Francis Dojun Cook, *How to Raise an Ox*. Los Angeles: Center Publications, 1978.

CB: Carl Bielefeldt, in *The Mountain Spirit*, ed. M. Tobias and H. Drasdo. Woodstock, N.Y.: Overlook Press, 1979.

YY: Yuho Yokoi, *Zen Master Dogen*. New York/Tokyo: Weatherhill, 1976.

HK: Hee-Jin Kim, *Dogen Kigen—Mystical Realist*. Tucson: University of Arizona Press, 1980.

NOTES

CHAPTER ONE

1. The monastery at Tassajara, California, was adapted from existing buildings.
2. Soyen Shaku, *Sermons of a Buddhist Abbot*, trans. D. T. Suzuki (New York: Samuel Weiser, 1971).
3. From *The Diamond Sutra*: "All composite things are as if a dream, a phantasm."
4. "Because Zen is fact and not 'religion' in its conventional sense of the term, the American mind with its scientific cast takes to it very readily. . . . Unlike European Buddhism, American Buddhism is not scholastic in character . . . the American mind is more inclined to practical activity than philosophical speculation. . . . Modern Americans are longing to reach the spirit of Buddha by engaging, if possible, in the actual practice the Buddha followed to attain enlightenment. Zen is the very spirit of Buddhism, the heart that beats and throbs with life . . . it can only be reached through practical action in one's everyday tasks . . . Zen emphasizes self-reliance and self-realization, rather than a dependence on the supernatural power of some god or Buddha; for this reason, it is the only teaching of Japanese Buddhism that has any hope of spreading in the future among Americans, for whom self-reliance is the essence of their way of life." Nyogen Senzaki, in *Namu Dai Bosa* (New York: Theatre Arts Books, 1976), pp. 89–91.
5. Soyen Shaku, *Sermons of a Buddhist Abbot*.
6. Ruth Fuller Sasaki, Sokei-an's wife (co-author, with Isshu Miura-roshi—whom she brought to New York—of *The Zen Koan* [New York: Harcourt Brace, 1965]), eventually persuaded him to encourage zazen among his American students.
7. Snyder was (and is) a Zen practitioner who once studied at Daitoku-ji, in Kyoto, and leads his own Zen community in California; in recent years, Ginsberg has become a formal student of Tibetan Buddhism. Other distinguished Zen student-poets include Jim Harrison and William Merwin. Merwin is a student of Robert Aitken-roshi (himself a poet), who is working with Aitken, Kazuaki Tanahashi, and others on new Zen translations.
8. Perceptive introductions to Zen such as *Zen in the Art of Archery* by Eugen Herrigel were obscured by ego-ridden and pretentious imitations, and also a rash of do-it-yourself Zen treatises on arts and sports; other diminished versions of the

teachings were transmitted to the West through the television adventures of a "Zen" knight-errant called Kung Fu.

9. From Daio. Kokushi, *On Zen*, trans. D. T. Suzuki in *Daily Sutras*, (New York: Zen Studies Society, undated).

10. "If I understand correctly, this is what I have been trying to say in all my writings." Martin Heidegger, quoted in foreword to *The Three Pillars of Zen*, ed. Philip Kapleau (Boston: Beacon Press, 1967).

11. "True Man of No Rank." See *Rinzai Roku* (*The Record of Master Rinzai*), trans. Ruth Fuller Sazaki and Dana Fraser, (New York: Zen Studies Society, undated).

12. These wishes echo the final instructions to his students of Japanese Zen master Takuan (1573–1645): "Do not recite sutras . . . Do not make portraits of me. Just bury my body in the back mountains. It is enough that you cover me with earth."

CHAPTER TWO

1. Kandida Boatwright, Marsha Feinhandler, and Sheila Curtis.

CHAPTER THREE

1. Having no real vocabulary for what science cannot define, we tend to dismiss all unexplainable experiences as "supernatural," i.e., impossible, and the many who have had them—and dare say so—are jeeringly condemned to a halo of fatuity or downright foolishness. Mostly these halos are deserved, and yet, and yet . . . As Rilke said in his *Letters to a Young Poet*, "That mankind has in this sense been cowardly has done life endless harm; the experiences that are called 'visions,' the whole so-called 'spirit-world,' death, all those things so closely akin to us, have by daily parrying been so crowded out of life that the senses with which we could have grasped them are atrophied. To say nothing of God."

CHAPTER FOUR

1. Hakuun Yasutani-roshi, in *The Three Pillars of Zen*, ed. Philip Kapleau (Boston: Beacon Press, 1967), pp. 29–30.

CHAPTER FIVE

1. From *The Record of Master Rinzai* (*Rinzai Roku*), trans. D. T. Suzuki, in *Daily Sutras* (New York: Zen Studies Society, undated).

CHAPTER SIX

1. The eleventh-century Soto master Tanka Shijun.

2. Quoted by Dogen Kigen Zenji in *Shobogenzo Raihai Tokuzui*. See Dr. Francis Cook, *How to Raise an Ox* (Los Angeles: Center Publications, 1978), p. 134.

3. Rick Fields, *How the Swans Came to the Lake* (Boston: Shambhala Publications, 1981).

4. The Himalayan journals are essentially composed of brief excerpts on Buddhism and Zen practice from Peter Matthiessen, *The Snow Leopard* (New York: Viking Press, 1978).

CHAPTER SEVEN

1. Lama Angarika Govinda, *The Way of the White Clouds* (Boston: Shambhala Publications, 1971).
2. David Snellgrove, *Himalayan Pilgrimage* (Oxford: Cassirer, 1961).
3. It has been suggested that the yogas were a kind of synthesis of Aryan physical austerity and the intricate psychic lore of the Dravidians . . . not the passive fatalism of which Eastern religions are so commonly accused but acceptance of each moment, resilience and serenity, calmness in action and intensity when calm. The yogi in seated meditation was called "the flame in windless spot that does not flicker." A. K. Coomaraswamy, *Buddha and the Gospel of Buddhism* (New York: Harper and Row, 1964).
4. Lao Tzu, *Tao Te Ching.*
6. *Rig Veda.*
6. Werner Heisenberg, quoted by L. LeShan in "How Can You Tell a Physicist from a Mystic?," *Intellectual Digest*, February 1972.
7. Lama Govinda, *The Way of the White Clouds.*
8. Carl Sagan, in I. S. Shklovsky and Carl Sagan, *Intelligent Life in the Universe* (San Francisco: Holden and Day, 1966).
9. Harlow Shapley, *Beyond the Universe* (New York: Scribner's, 1967).
10. W. Y. Evans-Wentz, *Tibet's Great Yogi, Milarepa* (New York: Oxford University Press, 1969).
11. Sanskrit terms are differently defined by Hindus and Buddhists, and even within Buddhism, they overlap a little, like snakes swallowing their own tails: *samadhi* (one-pointedness, unification) may lead to *sunyatta* (emptiness, void) which can open out into *satori* (glimpse) which may evolve into the *prajna* (transcendent wisdom) of *nirvana* (beyond dualism, delusion, beyond the relative world of life and death, beyond becoming) which might be perceived as eternal *samadhi*. Thus the circle is complete, every state is conditioned by each of the others, and all are inherent in meditation, which in itself is a realization of the Way.
12. W. Y. Evans-Wentz, *Tibetan Yoga and Secret Doctrines* (New York: Oxford University Press, 1967).

CHAPTER EIGHT

1. Thomas Traherne, *Centuries of Meditation* (seventeenth century).
2. Ibid.
3. Chögyam Trungpa, *Cutting Through Spiritual Materialism* (Boston: Shambhala Publications, 1973).
4. Dogen Zenji, *Shobogenzo* (San Francisco: Japan Publications, 1977).
5. *Bhagavad Gita.*

1. Note that Zen masters of the Soto school use their family names with the title *roshi*, whereas Rinzai masters—such as Soen-roshi and Eido-roshi—use their Dharma names.

2. See Ruth Benedict, *The Chrysanthemum and the Sword: Patterns of Japanese Culture* (New York: New American Library, 1974 [1946]).

3. "In shikan-taza," says Yasutani-roshi, "the mind must be unhurried yet at the same time firmly planted or massively composed, like Mt. Fuji . . . but it must also be alert, stretched, like a taut bowstring. So shikan-taza is a heightened state of concentrated awareness wherein one is neither tense nor hurried, and certainly never slack. It is the mind of somebody facing death. . . . In the beginning, tension is unavoidable, but with experience this tense zazen ripens into fully relaxed yet fully attentive sitting. And just as a master swordsman in an emergency unsheathes his sword effortlessly and attacks single-mindedly, just so the shikan-taza adept sits without strain, alert and mindful. But do not for one minute imagine that such sitting can be achieved without long and dedicated practice." See *The Three Pillars of Zen*, ed. Philip Kapleau (Boston: Beacon Press), 1967, p. 54.

4. The traditional equation of the Southern and Northern schools of early Chinese Zen with "sudden" and "gradual" teachings may always have been more political than philosophical, and remains to be clarified by scholars. In any case, the Northern school later died out, and the sudden and gradual factions represented by Rinzai and Soto, respectively, both had their origins in Eno's Southern school, which provided all of the Zen lineages in existence today.

5. Thomas Cleary, *Timeless Spring* (San Francisco: Wheelwright Press/Weatherhill, 1980).

6. Probably this rivalry was more important to the priesthood—the bureaucracy—than to the teachers. One master in the Soto lineage (Toshi Gisei) was originally a leading Rinzai disciple who agreed to be the Dharma heir of Soto master Taiyo Kyogen in order to perpetuate Soto transmission. Similarly, the twelfth-century Soto master Tendo Shogaku was a close personal friend of the Rinzai master Daei, a leading exponent of "sudden" teachings. It was Tendo Shogaku who assembled a great koan collection called *Shoyo Roku* (*The Book of Equanimity*), which is still used in the Soto school, and resembles in style the tenth-century Rinzai collection made by Master Setcho and known today as *Hekigan Roku* (*The Blue Cliff Record*). A third well-known collection, *Mumon-kan* (*Gateless Gate*), assembled by Master Mumon in the thirteenth century, contains many koan well known in both schools.

7. Excellent teisho collections available in English include Koun Yamada-roshi, *The Gateless Gate* (Los Angeles: Center Publications, 1979); Shunryu Suzuki-roshi, *Zen Mind/Beginner's Mind* (New York: Weatherhill, 1970); Shimano Eido-roshi, *Golden Wind* (Tokyo: Japan Publications, 1979).

8. *Sensei* means "teacher," *roshi* is "elder teacher." Within a Zen community, teachers are usually addressed and referred to by these titles.

9. See the ox-herding pictures in *The Three Pillars of Zen* and elsewhere. See also Dogen, *Everyday Life* (*Shobogenzo Kajo*) in Dr. Francis Cook, *How to Raise an Ox* (Los Angeles: Center Publications, 1978), p. 209.

CHAPTER TEN

1. *Mu Ryo*, "No Limit" or "Boundless," from the third of the Four Vows: *Ho mon mu ryo sei gan gakuu*—"The Dharma is boundless, I vow to perceive it"—which I was chanting with Eido-roshi at the moment of my wife's death.
2. From *Hekigan Roku* (*The Blue Cliff Record*). A monk asked Hyakujo, "What is the best thing of all?" Hyakujo answered, "Doing zazen alone on Daiyu Peak." (Dogen Zenji comments, "Doing zazen alone on Daiyu Peak is the same as eating rice and drinking tea." *Everyday Life* (*Shobogenzo Kajo*), in Dr. Francis Cook, *How to Raise an Ox* (Los Angeles, Center Publications, 1978, p. 207).
3. Translated by Hakuun Yasutani-roshi and Koun Yamada-roshi in *The Three Pillars of Zen*, ed. Philip Kapleau (Boston: Beacon Press, 1967).
4. Taizan Maezumi-roshi, in foreword to *How to Raise an Ox*, p. xi.
5. Dr. Francis Cook, in introduction to *How to Raise an Ox*.
6. Dogen Zenji, *Shobogenzo Genjo-koan*, in Taizan Maezumi-roshi, *The Way of Everyday Life* (Los Angeles: Center Publications, 1978).

CHAPTER ELEVEN

1. *Zen Flesh, Zen Bones*, ed. Nyogen Senzaki and Paul Reps (Rutland, Vt.: Charles E. Tuttle Co., 1958).
2. Koun Yamada-roshi is the translator of Dogen's *Being-Time* and many other passages for *The Three Pillars of Zen*, ed. Philip Kapleau (Boston: Beacon Press, 1967), and also author of a collection of teisho on *The Gateless Gate* (Los Angeles: Center Publications, 1979).
3. Soen Nakagawa was ordained by Katsube Keigaku-roshi at Kogaku-ji, the temple of the great teacher Bassui at Dai Bosatsu Mountain, near Mount Fuji, from which the first Zen monastery in America got its name.
4. *The Three Pillars of Zen*, p. 204.
5. Preface to *Gateless Gate*.
6. Adachi-roshi, Miyazaki-roshi, and Kubota-roshi.
7. *Namu Dai Bosa*, by Nyogen Senzaki, Soen Nakagawa, and Eido Shimano, ed. Louis Nordstrom (New York: Theatre Arts Books, 1976).

CHAPTER TWELVE

1. Basho, *The Narrow Road to the Deep North* (Middlesex, England: Penguin, 1970). (Also known as *The Narrow Way Within*, a title which better reflects the poet's Zen quest and is more accurate as well. See Robert Aitken, *A Zen Wave* [New York and Tokyo: Weatherhill, 1978], p. 45.)
2. Other Hakuho period buildings at Nara and elsewhere are replicas of the originals, which is also true of most great temple edifices in Japan. Every few centuries a

candle overturns or lightning strikes, and the ancient wood structures go up in fire.

3. In these early temples, the Yakushi *nyorai*, or "medicine Buddhas," used in healing ceremonies adapted from the Shinto faith, were very prominent, and so were Nikko and Gakko, bodhisattvas of the Sun and Moon, whose influence waned with the decline of Shinto to the status of a traditional cult.

4. Meanwhile, the Buddhist priesthood was taking part in Shinto rites, usurping the functions of the traditional holy men. Officiating at the Shinto nature-worship festival of the first fruit harvest in 765, in which Buddhist priests and nuns also participated, the empress declared that her duties were "first to serve the Three Treasures [the Buddha, the Dharma, and the Sangha, or Buddhist community], then to worship the Shinto gods, and next to cherish the people." To this day, many Japanese Buddhists (Eido-roshi was one) are married in a Shinto ceremony. See G. B. Sansom, *Japan: A Short Cultural History* (New York: Appleton-Century-Crofts, 1962), p. 132. See also historical material in Hee-Jin Kim, *Dogen Kigen—Mystical Realist* (Tucson: University of Arizona Press, 1975), and Yuho Yokoi, *Zen Master Dogen* (New York: Weatherhill, 1976).

5. Genko-ji.

6. The eleventh-century novel *Genji Monogatari* or *Tales of Genji*, by Lady Shikibu Murasaki, provides a deft and marvelous account of the exquisite court life of the Heian period.

7. *Heike Monogatari*, written anonymously in the thirteenth century, is the great war epic of Japan and the source of innumerable samurai films and dramas.

8. In *Daily Sutras*, trans. D. T. Suzuki (New York: Zen Studies Society, undated).

9. Quoted in Ruth Fuller Sasaki and Isshu Miura-roshi, *The Zen Koan* (New York: Harcourt Brace, 1965, p. 38).

CHAPTER THIRTEEN

1. A thousand people did zazen together in Tofuku-ji's great zendo, a national treasure. This room inspired the zendo at Dai Bosatsu in America.

2. As Toyan-ji's abbot Matsakura has written, "In Zen, everything, even a leaf of grass, expresses ultimate reality. Thus this simple garden suggests to us absolute value . . . [it] might better be called Mu-tei, Garden of Nothingness. . . . We can view the garden as a group of mountainous islands in a great ocean, or as mountain tops rising above a sea of clouds. We can see it as a picture framed by ancient mud wall . . . or sense the truth of this sea stretching out boundlessly. . . ."

3. Maitreya, the so-called future Buddha.

4. The other is the Sen Rikyu tearoom at Urasenke Tea School in Kyoto.

5. Sen Shositsu.

6. In Japan, the lunar New Year's Day (which changes every year) is around February 4, hence all dates used for Dogen's life are approximate.

7. *Genko Shakusho* (1322). For accounts of Dogen's life, see *Shobogenzo Zuimonki, Shobogenzo Bendowa*, etc.; also Hee-Jin Kim, *Dogen Kigen—Mystical Realist* (Tucson: University of Arizona Press, 1980); Yuho Yokoi, *Zen Master Dogen* (New

York: Weatherhill, 1976); Kazuaki Tanahashi, *Moon in a Dewdrop* (Berkeley: North Point Press, 1985); and T. J. Kodera, *Dogen's Formative Years in China* (Boulder: Prajna Press, 1980).

8. *Genko Shakusho.*
9. *Shobogenzo Zuimonki,* quoted in *Zen Master Dogen,* p. 28.
10. Ibid., quoted in *Dogen's Formative Years in China.*
11. See D. T. Suzuki, *Shin Buddhism* (New York: Harper and Row, 1970).
12. *Shobogenzo Zuimonki,* quoted in *Dogen's Formative Years in China,* p. 23.
13. From Dogen's China journals, called *Hokyo-ki,* quoted in *Dogen's Formative Years in China,* p. 35.
14. "Japan is very far from foreign lands, and people here are extremely deluded. From ancient times until now, no saintly people have been born here, nor have there been any naturally intelligent people. Need I say that there have been no true followers of the Buddha's Way." Dogen, *The Sounds of Valley Streams, The Form of Mountains* (*Shobogenzo Keisei Sanshoku*), quoted in *How to Raise an Ox* (Los Angeles: Center Publications, 1978), p. 108.
15. *On the Clarification of the Way* (*Shobogenzo Bendowa*), quoted in *Zen Master Dogen,* p. 28.
16. *Precautions for the Tenzo* (*Shobogenzo Tenzo Kyokun*), quoted in *Zen Master Dogen,* pp. 29–30.
17. Ibid., quoted in *Dogen's Formative Years in China,* p. 38.
18. Quoted in Thomas Cleary, *Timeless Spring* (San Francisco: Wheelwright Press/ Weatherhill, 1980), p. 26.
19. In *Face to Face Transmission* (*Shobogenzo Menju*) Dogen wrote that he received Dharma transmission on the same day he met his teacher. This is less "poetic license" than an expression of this mutual recognition of attainment.
20. *Denku Roku* (*The Transmission of the Light*), by Keizan Zenji, case no. 51.
21. Trans. by Koun Yamada, *The Gateless Gate* (Los Angeles: Center Publications, 1979), p. 13.
22. Ibid., p. 179. See also "Rules for the Auxiliary Zendo" (*Shobogenzo Juundo-shiki*), quoted in *Zen Master Dogen,* pp. 34–36.
23. D. T. Suzuki, *Zen and Japanese Culture* (Princeton: Princeton University Press, 1959), p. 275. Perhaps Dogen's spirit was not yet tender. In *Shobogenzo Zuimonki,* a record of his later sayings set down by his disciple Koun Ejo, Dogen seems relentless as ever: "To offer a diet of beans and water in an effort to save the old and infirm merely caters to the misguided love and deluded passions of this brief life. If you turn your back on them and study the Way of liberation, even though you may have some regret, you will have a good opportunity for an enlightened life." Quoted in *Dogen Kigen—Mystical Realist,* p. 288.

CHAPTER FOURTEEN

1. Thomas Kirchner, Shaku Yuho.
2. *Takuhatsu* has nothing to do with begging. The citizens support the spiritual practice by placing food or money in the bowl, but there is no giver and no

receiver, and no thanks; monk and layman bow to each other simultaneously.

3. From *Eihei Koroku* (*The Extensive Record of Eihei Dogen*).
4. *Denko Roku*, case no. 52.
5. *The Practice of the Way* (*Shobogenzo Bendowa*), Abe and Waddell, *Eastern Buddhist* 4, no. 1, p. 124.
6. Taizan Maezumi-roshi, *The Way of Everyday Life* (Los Angeles: Cener Publications, 1978).
7. "Treasury of the True Dharma Eye: Record of Things Heard—in effect, "*Shobogenzo* Simplified." (See Reiho Masunaga, *A Primer of Soto Zen* [Honolulu: East-West Center Press, 1971]).
8. See also case no. 60 of *Hekigan Roku*: Unmon showed his staff to the assembly and said, "This staff has become a dragon. It has swallowed the whole universe. The mountains, rivers, and great earth—where do they come from?" See also case no. 100 of *Shoyo Roku*.

> "Emptiness is a name for nothingness, a name for ungraspability, a name for mountains, rivers, the whole earth. It is also called the real form [as in "form is emptiness, emptiness is form," in the *Heart Sutra*]. In the green of the pines, the twist of the brambles, there is no going and coming; in the red of the flowers and the white of the snow there is no birth and no death" (Master Ryusui).

9. *Mountains and Rivers Sutra* (*Shobogenzo Sansui-kyo*), Carl Bielefeldt in *The Mountain Spirit*, ed. M. Tobias and H. Drasdo (Woodstock, N.Y.: Overlook Press, 1979), pp. 43–44.
10. *Meeting the Buddhas* (*Shobogenzo Kembutsu*), in Hee-Jin Kim, *Dogen Kigen— Mystical Realist* (Tucson: University of Arizona Press, 1980, p. 35).
11. *The Practice of the Way* (*Shobogenzo Bendowa*), Abe and Waddell, *Eastern Buddhist* 4, no. 1, p. 139.
12. *Arousing the Supreme Thought* (*Shobogenzo Hotsu Mujo Shin*), in Dr. Francis Cook, *How to Raise an Ox* (Center Publications: Los Angeles, 1978, p. 119).
13. *The Moon* (*Shobogenzo Tsuki*), in Kazuaki Tanahashi, *Moon in a Dewdrop* (Berkeley: North Point Press, 1985), pp. 178–80.
14. *Twining Vines* (*Shobogenzo Katto*), ibid., pp. 237–40.
15. *Document of Heritage* (*Shobogenzo Shisho*), ibid., pp. 263–64.
16. *Unbroken Practice* (*Shobogenzo Gyoji*), in *How to Raise an Ox*, p. 197.
17. It was reconstructed in its present form in 1649.

CHAPTER FIFTEEN

1. Most of the renditions of Dogen's poems used in this book are copied or adapted from translations by Kazuaki Tanahashi, whose *Moon in a Dewdrop*, an excellent compilation of Dogen's writings, was published in 1985 by North Point Press in Berkeley, California.
2. Ibid.
3. *Unsui* literally means "cloud, water," from an old Chinese verse, "to drift like clouds and flow like water"; see Gary Snyder, "Spring Sesshin," in *Earth House*

Hold (New York: New Directions, 1969).

4. *Shobogenzo Zuimonki*, quoted in Hee-Jin Kim, *Dogen Kigen—Mystical Realist* (Tucson: University of Arizona Press, 1980).

5. This story is perhaps apocryphal, since it does not turn up in the texts until the sixteenth century.

6. Kim, in *Dogen Kigen—Mystical Realist*.

7. The most recent gravestone in the Eihei-ji cemetery (as of April 1982) is that of Yamada Reiun Zenji, a noted Dogen scholar who was abbot of the Soto temple in Los Angeles when a young monk named Taizan Maezumi first arrived there in 1958.

8. It was Tokiyori's son who ordered the construction of Engaku-ji, later the temple of Soyen Shaku-roshi.

9. Waka poems no. 50 and no. 60, adapted from Heinreich Dumoulin, *A History of Zen Buddhism* (New York: Pantheon, 1963), p. 159.

10. Again, an approximate date; the solar calendar was unknown in thirteen-century Japan.

11. From a Dogen poem entitled "Zazen Practice."

CHAPTER SIXTEEN

1. Extracts from *The Original Stream*, quoted in Thomas Cleary, *Timeless Spring* (San Francisco: Wheelwright Press/Weatherhill, 1980), p. 108.

2. Ibid., p. 112.

3. G. B. Samson, *Japan, A Short Cultural History* (New York: Appleton-Century Crofts, 1962), p. 335.

4. D. T. Suzuki, *Zen and Japanese Culture* (Princeton: Princeton University Press, 1959), p. 346.

5. See "Japanese Zen: A Symposium," *Eastern Buddhist* 10, no. 2 (October 1977); 76–101.

6. R. Y. Blyth, *Zen and Zen Classics*, vol. 5 (Tokyo: Hokuseido Press, 1962), p. 156).

7. See Omori Sogen, "Zen Sword," *Chanoyu Quarterly*, no. 30.

8. *So* means "grandfather" or "patriarch"; *in* means "hall" or "house," with a connotation of "sanctuary."

CHAPTER SEVENTEEN

1. *Zen Flesh, Zen Bones*, ed. Nyogen Senzaki and Paul Reps (Rutland, Vt.: Charles E. Tuttle Co., 1958), p. 22.

2. Hakuin Ekaku, quoted in *The Zen Koan* (New York: Harcourt Brace, 1965, pp. 63–69).

3. In *Daily Sutras*, trans. D. T. Suzuki (New York: Zen Studies Society, undated).

4. Hakuin, quoted in K. Tanahashi, *Penetrating Laughter* (Woodstock, N.Y.: Overlook Press, 1984).

5. Ibid.

6. Tenkei Denson, in *Benchu*, 1730.

7. Trans. by K. Tanahashi and D. Leighton, in *Moon in a Dewdrop* (Berkeley: North Point Press, 1985). Ryokan (1758–1831) was revered in Japan for his "crazy wisdom" as well as for poems of *mujo* (impermanence) and *mushin* (no-mind; cf. free, nonclinging "Zen" mind).

8. Bamboo was brought from China in the seventeenth century by Master Ingen, founder of the Obaku Zen school. This near-Rinzai teaching asserts that the benefits of zazen and of the Amida *nembutsu* chanting of the Pure Land (Jodo) sect are essentially identical.

9. Kenchu Hantetsu.

10. See Sekito's teaching in *Shobogenzo Kajo* (*Being Ordinary*), "Everyday Life," in Dr. Francis Cook, *How to Raise an Ox* (Los Angeles: Center Publications, 1978), p. 206.

11. Thomas Cleary, *Timeless Spring* (San Francisco: Wheelwright Press/Weatherhill), p. 35.

12. It appears that Dogen's strictures against prejudice against women (see *Bowing, Penetrating the Marrow* [*Shobogenzo Raihai Tokuzui*]) are not yet heeded, since nuns are few.

13. In Soto tradition, the title *zenji* is reserved for past or present abbots of Eihei-ji or Soji-ji, the head temples or "mountains" of the Soto sect, and also for deceased patriarchs or major figures in the lineage, such as Sekito and Tozan; no other Soto teacher would presume to use this honorific title.

14. See *Hekigan Roku*, case no. 1, and *Shoyo Roku*, case no. 2. Perversely inspired by this Soji-ji custom, I would choose this classic koan as the basis for my first Dharma talk and Dharma combat, in November 1982.

15. A fifth brother, Yoshikatsu Kuroda, is a sculptor.

16. Hee-Jin Kim, *Dogen Kigen—Mystical Realist* (Tucson: University of Arizona Press, 1980).

Chapter Eighteen

1. The Meaning of Practice Enlightenment, *Shusho-gi*.

2. See *The Three Pillars of Zen*, ed. Philip Kapleau (Boston: Beacon Press, 1967).

3. Eido-roshi says that his teacher's eccentricity commenced with a head injury suffered in the early sixties. No one seems to agree on exactly what happened —a fall, a blow—but these days that accident is often blamed for his sometimes whimsical behavior.

4. Homio Shimada.

5. At Zenshin-ji Temple of the Zen Community of New York.

Chapter Nineteen

1. Dogen, "Inconceivable Mind of Nirvana," quoted in Kazuaki Tanahashi, *Moon in a Dewdrop* (Berkeley: North Point Press, 1985).

2. *Denko Roku* (*Transmission of the Light*) should not be confused with *Dento Roku* (*Transmission of the Lamp*), an ancient sourcebook of accounts of the Zen masters.

3. Tozan's Five Ranks: the esoteric teaching in the *Goi Kenketsu* and *Hokyo Zammai*,

praised so highly by Hakuin Zenji. See Ruth Fuller Sasaki and Isshu Miura-roshi, *The Zen Koan* (New York: Harcourt Brace, 1965), chap. 7.

4. Harada-roshi's talks, transcribed by Yasutani-roshi and translated for Zen students in the United States by Yasutani's disciple Koun Yamada-roshi, are the foundation of *The Three Pillars of Zen.*

5. "Japanese Zen: A Symposium," *Eastern Buddhist* 2, no. 2 (October 1977).

6. *Deep Faith in Cause and Effect* (*Shobogenzo Jinshin Inga*), in Francis Cook, *How to Raise an Ox* (Los Angeles: Center Publications, 1978), p. 163.

7. "Japanese Zen: A Symposium."

CHAPTER TWENTY

1. See R. H. Blyth, *Zen and Zen Classics* in five volumes (Tokyo: Hokuseido Press, 1962). See also Blyth's four volumes on haiku and his valuable *Zen in English Literature and Oriental Classics* (Tokyo: Hokuseido Press, 1975).

2. *Zen and Zen Classics*, vol. 5, p. 144.

3. *San* here signifies "mountain," not "honorable."

4. Ryokan, "Chinese Poems," in *One Robe, One Bowl*, trans. John Stevens (New York: Weatherhill, 1977), p. 59.

5. *Mountains and Rivers Sutra* (*Shobogenzo Sansuikyo*), Carl Bielefeldt, trans., in *The Mountain Spirit*, ed. M. C. Tobias and H. Drago (Woodstock, N.Y.: Overlook Press, 1979, p. 41).

6. See also the story of Chokei and Hofuku, in *Hekigan Roku.*

7. See the fine discussion of this haiku by Robert Aitken-roshi, chap. 1 of *A Zen Wave* (New York and Tokyo: Weatherhill, 1978).

8. Monks Rin-san, Ho-san, and Do-san (Ho-san had been our interpreter throughout our travels), all of whom had studied with us at the New York Zendo, took pains to see that our sesshin went as smoothly as possible.

9. Haiku by Nakagawa Soen-roshi.

10. In the summer of 1982, Soen-roshi made his last visit to America, and we welcomed him briefly at a kabuki performance in New York City. On the fourth of July, six years to the day after the opening of Dai Bosatsu, he gave his final teisho to American students:

There are so many pleasures in life! Cooking, eating, sleeping, every deed of everyday life is nothing else but This Great Matter. Realize this! So we extend tender care with a worshiping heart even to such beings as beasts and birds— but not only to beasts, not only to birds, but to insects, too, okay? Even to grass, to one blade of grass, even to dust, to one speck of dust. Sometimes I bow to the dust. . . .

Nakagawa Soen-roshi died in the baths of Ryutaku-ji in March 1984. Eido-roshi discounted his past difficulties with his teacher, relating that on that final visit, Soen-roshi had sunk to his knees with tears of gratitude at Eido's suggestion that part of his bones might eventually be buried in America.

In the autumn of 1984, Etsudo Nishiwaki-roshi visited Soen-roshi's New World grave (part of Soen's bones are at Ryutaku-ji). Weeping, he bent to kiss the stone, crying out, "My old friend! My old friend!"

GLOSSARY

ango: a ninety- or one-hundred-day intensive training period, at the end of which the head monk (*shuso*) gives his first dharma talk and participates in "dharma combat," a testing ceremony and rite of passage that initiates him as a senior monk.

bessu: white ceremonial footwear used by Soto monks for formal services.

bushido: literally "the way of the warrior," or *samurai*; also the spiritual essence of martial arts.

chanoyu: the art of ceremonial tea.

daikensho: ordinary *kensho* still leaves some doubt, some questions remain as to what life is; *daikensho*, or "great opening" leaves one free of doubt with no questions remaining.

dojo: meditation training or practice center.

dokusan: the private, face-to-face study with a roshi, the spirit of which penetrates the essence of life. In the Rinzai tradition it is usually called *sanzen*.

gaijin: non-Japanese person.

gassho: the gesture (*mudra*) of putting one's hands together to express respect, reverence, and gratitude; in itself, an expression of the essence.

honzan: literally means "root mountain"; refers to main or root monasteries of a sect of Zen Buddhism. In the Soto sect, they are Eihei-ji and Soji-ji.

inka: literally, *in* means "seal" and *ka* "approval." In the Rinzai tradition, *inka* is equivalent to dharma transmission and is bestowed upon completion of formal study; in Maezumi Roshi's lineage, dharma transmission (*shiho*) and *inka* (receiving the formal approval) are distinguished, the latter usually taking place considerably later than dharma transmission.

inochi: life "integrity" of a given thing.

jihatsu: the set of formal bowls for meals.

jisha: personal attendant of a sensei or roshi.

junkei: the zendo monitor who uses the *kyosaku* or "encouragement-stick."

kaiseki: a light meal.

keisaku (kyosaku): long wooden stick applied to the shoulders to offset sleepiness and/or stiffness, and generally encourage people's zazen practice.

kensho: literally, *ken* (seeing into) *sho* (the original nature, one's true nature). Enlightenment-experience, the opening of the Buddha-eye; not yet true enlightenment, which requires the maturing of this opening and the shedding of all traces of it.

kesa: the full seven- or nine-striped formal monks', priests', or teachers' robe of which the *rakusu* is the abbreviated, shorter version. "The vast robe of liberation."

kinhin: period of walking meditation coming after seated zazen; or, the practice of walking meditation as the expression or embodiment of meditation-in-action.

Kokushi: honorific epithet or title awarded to Zen masters, meaning "national teacher," in the sense of teacher of the Emperor.

koan: literally *ko* means "public" and *an* means "document" or "standard." Usually a *mondo* (dialogue or encounter between a Zen teacher and a student or another teacher), anecdote or statement that vividly manifests some aspect of the enlightened way, often in an unintelligible, paradoxical manner. In the Rinzai tradition, *koans* are seen more in terms of their use as vehicles of realization, insight, and *kensho*, while for Dogen Zenji the other aspect is emphasized, that whether one realizes anything or not, koan study is the manifestation of the enlightened way. In an unrestricted, boundless sense, as in Dogen Zenji's expression *genjokoan*, the koan is nothing but this very moment, this very life.

mokugyo: fish-shaped wooden drum used in the service hall to maintain rhythm during sutra chanting.

muji: mu practice, which takes two main forms: an intensive questioning, What is Mu? and the intensive practice of being one with the sound *Mu*—that is, seeing or realizing what this state of oneness is. Mu first appears in the koan "Joshu's Dog" in the *Gateless Gate* (Mumonkan, case 1).

mujo: impermanence; the condition of no inherent permanence. One of the three fundamental "marks" or "characteristics" of things *just as they are*. Often associated with raising the Bodhi-mind, or igniting the aspiration to realize what this life is.

nembutsu: the practice of the recitation and invocation of the name of Amida Buddha ("Namu Amida Butsu"); the practice of being one with Amida Buddha associated with the Pure Land schools of Buddhism in Japan.

prajna: (hannya, J.): the "empty" wisdom of no-separation. Because *prajna* is "empty" wisdom, it should not be confused with "knowledge."

rakusu: a seven- or nine-striped abbreviated (apron-like) monk's or priest's robe representing the formal *kesa*, used on less formal occasions. In the Rinzai tradition, the *kesa* is worn only for special occasions; in the Soto tradition, the *kesa* is worn more frequently than the *rakusu*.

roshi: literally "elder teacher." In the Rinzai tradition, one takes the title after receiving Dharma transmission; in the Soto tradition, the title is generally reserved for older teachers.

samadhi: experientially, the state of oneness of subject and object: intrinsically, the fact of such oneness, which is the fact that everything just-as-it-is is the enlightened way. The "power" of things *just* as they are. Colloquially, strong, concentrated sitting meditation.

samsara: the relative, phenomenal world of ceaseless becoming and suffering (in Japanese, *shoji*, or "birth-death"). Usually contrasted with *nirvana*, a state or condition of no suffering. In the Zen tradition, we say that samsara is nirvana, nirvana is samsara, which means that nirvana is one with samsara, (as liberation is one with bondage), and also that there is no samsara, in the sense that this very moment—*no matter what it is*—is the enlightened way.

satori: enlightenment experience, synonymous with *kensho.*

sensei: teacher. In Maezumi Roshi's Zen lineage it refers to one who has completed formal study and received *shiho* (dharma transmission), but has not yet received *inka* (final seal of approval) and the title of roshi.

sesshin: literally, "to unify the mind"; a Zen meditation retreat, usually lasting three to seven days, the purpose of which is the intensification of practice.

shiho: dharma transmission; face-to-face recognition and approval of the disciple's realization and actualization of the teachings.

shikan taza: literally means *"just* (nothing but) sitting". This purest form of zazen relies on no devices such as breath-counting or koan practice, and disowns any goal, as well as any interest in realization or attainment; the practice of *just* being one with this very moment, moment after moment, which is the manifestation of "original enlightenment."

shuso: head monk or head of training for a designated training period. See *ango.*

takuhatsu: Zen monastic daily "begging" practice.

teisho: literally *tei* means "to carry" and *sho* means "to declare." Usually refers to Dharma talks by Zen teachers, but can refer to anything that vividly and directly presents the Buddha Dharma, in a way that attacks the student's attachment to ideas and opinions.

tenzo: the cook in a Zen monastery; usually a senior student.

tokudo: the monk-ordination ceremony.

unsui: novice monks (from *un,* "cloud," and *sui,* "water").

zazen: sitting meditation. Experientially, the elimination of separation between subject and object; the unification of body, breath and consciousness.

zazen-kai: group of persons practicing zazen.

zenji: formal title meaning "Zen teacher"; term of respect for deceased priests of superior accomplishment. In the Soto tradition, the term is also used for the abbots of Eihei-ji and Soji-ji, the dual centers of the Soto school.

zuise: in the Soto tradition, a ceremony at Eihei-ji and Soji-ji which takes place after completing formal study and receiving Dharma transmission.

INDEX

284

Mii-dera, 162, 171
Milarepa, Lama, 80–82, 86, 91
Minamoto, 155, 156, 161, 162, 202
Minamoto, Yoritomo, 155, 163
Mind, v, 11, 14, 30, 31, 33, 42, 44, 74, 76, 78, 81, 90, 117, 120, 130, 137, 144, 156, 158, 163, 189, 196, 199, 233–235, 245, 267, 270, 276; mirror, 221; monkey, 42, 160; ordinary, 199; universal, 5, 16, 33, 56; Zen, 5, 14
Miroku Bodhisattva, 159
Mishima, 147, 252
Miura-roshi, Isshu, 18, 267
Moon in a Dewdrop, 273, 274
Mountains and Rivers Sutra. See *Sansuikyo*.
Mu, 21, 25, 28, 32, 35, 39, 40–42, 46, 50, 57, 63, 65, 123–125, 127, 129, 135, 168, 210, 211, 229, 255, 256
Mu-ji, 125
Mujo, 153, 163, 195, 276
Mumonkan, The, 175, 192, 203, 242, 270, 273
Muromachi period, 202
Muso, Zen Master Soseki, 188
Myozen, Zen Master, 163–165, 168, 172, 177, 198
Mystic, 78, 79, 82, 269

Nagasaki, 235
Nakagawa-roshi, Soen, xv, 3–6, 15–19, 22, 23, 30–36, 39, 40, 41, 46–52, 57, 61–67, 82, 102, 109, 119, 124, 128, 129, 135, 137, 143, 144, 146, 147, 152, 210, 228, 229, 246–259, 270, 271, 276, 277
Names of the Patriarchs, 191
Namu Dau Bosa, 52, 271
Nansen, Zen Master, 121
Nara, 63, 137, 147–149, 151–155, 163, 173, 200, 201, 271
Naropa, 91
Narrow Road to the Deep North, 186, 236, 271
Namu-myoho-renge-kyo, 201
Nembutsu, 201, 276
Nepal, 47, 72, 83, 112
New York Zendo, 4, 18, 19, 20, 21, 35, 47
Nichiren, 170, 201
Nichiren Buddhism, 201, 202
Nightingale, 213, 241, 250, 252, 257
Nihon Daruma school, 173
Nine-Headed Dragon River, 186, 191, 194, 216
Nirvana, 30, 81, 83, 109, 168, 218, 269, 280
Nishiwaki-roshi, Etsudo, 227–230, 234, 277
Noh play, 62, 202, 259
Non-discrimination, 56
Non-duality, 7
Nordstrom, Lou, xv, 54, 136, 271
Not-knowing, 9, 11, 16, 226, 227
Noto Peninsula, 199, 205, 216, 230

Nun, 143, 217, 218, 272, 276
Nyingma sect, 91
Nyogen-sensei. *See* Senzaki-sensei, Nyogen.
Nyojo-zenji, Tendo, ix, x, 166–168, 177, 182, 185, 195, 199

Obaku sect, 205, 276
Obaku, Zen Master, xiii, 57, 63, 121, 176, 276
Obama, 224, 225, 232
Ojibwa Indian, 10
Old sect. *See* Nyingma sect.
Om, 21, 83
Om Mani Padme Hum, 82, 83, 85
"On a Portrait of Myself," 184
"On the Treasury of the True Dharma Eye," 206
"On Zen," 156, 268
One Robe, One Bowl, 276
One Thousand Cranes, 142, 222
Open Court, 11
Ordination, lay, 36; monk, 123, 127, 136, 145, 154, 171, 174, 225, 245, 246
Oriental, 4, 12, 13, 236
Original face, 38, 194
Oryu branch of Rinzai sect, 155, 163
Otawara, 237–239
Outlines of Mahayana Buddhism, The, 12
Ox, 132, 271

Padma Sambhava, 86
Pain, 58, 129, 130, 255, 256
Patriarch, ix, 6, 50, 71, 145, 162, 167, 169, 176, 183, 205, 210, 217, 245, 276
Penetrating Laughter, 275
Pilgrimage, 17, 47, 71, 72, 85, 133, 137, 155, 163, 226, 265
Plum Blossoms. See *Baika*.
Po Chang. See Hyakujo, Zen Master.
"Portrait of Dogen Viewing the Moon," 195
Posture, 4, 93
Practice, v, ix, x, xi, 5, 14, 15, 40, 43, 45, 60, 64, 81, 92, 93, 104, 108, 119, 123, 128, 134, 154, 162, 163, 166, 173, 174, 177, 178, 190, 193, 210, 221, 232, 233, 239, 246, 250, 255
Practice of the Way, The. See *Bendowa*.
Prajna, 57, 75, 137, 269
Prajna Paramita literature, 191
Precepts, Buddhist, 23, 34, 35, 150, 154, 157, 162, 163, 194, 200, 217, 242
Primer of Soto Zen, A, 274
Propagation of Zazen for the Protection of the Country, The, 155
Pure Land School. *See* Jodo sect.
Purification, 34, 35, 52
Purification Gatha, 34, 246, 256